FROM
THUG
TO
SCHOLAR

An Odyssey to Unmask My True Potential

Religion, Drugs, Sex,
Violence, and Mental Warfare

Elaine, I appreciate your support, pleasant smile, and huge heart. I wish you the best Dr. keep smiling and changing lives!

DR. JAMES A. WILLIAMS

252-412-4077
jwill316@utk.edu

Praise for *From Thug to Scholar*

"*From Thug to Scholar* is the true account of James Williams's journey in life, the process of losing the mask he wore to fit in with the crowd and becoming a role model for young people of all races. Read it and be inspired."

—**Linda Jacobs,**
Spur Finalist and WILLA Award winning
author of Jackson Hole Journey.

"James excelled in our doctoral program at ISU. He was the leader of our graduate students. We're thrilled to see his career flourish, and I am sure the students at James Madison appreciate him. His life story is one that opens your eyes to the resilience of the human spirit. He is a role model for young men and women who find themselves searching for a direction."

—**Dr. Bob Bosselman,**
Chair-Department of Apparel, Events, and
Hospitality Management at Iowa State University

"Not only does Dr. James Williams present a compelling story about the struggles and triumphs of his life; but interwoven, amidst every page, are life-principles destined to positively impact every generation. This book should be in the hands of every person who has a dream . . . and is dogmatic enough to do what it takes, to make those dreams come true!"

—**Savaslas A. Lofton, author**
"At a Mirror's Glance" novel

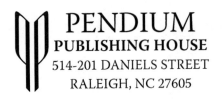

PENDIUM
PUBLISHING HOUSE
514-201 DANIELS STREET
RALEIGH, NC 27605

For information, please visit our Web site at
www.pendiumpublishing.com

PENDIUM Publishing and its logo
are registered trademarks.

From Thug to Scholar
An Odyssey to Unmask My True Potential
By Dr. James A. Williams

ISBN: 978-1-936513-72-7

PUBLISHER'S NOTE

This book is printed on acid-free paper.

For my wife,

LaToya, thank you for believing in me and inspiring me throughout my life; you kept me motivated during my maturation process and my low points in life. You believed in me when I questioned myself at times. You demonstrated that belief in me by uprooting everything and following my dreams all over this complex world. I love you, and I am honored to be your husband and friend!

Dedication

To family and friends who have passed on and who have inspired me through personal encounters: Cedric Barnes, Linwood Richardson, Chubby, Nate Poole, Derrick Liles, Melvin Wooten, Mike Honey, Maurice Faison, Cameron Scotty Wayne, Patricia-Maye Wilson, Robert Battle, Catherine Williams, and millions of people who died before there time living under a masked identity. I would also like to dedicate this book to everyone still struggling to find his or her identity and his or her purpose in this life.

Acknowledgements

I offer special acknowledgements to my $50 or more backers through Kickstarter Funding: Shon Ford, Starfela Speight, Maria Cox, Erin Breen, Vicki Rodriguez, Miranda Lynch, Michele Teel, Dr. Mark Warner, Dorothy Johnson, Elizabeth Albin, Cameron Beatty, Kelsie Langston, Andy Anderson, Gayle Gardner Lin, Samantha Durden, Elizabeth Nocito, Torey Barnes, Kelly Mayfield, Brenda Martinez, Desmond Prosper, James Newton, Ryan Giffen, Donald and Heidi Schoffstall, Neil Marren, Lawanda Blount, Eric Brown, and my mom, Dorothy Williams, and dad, Jimmy Williams.

Dr. Chris Loudermilk was a financial backer that went above and beyond, and I am extremely grateful for his financial support. Further, he served as a great mentor and role model while I served proudly with him in the United States Air Force (USAF) at Holloman AFB, NM. His warm words and belief in me helped to inspire me in and out of the armed services. I am honored to call you my friend, Chris, and I truly appreciate all of your love and support!

Tonya Ford, my cousin, was another backer who went above and beyond, and she did not waste any time providing her hard earned money to make this project a success. I have admired Tonya throughout my short existence, and she is the epitome of family; her love is genuine, and her support is authentic. I am grateful to have her as a cousin, and I am overjoyed for her support and belief in me. I love you, Tonya! Thank you so much!

Rodger Boot was an angel sent from God because I do not know him. But he decided to pay the remaining balance of my Kickstarter to reach the set pledge, and he demonstrated the love that still exists in this world. He cared enough to invest in my book, and I am very appreciative for his over-the-top donation. Thank you, and I ask God to grant you much happiness and many future blessings.

I owe a debt of gratitude to the many mentors who played a significant role in my maturation to manhood and my evolution into a scholar. Special acknowledgement to Dr. Robert (Bob) Bosselman, Dr. Chris Roberts, the amazing faculty and excellent students at James Madison University School of Hospitality Sports Recreation Management, Iowa State University AESHM faculty, former colleagues and students at Rocky Mount Preparatory, and Wilson County Public Schools colleagues and students.

I am also grateful to the multitude of friends whom I have acquired through my brief life experiences in New Mexico, Texas, Virginia, Iowa, Massachusetts, and North Carolina. I would like to acknowledge the negative and positive situations because both led me to my hidden self and my true potential. I am grateful for Linda Jacobs, an award-winning author who took time out of her very busy schedule to read my book and to provide some very sage advice, thank you my friend. I am grateful to my friend and colleague Dr. Benjamin Carr who took the time to assist me on the introduction section of my book, thank you buddy.

I offer my love and gratitude to my loving wife, Toya, my beautiful kids, Tia, Jas, Jay, and Joce, my parents, Dorothy and Jimmy Williams, and my robust brothers, Deon Williams, Mack Williams, Ajay Williams, Torey Barnes (cousin), and Tony Mendez (brother from another mother).

I want to send a special thank you to Robin Wolstenholme, who provided some beneficial ideas for the cover of my book. I want to provide another special thank you to Edward Arnold and

Pendium Publishing for their dedication and diligence toward producing this work. I want to recognize three excellent editors, Lauren Jones, Lauren Marlene, and LaToya Williams (wife); and a special thank you to my friend, Jermaine Jones, who supported me.

Finally, I would like to acknowledge my resounding faith and belief in God for assisting me with unimaginable insight and perspective toward completing this manuscript, and I would like to thank the random people whom I meet and who inspire me through words and actions. I am grateful and love you all . . . be blessed and enjoy!

Important Terms For This Book

World English Dictionary defines a **thug** as a tough and violent person. A thug should never be defined by how they look or dress; a thug should be defined by how an individual thinks and acts in a given situation. Being a thug is a mentality and can never be defined by a profile.

A **scholar** is a learned person who is highly educated in a particular branch of study (World English Dictionary). A scholar is a seeker of applied knowledge in thought and in action. Both of these terms require an in-depth way of thinking that alters one's paradigm and demonstrates the power of thought.

Disclaimer

I have tried to recreate events, locales and conversations from my memories of them. In order to maintain their anonymity in some instances I have changed the names of individuals and places, I may have changed some identifying characteristics and details such as physical properties, occupations and places of residence.

Table of Contents

Introduction

Everything happens for a reason and everything has a purpose, so as you read this introduction page or reflect on the title of this book, realize that you were led to read this book for some distinctive reason. Some of you are reading to support me, and I am thankful for that. Some may have faced struggles similar to mine, while some are intrigued by the triumph within the book's title. Others are embarking on their own odysseys to unmask and to tap into their true potential. Whatever the motive or the specific reason, I believe something higher (i.e., God, love, intuition, or positive energy) than me led you to read this book at this particular season or pivotal time in your life. At the end of the day, if you are in pursuit of personal growth or if your aim is professional success, this book might serve as an awakening experience to help you discover your hidden, internal treasures. Some of our internal treasures lie dormant behind the well-crafted masks of others' perceptions of us, and those treasures wait patiently for us to grasp them firmly and saunter happily to our true purpose and our true potential.

Some of you may be considering the previous sentence while reflecting on your accomplishments, scoffing at the notion of being masked because you have acquired a multitude of successes and have lived the so-called "American Dream." But the harder you ponder my idea of being masked, the more you might realize that you might be living a lie and you might be masked at this very moment.

The successful life is not about our titles (i.e., MD, PhD, lawyer, professor, engineer, or etc.), our high-incomes, our visible service performed in front of others, or other laurels; the successful life is about maximizing our lives and living every single day happy and in a state of tranquility.

Consider this: a confused and unhappy professional is no different than a confused or unhappy thug or criminal, in theory; the distinction is that one lifestyle is legal, and one lifestyle is illegal. Both lifestyles are lived by individuals who are blinded to their true potential and inner world of happiness. If you are living to appease others rather than yourself, you are masking your true self and this book is written specifically for you.

The purpose of this book is to take a journey and to raise awareness of our masked lives. This book will also serve as an example of how to open ourselves to the unique experiences available to us in this universe and how to live more fully through those unique experiences, and how to live an existence of abundant successes and permanent happiness by thriving in our true potential.

The journey begins.

Transformation

"Transformation means literally going beyond your form."

~ Wayne Dyer

I stood there breathing hard, my jaw clenched, with bloodstained knuckles and a swollen, fractured right hand from the violent barrage of punches that had rendered my battered opponent crawling and moaning on the ground. At 14 years old and in the sweltering humidity of Wilson, North Carolina, I stood there frozen in time, as my adrenaline filled my body with energy that seemed to beg me to hit him again. I felt like a giant standing over an ant because I compensated for my small and wiry stature with a big and fearless heart. This gorilla-sized heart propelled me to saunter around my opponent's balled up body with a menacing stare that let him know I aimed to do him harm. Fueling my masked hardcore exterior were chants of "stomp him out" from the small, chaotic crowd of peers who witnessed my prowess as a fighter. I was awash with a euphoric sense of pride.

I wore the mantle of this thug life proudly, and I emphasized my commitment to that life with two vicious stomps of my Timberland boots that cracked the other boy's underdeveloped ribs. In my mind, at that moment, I had arrived. I epitomized the hardcore life portrayed in some of Tupac Shakur's songs. I had just badly beaten a 16-year-old guy because I told my friends I would hit him. I had to stay true to my words and honor, and perpetuate that life and way of thinking.

I would be committed for most of my first 19 years to win the approval of the only people who mattered. Not my father, not my mother, and not other loving family members who had my best interest at heart. The only people who mattered were friends who perpetuated this life and considered me a real man.

But that was many years and many revelations ago. Today, I write with a Ph.D. framed on my wall and a cushy job as a university professor, which allowed me to join the less than one percent of African Americans with a doctoral degree rather than 37.1 percent of African Americans who represent our nationwide prison population (Federal Bureau of Prisons, 2013). During those years I had become a man, or at least I thought I had. I would have laughed at the notion of having a college degree because I thought life was all about fighting, getting high, sports, and screwing girls. What I did not understand until much later was that the life I had led was only a mask covering the person I was afraid to become.

In the brutal world in which I lived, I did not confess to any weakness. I did not aspire to any greatness. I only aspired to survive and live in the moment. My education was what I learned on the street from others who wore some type of thug persona. My respect was measured by the severity of the indignities I was willing to inflict upon others. My life was measured by days, not years. And my future . . . well, nobody thought of the future, only satisfying whatever we happened to want at that particular moment. On the streets, we were either with them or against them, and by them, I mean the thugs . . . the criminals . . . the bad boys . . . the people I deemed as real men.

In that dark and polarized world, even if we didn't want to be one of them, we had better mimic other characters in the street game and act like one of them. We had better put on the mask . . . or we would become their victims. But beyond the sadness of the ultimate emptiness of our lives, the real tragedy was when the mask became the man . . . or we became the mask. Either way, a true self had been lost to the viciousness of the world.

Thankfully, I was one of the few blessed ones. I was not lost to my mask. Ironically, I do not know or recall the exact day that I looked into the mirror and saw it, but I know that it happened, and I know that I despised what it looked like on my face and the values that came with it. I found the internal strength to take it off. I am not writing this to glorify the things I did during those years, which I now regret, but instead, I write with the sincere hope that I can inspire or help at least one person find the courage to see his or her mask, to take it off, and to embrace his or her true self. It is my desire to help others know they have a future and to pursue it fearlessly. If that happens, then every step of my personal journey would have had meaning.

Chapter 1

Donning the Mask

The Beginning

"Life is really simple, but we insist on making it complicated"

~ Confucius

There are multiple factors that play meaningful roles in our lives as we don our masks: environment, friends, parents, religion, confidence, and acceptance, to name a few. An imbalance of time and effort in any of these areas can lead any of us to don fictitious identities that are contrary to our true identities, and this causes inauthenticity in us—propelling us to maintain our masked identities to appease others. It is impossible to pinpoint the moment I decided to don a mask that emulated "thug life" or the development of actions and behaviors that would lead to future criminal-minded behaviors.

Everything in life is a process, and at the age of five in Fall River, Massachusetts, my mind was formulating and building the notion that a strong, revered, and feared young man earns the admiration of many.

This idea was skewed because I attempted to equate street

successes and confidence to the majority's ideal of successes (i.e. likeability factor, luxury cars and homes, and a wealthy income). When I reminisce over my formative elementary childhood years, I realize that I experienced or witnessed so many flashes of evil deeds that led me to believe that the toughest and most ruthless individuals prevailed in our society. I started off focusing solely on making excellent grades and being known as an intelligent boy, but students picked on my height and my academic successes. However, when I started acting out in class and scrapping with other students in classrooms and schoolyards, I won the respect and admiration of my peers, who saw no value in positive success.

Remember, this perspective was being developed while I was observing a structured-wall society where people bragged and boasted about what little they truly had. People showed off their designer clothes, chromed out cars, and expensive jewelry to pose as ghetto kings and queens. In my impoverished environment, the local street fighters, womanizers, pimps, and dope dealers were well respected by everyone. Secretly, I wanted the praise and negative attention the criminals and so-called bad guys got because I unfairly compared their lives to my parents' lives; my parents were meek and humble, viewed as saints, but among my friends they were viewed as uncool and weak.

Reflecting back, my parents displayed resolve to make progress toward long-term success, and they were robust in their faith; I yearn for that life now. Yet, as a child, your mind tends to expand no farther than a day, so it was impossible for me to visualize any patience or resolve for the future like my parents. I had a strong desire to be perceived as cool among my peers, and I desired the respect of the neighborhood bad guys. I was fixated on acquiring attention from others, and I learned throughout my short life that attention seeking could be a very dangerous endeavor. I have known people to lose their lives to gun violence in an attempt to be accepted; they joined gangs or neighborhood cliques to be a part of an accepting circle of peers. My parents tried to influence me with Bible scriptures and rehearsed stories about educational successes to sway me from the lure of drugs and negative situations. My mom painted very vivid pictures of drugs that could lead to a horrific life in prison or to death, and her imprinted images scared me away from the idea of coexisting with other aggressive inmates in prison.

I feared prison, and I had no intention of ever getting locked up or spending time in a jail or prison—I was driven to be a smart criminal and never get caught. I felt trepidation and some unexplainable hidden excitement when I walked by neighborhood tough guys who lurked on street corners. When I walked to the local convenience store, I found my eyes fixated on them; I studied their loud banter, their walk, their swagger, and their clothes. The logical left hemisphere of my brain held onto my mother's admonitions, but the right hemisphere of my brain generated creative opinions about these people that opposed my logical way of thinking.

I recognized as top quality the beautiful exterior appearance of the women the street guys possessed, and I noticed the litany of luxury cars they drove. At that time, my parents' words were stronger than my heightened interest about the apparently affluent lifestyles of the people I saw on the streets; but trouble starts with selfish thoughts of satisfying the flesh. Those thoughts would grow over the years, and those thoughts propelled me to seek the attention of similar negative individuals I had observed quietly as a child.

My parents loved me, and they would try their best to make sure I understood the depths of their love. They wanted me to live a life that included the pursuit of a college degree, but I spent the majority of my time around uneducated individuals who subsisted for their little scraps passively acquired through government assistance, making it hard for me to grasp the true value of a college degree. My parents tried to inspire me with words, but they did not have a tasty tangible recipe for motivating poor black males to understand the importance of an education.

I watched a lot of PBS educational shows, but I was not forced to read a vast amount of books or to build my writing skills outside of the classroom. My parents did not understand the importance of requiring me to do additional educational work outside of school. My parents worked out in the cotton and tobacco fields as teenagers, so they never learned the true value of education; they learned the value of sweat and hard work. Hourly wages appeared to be the common pay format for family members, so the concept of salary meant nothing to me; salary was a foreign term or topic in my small, inclusive world. Furthermore, earning a college degree appeared more difficult to achieve than playing professional sports or being some mega television star. I witnessed more blacks on television doing well compared to blacks I knew working hard with no degrees.

Some common facts suggest that an individual's chances of playing professional sports is less than one percent compared to approximately 35 percent of the population who obtained a bachelor's degree. We can control the 35 percent, but we must rely on timing or impressing the right people to fall into that lofty one percent. As a child, I didn't understand the statistical probabilities of playing professional sports or acquiring a college degree, and I probably would have been unable to grasp the statistical findings anyway as my professional dreams formed in my immature mind.

I viewed college-educated people as gifted-thinkers who possessed some unique intellectual qualities that I probably lacked due to my circumstances. However, at that age, I had no appreciation for being perceived as an intelligent student since I lived for the moment and desired the respect of my peers for instant gratification. As I reflect on who I was at that time, I realize I wanted to be respected among my peers for my talents (e.g., athletic abilities, charisma, fighting skills), and my willingness to go above and beyond and to pursue a victory in any given situation, negative or positive.

In the hood, projects, or ghetto, I recognized that respect came from being a great athlete, funny, or a tough boy; my competitiveness and drive to be liked and accepted spurred me to be great in all three. Throughout my school years, I worked diligently to entertain classrooms as the class clown, to "wow" football stadiums, basketball gyms, and wrestling arenas, and to engage in criminal activities to appear tough. Constantly, I competed in random activities: who could win street races with no shoes; who could eat macaroni and cheese the fastest at dinner; or who could stand the longest without moving while receiving knuckle penetrating punches to our scrawny shoulders.

Mental challenges, directly and indirectly, became my most formidable opponent; sparring with conflicting thoughts in my mind on a daily basis, my mind was never at rest and always battling the right and wrong decisions. Foundations of positive and productive living are developed during the formation of right and wrong because ethical decision-making can be altered throughout these stages, and a maturing mind can rationalize to embrace negative behaviors or role models (i.e. fighting to prove a point or impress friends and desiring the life of neighborhood drug dealers) as a display of success.

I built a stoic demeanor around my sensitive soul as a defense against taunts I endured from Deon, my brother who is five years my senior, and my two cousins, Torey and Ced. They all called me "Darla," a female character from the 1922 Our Gang movie shorts that later became known as The Little Rascals because I had pointy nipples. I was tormented by that name, and their laughter haunted me, playing over and over in my mind like some annoying song stuck on repeat in a modern-day CD player.

These taunts would infuriate and compel me to fight with Deon to no avail. Deon would make easy work of me when I attempted to fight him, and this irritated me even more. These constant verbal and physical battles transformed me into an individual who lacked fear when engaging in fights with other opponents. These experiences made me stoic in confrontations, and not afraid of other so-called tough kids or bullies. I welcomed any challengers in the schoolyard or within our neighborhood.

The busted lips, bruises, and scrapes I received from

Deon, prepared me mentally and physically for the biggest and roughest of my school-aged peers. I perceived toughness as a way to escape the name-calling and ridicule I experienced from others, so I prided myself on excelling at macho activities. I was always striving to do the most push-ups, pull-ups, and sit-ups among my classmates during physical education assessments. I thought machismo would protect me from insults and create a sense of inner personal pride. However, I learned that those accomplishments only gave me temporary satisfaction, not the lasting happiness I was desperately seeking in an ambiguous world.

I was confused about the purpose of life because I was stuck on the notion that everything is temporary and leaves you sooner or later. As I child, I was always thinking about the purpose of life. I would become pensive about the idea that we live for awhile, purchase a house or a car, get married, have some kids, and eventually die—it made no sense to me, and this idea of life left me perplexed and stressed about heaven and hell. I would challenge God with questions of "why was I ever born" because I perceived being unborn to be a greater blessing than being born and facing the unexpected future challenges and obstacles—my mind was all over the place. I am sure many of us struggle or have struggled with the question: "what is the purpose of life if it all ends anyway?" This book addresses my solution to that very difficult question and how the elements of life can force us to mask ourselves unintentionally with fictitious identities.

My parents were nurturing and supportive and exhibited love to all of us equally, and they anchored their faith and actions in their fervor for serving God. But they struggled financially, and I could not fathom why God would not bless them with more than enough money since they devoted their lives to being a blessing to others and serving him. I observed their struggle while watching local dope dealers and criminals appear to prosper financially from their illegal activities in our impoverished Fall River, MA neighborhood. This observation created an imbalance in my philosophy and approach to life, and it left me confused about the benefits of serving God. I wanted God to be a magical genie who would deliver us monetary fortunes and blessings, but it never happened. I grew angry, and I wanted to display a fighting prowess.

I couldn't beat Deon, and I couldn't change my situation, but I thought I could definitely beat up some of my classmates. I was never a bully, but I started to yearn for the competition that was part of the foundation of street fighting. I have been fighting since kindergarten, but I also exhibited intellect within those bland classroom walls. I was not going to be the dumb black kid in any class; my pride would not allow me to be labeled as a "dummy." During my Susan H. Wixon Elementary School years, I received "Satisfactory (S)" in subject areas, but on the flipside, I always received "Unsatisfactory (U)" for "talking too much," "disruption," and "not following directions."

My report card was filled with comments about poor classroom behavior. Still, it felt great being recognized for doing something positive and exceptional in the classroom rather than receiving only reprimands and suspensions. I adored attention, and in the future, attention would become a blessing and a curse for me. Attention served as an impactful factor that led me to don the mask of a thug. My parents praised my high marks in content areas, but chastised me about my negligent behavior within my learning environment.

Kindergarten was more structured than the less structured Head Start Program from which I had transitioned. Head Start was designed to provide basic education, nutrition, health, and parent involvement to low-income students. I had a difficult time adjusting and adapting my behavior to the new learning environment, but learning was never a real issue for me. My grades suffered later on in life when I lacked interest or focused my interest on other temptations, such as drama, fighting, sports, and girls, which were contrary to academic success.

However, in elementary school, I rode the high tides of

compliments from my mom and dad about my grades, and I adored the acknowledgement from our church congregation as my mother bragged about my grades. Yet, she never seemed to elaborate too much on my quick temper and poor classroom behavior; moms love to focus on the great qualities of their kids, you've got to love them for that. I must admit attention was, for me, like a drug to which I was addicted completely. I thought about attention often, and I basked in the happiness I felt when I received attention. I have no doubt that the need for attention has probably led many people to mask themselves in passionless careers, destructive relationships, criminal lifestyles, or unhappy lives in general.

I lived for self-gratifying feedback because it validated my significance on earth and within my secluded world. I believed if I earned other people's respect, it would validate my existence. Television shows and my poor community were filled with people who spoke about the importance of respect, and my young mind could not discern the difference between productive and destructive respect, so I sought both. I respected and adored when classmates raved about my fighting skills or ability to tell a joke and disrupt class; I also loved when teachers praised my ability to solve mathematical problems. Positive comments and smiles inspired me to pursue positive endeavors and enhanced my confidence, but the negative comments dissipated my confidence and generated demons that I wrestled within my mind.

Being perceived as smart was self-rewarding and exhilarating at times, but it did not gain me the respect I sought from my peers; instead, they talked about my academic success in ways that I perceived as insults. My mind translates their comments into a litany of insults: "you are ugly, you are short, you have girly nipples, you are not really smart and people will find out, you know those people are laughing at you, and you will never amount to anything." I had an uncontrollable desire to please people, and I yearned to feel accepted by my school-age peers. I was convinced that this was the only way I could win those mental battles in my confused and perplexed mind.

When I was between the ages of four and eight, the Maple Gardens "projects" or "ghetto" in Fall River was my home, and during my time there, I formulated many bad habits and developed a distorted view of success and winning. I learned that a nonexistent fear of fighting could gain me much respect among peers who shared similar experiences in that stone-brick, drug-infested community, making me an instant neighborhood superstar. I soon developed an ardent attitude toward fighting, while developing a cocky or arrogant way of communicating to challengers.

I was a wiry, yet quick individual, who exhibited impressive grappling and boxing prowess. I would shadow box daily in the tight corners of my closet, using the hangers as a tight rope to duck under while maneuvering swiftly corner-to-corner with an abundance of jabs and crossovers—I taught myself to box by watching Tommy Hearns and Mike Tyson's training videos. I would also box my brothers, friends, and cousins, wearing socks as low-budget boxing gloves that barely protected our tiny knuckles which tended to slip underneath the socks' imaginary knuckle buffer. Grappling was another daily practice because my brothers and I were always trying to hone our judo skills with swift takedowns and submission holds.

We took street fighting seriously by treating it as a neighborhood sport because we understood the benefits of being perceived as a great fighter. Conversely, we never considered the dangers of punches to the face and body slams to the unforgiving concrete, mainly because we never considered the possibility of losing a street fight or even being challenged to the brink of losing a street fight. My immature mind had me convinced that I would always walk away as the victor. I wonder how many young kids or teenagers have brandished knives and guns thinking they would walk away victorious but who now lay six feet deep deteriorating in their early graves?

Kids within the neighborhood would ridicule you and label

you as a "punk" if you exhibited any fear or backed down from bullies, making it extremely difficult to walk home from school or play peacefully at the shared playground. There was no way to escape the taunts because words traveled fast within my unstructured, danger-filled environment. Those words were sharp and intimidating at times, but fear had to be managed if I planned to function without worries in that environment.

Once your peers branded you as a punk, bullying was sure to follow. Even kids who were also bullied by others would try to fight the person identified as a punk, in an attempt to build their individual fighting reputations. I did not want the "punk" label, so I was determined to be among the best street fighters for my young age of five. I viewed this as some kind of desirable competition rather than as the practice and adoption of disruptive and destructive behavior that would haunt me throughout my formative teenage years. We started fighting when we were young, very young. Eventually, I gained the respect of my peers, but I was unaware that I was masking myself with a fictitious identity in the process that repudiated my religious training and the positive moral teachings of my parents.

Acceptance and fitting in became my long-term goals, and those goals replaced my true potential of valuing a sound education and conducting me as a positive citizen. My parents had the best intentions, but their religious teachings and positive morals were no match for an environment that functioned on a different set of principles that were opposed to their beliefs. There were too many factors that met my observant eyes and stimulated my critical and creative thinking. Why does God place those who love him in impoverished environments? Why do the good get picked on and bullied? How is being bad or violent bad when one gains the respect of those he admires? I wanted to be good, but my flesh witnessed success in wrongdoing; I was starting to don the mask in elementary school as a small child, and I was traveling toward a destructive path.

"I don't really understand myself, for I want to do what is right, but I don't do it. Instead, I do what I hate"

~ (NIV) Romans 7:15

Lessons Learned

People enroll in college every year to appease their parents, but their inner potential or true desires are outside the realm of college. I have witnessed students struggle to complete degrees since their parents forced them into those degree fields for prestige. Some people join churches to obtain titles or positions, and they become more driven for recognition in church rather than committed to pleasing God. These situations describe masked individuals, so we must protect ourselves from factors that trap us into an identity that fights against our inner passions and desires.

Challenge yourself with these questions on a daily basis: Who am I? Do I resemble my inner beliefs or the beliefs of family members? Are my actions aligned with my purpose? What is my true purpose? If you cannot answer any or all of those questions, you are probably masked in some aspects of your life.

Chapter 2

Humble Beginnings

Biological Father Did Not Bother

"Fathers, do not exasperate your children; instead, bring them up in the training and instruction of the Lord."

~ (NIV) Ephesians 6:4

My parents tried their best to protect and shelter us from negative influences and a hopeless method of viewing life. They wanted us to obtain fancy college degrees and to have life experiences that were not as readily available to them as they grew up. My parents worked common share cropper jobs to assist the family with money, and other nonpaying household chores at the direction of their parents. My mom impulsively got married at the tender age of 17 to Will Crumel, and gave birth to three children by the age of 25 with my biological sperm donor, Will. She probably wanted a life that appeared more exciting than her mundane life, which included working long hours in humidity that consisted of 90-to 100-degree temperatures to help maintain her shared household.

My mom's youthful marriage was very tumultuous, and the union would leave my mom and my brother Deon mentally and physically scarred. She admitted to being too immature for marriage, and in my opinion, from stories told to me over the years, she sought a man who possessed charismatic qualities similar to her father. My grandfather, AJ Battle worked extremely hard to assure his family was financially secure as a coast-to-coast truck driver. They never wanted for food, shelter, or money. However, I suspect that his children lacked an appropriate father figure to instruct his sons about how to treat young ladies and to instruct his daughters about how young men should treat them.

Money is not the key to teaching children how to live productive lives, but many parents, especially those living in impoverished conditions such as my family did, viewed money and materialistic items as a panacea for their personal struggles.

> *"If money is your hope for independence you will never have it. The only real security that a man will have in this world is a reserve of knowledge, experience, and ability."*
>
> ~ *Henry Ford*

My mother adored her father, but his struggles with adultery, left a negative legacy for his family members for generations. He was a robust man with a lustful spirit, a weakness to which many great men succumb. I am a firm believer in recycled behavior and generational curses. I also believe that generational curses remain until those curses are properly addressed with goal-oriented and committed solutions. If a legacy of negative behavior goes unaddressed, that history merely repeats itself and negative behavior is perpetuated.

My twin brother Mack and I were two-year olds and too young to develop any sound memories of our biological father during my mom's volatile union with him. Yet, Deon was affected by the negative treatment he and my mother endured. According to a psychologist who would treat Deon later in his life, the abuse he suffered played a significant role in the poor choices Deon made.

But, as Kirk Franklin tells us in his song, "There's is a blessing in the storm."

According to my mother, her situation became so dire that she contemplated suicide while she was pregnant with Mack and me. My mom hates reflecting on that brief moment of desperation, so I joke that she must have felt compelled to live and to deliver two packages of greatness to this world—speaking as if her belly was glowing with a spiritual force field. When suicide was no longer an option, my mother stood lurking in the dark shadows of her four-cornered bedroom with a stainless steel knife, trying to decide if she would slit Richard's throat and trade her freedom for a cold and hollow prison cell.

She was fed up with the pain of her husband's physical and mental abuse and the betrayal, but she also realized that it was her choice to walk away or to continue living in this turmoil. The hard choice requires faith, and sound faith to create some type of personal growth. My mom believed God would bring her peace, if she could find a way to muster up the strength to leave her bad marriage. She chose peace and happiness and walked out of Richard's life forever. Through pain and dark storms, joy and sunshine will ultimately prevail over our seemingly dark situations. My mother made the difficult decision to leave my father and to pursue a divorce. Like millions of people contemplating divorce, she realized that change started with her, not Richard.

Shortly after her divorce, my mother met an amazing man who fell in love with her, and who loved her kids as his own kids. Jimmy Williams was the new king in her life, and after some courting and wedding bells, he became my father, the man who taught me true leadership throughout my existence. He led by example and supported his godly words with consistent actions and examples. His actions inspired me more than any prolific sermon spoken by a gifted pastor; my father lived the life pastors preached.

When Will decided to relinquish his parental rights to avoid paying child support, Jimmy, my mother's second husband, stepped up with no hesitation to adopt all three of us as his own children. I felt an instant connection to his bloodline, prompting me to reject that Crumel bloodline because I felt my biological father rejected me. I mean no disrespect to my cousins and family members on that side, but rejection brings pain or change. I felt no malice toward Will, but the confusion I felt from Will's rejection drew me even closer to Jimmy Williams, the man who is my father. Our last name changed from Crumel to Williams, and I felt proud of my new name. I practiced writing Williams on a daily basis to capture the significance of this momentous event. Jimmy Williams not only adopted all three of us, but he exhibited godly love throughout our entire household, treating my mother like a queen and preparing us to be future kings of our lives and households.

While I gravitated toward bad habits in my donning mask stages, my parents planted seeds that sprouted and provided wisdom at different stages in my life. Sometimes seeds sprout much later on in life, so we should always seek those planted seeds and also spread positive seeds in the lives of others. These humble beginnings were composed of joy and pain, and both joy and pain affected my development. It seems I had to experience pain before I felt joy in my psyche; I had to acknowledge pain before I could truly conceive or accept joy. I thrived on failures, and I still do to this day. Failures force me to analyze and critique my shortcomings, which propel me to repair weak areas, personally and professionally.

My competitiveness fed my desire to be a winner in all things, and my desire to be victorious came from my father's rhetoric that "If God is for you, it is more than the whole world against you." I allowed those words to pierce my heart and serve as a mantra in my life; I felt like God hovered over me at all times, even as a sinner or worshiper of the world. My mother and father worked well as a cohesive unit, and they tried hard to raise us according to biblical principles and to old African American philosophies or sayings (i.e., "I told you so, do as I say, or I am going to get the belt"). They were very young, and they were trying to raise us the way they were taught by their own parents. Their parents were raised to work with limited education, so they encouraged us to work hard always, regardless of how much education we had.

Because of the way they were reared, my parents were not well equipped to prepare their children for modern-day temptations and pressures. We lived in a vastly different society compared to their childhood experiences. My father became a provider for three children at the young age of 23. He had to manage a new marriage, a unique and complex household, and an extremely demanding naval career, while living in a new state about 600 miles north of the familiar slow pace of Wilson, North Carolina.

My father was stationed in Rhode Island on the USS Capadonna, so his military orders brought us to the home of the New England Patriots, Boston Red Sox, and Boston Celtics. At that time, my father was the sole financial provider, while my mom utilized her spare time pursuing her associate's degree at Bristol Community College. My father would deploy for sea duty in conflict areas for six to seven months at a time every year of his four-year enlistment. This periodic deployment placed added and unwarranted stress on my young and docile mother; she had to contend alone with the dreaded worries of our impoverished environment and paucity of income. My mother also dealt with the pressure of raising us, maintaining the household, completing difficult college courses, and managing the concerns of my father possibly dying while he was out on sea duty.

They worked together to establish parental guidelines, so they could raise us from a cohesive perspective while dad was at home or at sea. They tailored their teachings from their Christian values and high moral beliefs because they viewed a sound understanding and relationship with God as the most important value. My parents raised us to fear God and to keep God first in our beliefs. However, they were naïve and too trusting of me, assuming that their positive teachings would inspire me to do the right thing at all times, not realizing the powerful influence my peers, cousins, and Deon had upon me.

Throughout my life, my parents would allow me to visit friends who, unbeknownst to them, had poor parental guidance, and I became exposed to images or entertainment that my parents would not allow me to indulge in under their supervision. This exposure to inappropriate material altered and warped my perceptions about life. Some studies have shown that inappropriate images can impact viewers positively and negatively, and most children spend about 28 hours a week watching inappropriate images on television and on computers without their parents knowledge; I was one of those children.

We have 168 hours in a week, and we spend about 35 of those hours sleeping, approximately five hours eating, about 35 hours at school or involved in learning activities, and about 28 hours watching television. All these activities take up about 103 hours in a week. This distribution of time demonstrates that most Americans, primarily disadvantaged citizens from my observations, allow television to consume too much of their time and their children's time.

Television consumed a lot of my individual time—time during which I should have been reading and thinking. I watched violent shows and movies that glorified drug dealers, murderers, and tough guys who had a slew of beautiful and sex-driven women. Far from improving or broadening my mind, I spent my free hours feeding my young and impressionable mind with negative images that incited negative behavioral responses. The general rule in mathematics is that a negative integer added to another negative integer produce an even larger negative integer, so small negative behaviors that are added to other small negative behaviors equate to more uncontrollable negative behaviors. Inappropriate images assaulted my young mind daily; those images took my created negative energy farther and farther away from my positive energy or a positive mental state. Even though I started to embrace detrimental behaviors and attitudes, I displayed respectable manners to most adults. I had the ability to mask my rough and robust exterior when communicating with adults because I was born to be a caring individual, and I was trained by my parents to put on the mask of respect for my elders. Additionally, I learned how to mask those positive qualities and limit my true potential with a hardcore persona that chased after negative drama-filled situations.

I was conflicted because I yearned for a negative lifestyle, while exhibiting courteous behaviors and speaking pleasantries around individuals whom I respected. Remember, a negative integer multiplied by a positive integer produces a negative result as well. Those bad behaviors had me secretly starting to mask myself and to embrace a subculture that was opposed to my parents' careful nurturing, spiritual teachings, and my humble beginnings. My humble beginnings trained me to call my elders "ma'am" or "sir" routinely, without being prompted by my parents to do so. I must admit I liked it when people acknowledged my courteous behavior. Those expressions of respect were engrained in my speech, and I added a charismatic smile to the façade to reinforce my shining image as a well-mannered young man. I was very talkative within my circle of true influence, but, due to the inauthenticity in my character, I played coy around adults, by whom I still desired to be perceived as a positive kid.

I was never completely comfortable in my own skin, and at times, I would not know how to act lovingly and pleasantly around adults without feeling awkward. I battled a conviction of feeling like a fraud, never comprehending what it meant to be real in my impoverished environment; this lack of understanding, left me questioning what was real or fake in all encounters with people. It was torturous being trapped in this mental prison, but I was ill equipped to handle the internal struggles that came with living my double life. My stoic demeanor kept others in the dark about these daily mental battles. I was always comfortable communicating with people about sports or topics unrelated to me, but my fraudulent behavior made me develop a lack of trust in others and within myself. I locked particular thoughts and internal moral conflicts away from other people's view.

My own fictitious demeanor had me assuming others were charlatans or frauds when attempting to evaluate their words and particular behaviors. At times, I would trust in the simple utterances of my parents, and their words would briefly challenge me to strive for higher expectations and goals, but their confidence in me also provoked creative and critical thinking processes within my young mind.

For a brief moment, they had me convinced that I would graduate from college and maybe even be the first black president, which was an extremely lofty and unimaginable goal for a black male in the late 1980s. It was a goal I found laughable at times, and personally, I never thought I would live to witness a black man being sworn in as the 44th president. It was a remarkable feat to witness President Obama becoming commander-in-chief, and, consequently, the most powerful man in the world. It signified a sign of true African American progress in our great country.

The moment also served to validate Dr. King's dream and vision of an integrated society that judges men by their character and content rather than their skin tone. Occasionally, as I traveled off into these deep mental states as a child and contemplated unimaginable careers of being a doctor, lawyer, or professor, a smile would grace my face as I imagined myself living in an affluent neighborhood, wearing expensive suits, and driving luxury cars. This escape would take me to a world vastly different from the ruptured pavements and half-paved streets throughout my impoverished locale.

There was a scarcity of money in my complex environment; however, we never had to worry about food, shelter, or love. We were definitely below middle-class status, and our parents were one missed paycheck away from some serious financial hardship. On most nights, we received quality home-cooked meals, but there were some nights that we made it work with Ramen noodles, sardines, Vienna sausage, and peanut butter and jelly sandwiches. I was never the best dressed according to my peers' standards, but my parents made sure I had quality apparel and was well-groomed prior to departing for school in the cold Fall River mornings.

My mom would lick her fingertips to remove hardened matter from my partially opened eyes to liven up my facial appearance, but I fought to remain cool by moving my head away from her stubby finger tips; she was determined to make me presentable in front of my teachers and peers regardless of how many times I turned my head away. Our parents focused on our controllable ability to look neat and personal hygiene rather than some fashionable clothing lines that sell expensive clothes to ascend some millionaire farther up the Forbes's most richest list.

My parents' inability to buy me top dollar designer clothes was one of the greatest gifts because I developed an attitude that clothes were something to wear for protection rather than for prestige. I never put much stock into my clothes, so I used creativity with my apparel to make some stylish combinations. I never strived to be the best dresser or utilized my clothes to build my self-confidence. My father was a modest dresser, and I viewed him as a high-quality individual; so I believe this circumstance probably strengthened my belief that clothes are to be worn for protection—I wanted to look presentable at all times though.

My parents gave me a lot of love to build my inner confidence, and it worked in some ways, though not in every form. My parents taught me to value character rather than build my self-confidence through expensive worldly possessions such as clothes, shoes, and electronics. Worldly possessions never truly impacted my confidence, but admiration and acceptance were key factors that tended to impact my decision-making process. Sometimes decision-making can be structured into a positive form of creativity when we are faced with unforeseen obstacles. Creativity was never far from me because I viewed the world from several perspectives, even at a young age.

When the heating system failed in our tiny apartment, I honed in on my innovative and survival skills to press bake on the oven while periodically heating my hands over electric burners turned on low. This strategy generated heat throughout my small body, and it became easier for me to don my school attire. I walked on my tiptoes to avoid the sudden shock of my feet making contact with the cold ceramic-style floors; I would stroll briskly throughout the apartment to shake the cold from my shivering little body to no avail. This is no indictment on my parents' ability to provide for us. In low-income locales, landlords are not the most reliable maintenance workers, and cheap apartments are not always maintained in adequate conditions.

I hid my emotions and protected my thoughts, adding fuel to the fiery rage that was already bottled up within me because I never opened up to communicate any issues that bothered me, thus I never allowed a release of this negative energy. Negative energy is counterproductive to positive energy; positive energy is utilized to take risks needed to unmask our true potential and to find our true identities. So conservation of my negative energy prevented me from tapping into my true potential. I kept my emotions in check because I thought real men controlled their emotions by remaining unresponsive in challenging situations. No pain, no gain, and no mercy for the weak were phrases I embraced even as an adolescent.

I was frustrated and appalled by the fact that my father deployed for extended periods of time for our great country and returned after sacrificing his life for our country to our poor state of living. I felt America did not value his daily sacrifice, and this notion infuriated me. I grew to resent the American-made system that I did not fully comprehend, and I repudiated this idea that patience was the true virtue of success. I desired immediate results, as do most immature kids, because tomorrow or waiting for the future felt like light years away.

Conversely, my parents displayed undeniable patience within what I saw as our destitute state of being, so they relied on prayer and belief rather than complaining about their undesirable living conditions. I felt like their perspective was a sign of weakness, and I despised their fervent prayers and their desire to wait patiently on God to deliver. Patience was not a concept I accepted. The majority of my peers in our neighborhood also desired instantaneous pleasure, but we failed to value education and taxing work as a realistic means of escape from our impoverished environment.

Most people whom I encountered in the projects failed to value a college degree as an avenue to long-term prosperity. Most valued sports and music as legitimate ways out of their poor living conditions, viewing education was an unreachable feat. Conversely, education is a more achievable feat than launching a career in professional sports, which often requires perfect timing or the ability to impress scouts. Injuries can also halt the quest of playing sports professionally.

A vast amount of individuals forfeit opportunities to play collegiate sports because they neglect their academic studies. Mainly African Americans and low-income individuals suffered in this particular area, from my personal observations. I have encountered many people who seem to have embraced the unfounded belief that "A college degree is just like a high school diploma these days," but most people making this ridiculous statement seemed to possess no college degrees.

I had a strong desire to be accepted in this subculture that rejected the notion of aspiring for a college degree, and I believed this negative lifestyle gave me the best advantage to exit the ghetto to more money. I often envisioned a better life outside of our poorly structured ghetto environment, but I was unsure about the best exit route. My parents instructed me to dream big, and I did; however, my positive dreams tended to clash with my negative and fleshly desires. In this ghetto subculture of unending negativity and violence, people found themselves jockeying for recognition and acceptance of others. Most displayed no regard for saving money or investing money because realistically, patience does not exist among the majority in most projects; behavior is predicated on the present rather than developing any thought of an auspicious future.

Some people whom I encountered self-medicated with drugs or alcohol to elude their mental battles. There was a beautiful woman upon whom I developed a strong crush in Fall River, but I later found out that she overdosed on heroin. Perhaps, she attempted to mask her problems with drugs, but the sad reminder was that she woke up to those same problems once her high dissipated. We cannot run from problems or mask our problems; we have to run to our problems and conquer those problems.

I learned many lessons through my ghetto life observations, and those lessons forced me to discern between ignorance and knowledge; however, I sought street knowledge that could make me more a sage to ghetto philosophies or principles. I learned the appropriate students to associate with, and the students to avoid within my complex school community. I learned quickly never to be caught hanging around a deceiver or someone perceived as weak; you become guilty by association.

My humble beginnings provided me with a solid foundation of biblical teachings; but I am a visual learner, and my eyes saw that it was more important to gain acceptance among my peers than to wait patiently on spiritual promises and prayers the way my humble, prayerful parents did.

Lessons Learned

Parents are responsible for constructing a foundation for success, while instructing their children on the principles of life. It is also crucial to understand variables that can counter parents' best efforts to guide their children to do what is right. My parents were the epitome of Christians, and they lived their religious teachings and reinforced those teachings by forcing us to go to church faithfully. My humble beginnings taught me to embrace their religious teachings, while my environment encouraged me to repudiate their instruction. My parents' instructions did not give me acceptance or respect among my peers. I was forced to trust my parents' rhetoric or to trust my observations of ghetto life. Once again, I am a visual learner, and their words failed to connect with what I was envisioning and encountering on a daily basis when I reflect back on my five-year old mind. We can have the best teaching method, but people have different learning styles. We must instruct others proactively from several perspectives to counter diverse learning styles and variables (e. g. environment, peers, school, and etc.) that are opposed to positive instruction. Humble beginnings can lead individuals to self-discovery, which propels them to successful futures, but confusion can also lead individuals to don masks or fictitious identities that focus solely on the moment rather than the future.

Chapter 3

Fighting is an E-Z Pass in the Ghetto

Survival Tactics

"Every man has a wild beast within him."
~ *Frederick the Great*

There were too many distractions to overcome when I was immersed with other ghetto minded peers in a tunnel of hopelessness. My parents raised me to respect God, respect myself, and then to respect others, in that order, while striving to become a productive student who rose above my temporary living circumstances. I tried diligently to embrace their glimmer of hope for a superior life, but it was hard to grasp their concepts when the majority of my life was consumed by our neighborhood and schoolyard interactions with the perceived "bad boys" who received most of the attention from the alluring girls. This observation of "bad boys" getting the attention from girls and respect from guys corresponded to and aligned with the story lines from famous movie scripts. My visual outlook taught me to reject my parents' positive and spiritual approach toward life and to gravitate toward the "bad boys" approach because that approach resonated with my desire to gain attention and acceptance from my school-aged peers.

My parents' words failed to connect fully with me because my eyes painted a more compelling picture of a more fulfilling life when I was acting inappropriately around my peers—distractions blind us from the truth and true happiness. I was too impatient to embrace my parents' godly approach because I still did not really understand and appreciate the purpose of serving God. I was very observant, and I watched people very closely, mimicking their mannerisms, the way they walked, and the way they moved their lips as they spoke.

If I was going to be a "bad boy," I wanted to be the most convincing and intelligent "bad boy," not one of the bad boys who reacted solely on emotions and who died early and often in well-scripted gangster movies. I learned at a young age that the more aggressive individual in combat normally wins the fight, unless the calm individual is highly skilled outside of the realm of typical wild arm swings and awkward standup wrestling maneuvers. My mind ran wild with multiple scenarios before every fight or confrontation. I had to convince myself that my hand speed and strength gave me an advantage over an opponent; this inner belief motivated me prior to engaging in combat.

The strategic street fighter with vast experiences typically dominated the more aggressive fighter with no tactical skills. As I came to understand this vital information, I embraced and applied this wisdom as part of my personal philosophy. I worked strenuously to be perceived as a "bad boy" among my peers because I was small in stature and needed leverage with some of the bigger students. I mastered the ability to speak in a confident and domineering fashion even when fear churned in my stomach, in the form of cramps or so-called nervous pains.

I also gained confidence from the fact that I have been fighting since the age of five, and I probably had well over 15 fights before the age of nine; I fought so much at a young age that I stopped getting nervous before engaging in physical combat. My brother Deon taught me to live by the mantra "no mercy for the weak." My twin Mack and I became ghetto prizefighters with no monetary purse for our brawls, but we gained invaluable respect from our peers. I considered this respect to be as precious as gold; in my mind, I was a king and becoming someone important in the projects. Deon and Eric (childhood friend) were the charismatic promoters of our fights, and they scheduled all fights in the heart of Eric's dilapidated neighborhood. Kids gathered in circles and urged the fighters on with various combative chants (e.g., kill him or break his jaw).

Eric's neighborhood had square brick buildings that formed in a distorted circle with a poorly paved basketball court in the middle of the buildings' circle. There was also one set of monkey bars that I frequented. Looking back now, I wonder if this housing project was constructed in a manner to trap us within this dirty environment and swinging on bars mirroring wild monkeys in zoo enclosures. We also got kicks out of using the Stop-N-Shop grocery carts to smash into each other at high-speeds, and the object of our game was to send our opponents flying haphazardly out of their shopping carts. We did anything for a great thrill and a demonstration of our toughness— we were the original "Jackass" crew long before the MTV series of the early 2000's.

We dived in high ditches that trapped in a vast amount of rain in an attempt to swim to the other side. The problem was that sometimes the ditches lacked depth, causing us to dive into the muddy ground. Deon and Eric coined these activities "ghetto games." We enjoyed taking those idiotic risks. Taking risk got me a lot of respect, or "props," but fighting gave me an E-ZPass in the ghetto. Deon became a living legend in Eric's neighborhood for his famous fight, in which he beat up Chris, the former informal teenage leader among other kids in Eric's housing complex. Deon received two black eyes in the fight, but he found a way to maneuver Chris's shirt over his head and drive his head into a protruding brick on the side of the concrete project building. As blood spewed from Chris's head, Deon began to pound his face with a barrage of right and left cross punch combinations. People quickly separated the two as blood poured from Chris's head. This monumental fight warranted Deon instant immunity from any future sanctioned fights in Eric's environment, and consequently granted me some immediate, though unproven respect in that neighborhood. The respect was critical for my success because we became permanent fixtures within Eric's neighborhood.

We spent a vast amount of time in Eric's projects because my mother and Eric's mom, Ms. Bessie, were extremely close friends. I viewed Eric as my brother, and his mom as my adopted mother. I lived across town in Maple Gardens, where crack invaded my neighborhood, like many environments in the late '80s. Drugs had people exhibiting odd and dangers behaviors at times, but I somehow found humor in my impaired neighbors who made snow angels in subzero temperatures outside my extra insulated windows.

My parents did not allow us to venture out much around Maple Gardens due to the excessive criminal activity. My parents did not worry as much when we traveled in Eric's neighborhood; but honestly, Eric's neighborhood was not much better than ours, just more ethnically diverse. His neighborhood was home to fewer African Americans, Puerto Ricans, and Cambodians than mine. Whites were in the majority there, but I saw no difference in the behaviors of whites or any other races that lived in impoverished living conditions. We were all struggling and mentally confused about our purpose in life. Even though African Americans were few in number, I never noticed bigotry from other races.

I learned between the ages of five and nine that my white brothers could brawl because I participated in many epic battles with them while I lived in Fall River. My sparring and grappling encounters took place frequently; we took turns fighting, normally on a bi-weekly basis, and a fight club was born. We had an unspoken fight club rule not to speak to adults about our fights. Only fighters within our group were privy to fighting information. I fought so much that I viewed fighting as a normal sporting activity, and I thought it was something kids did in all neighborhoods. I actually desired more fights, because the more I fought and showed a lack of fear toward fighting, the more I stood out among my peers. My adult knuckles still bear scars from fights I engaged in over two decades ago. My parents never thought much about our aggressive behaviors or brief discussions about fights until Mack was cracked over the head with a Transformers lunchbox during a casual snowball fight at school recess.

My father viewed our tussles as young boys just fooling around, but nothing too major to worry about. However, one day some kid slapped Mack upside his head with his plastic hinged lunchbox. Then some days later, in the carpool line, this kid actually had the gumption to demand that my mom buy him a new lunchbox. My mom was baffled by his demand. This request did not sit well with Mack and me, and we made a point to teach him a lesson, using our own forceful brand of corporal punishment, about the world of common sense and respect. He never spoke so candidly about that lunchbox matter again.

Fighting was a common occurrence for me, so I viewed fighting as an endeavor that real men engaged in; therefore, I came to believe that fighting was a strategy I must use to gain acceptance among peers and to solve problems. I valued and viewed fighting as a panacea for any conflicts with other people; they do not like you, fight them and resolve the issue—the truth is you cannot beat everybody and fighting never truly solve or eliminate the problem. My masked identity had me at odds with rational thinking because I masked myself with a thug persona and survival tactics rather than the positive long-term behaviors my parents taught me.

Deon taught me to settle disputes with forceful intimidation tactics like posturing in an imperious manner, speaking in a firm and demanding tone, and using direct and menacing eye contact. If the situation persisted after intimidation tactics were enforced, I was instructed to make an example out of that individual with combative measures. Deon warned me never to engage in combat when no spectators were around because spectators were needed to spread the outcome of the battle by word-of-mouth to others. When people perceived me as a winner in fights, my credibility was bolstered automatically among peers.

When no one was there to watch a fight, I utilized trickery to evade the fight; after all, there is no benefit in fighting without receiving credit. A smart man would avoid all physical confrontations by using clever speech to mitigate or diffuse the situation. All of my years of fighting never provided true resolutions to any conflicts; I was on guard for the retaliation I knew was inevitable. Normally, payback came in the form of group beatings, so I tried to always travel with a young pack of motivated fighters.

Even at my young age, I knew that fighting was futile, but I was willing to do anything to build my self-worth and to gain some form of recognition among my peers. When school dismissed each day, at 3 o'clock, Mack, Deon, and I packed into a small, stinky van with a stout middle-aged man, who drove us to an after school program called "Outreach." The program was designed to keep low-income kids in a safe environment while their parents were occupied with work or other tasks. Outreach was not a typical afterschool program because I never learned information needed to enhance my school experience or to create productive thinking. Outreach sharpened my street knowledge and squabbling repertoire.

The one positive consequence was that Outreach introduced me to contact football. There were young male and female workers who periodically monitored us throughout the facility, so with no real structured leadership in place, someone will emerge as a leader among a slew of followers. Deon happened to emerge as the leader of our miniature afterschool gang. Our focus was on terrorizing and controlling other Outreach members who failed to conform to our in-house demands.

Deon was an autocratic leader; he informed without reasoning, and we followed without resistance. He utilized cunning methods to influence other kids to perform his mischievous tasks. If they failed to comply, he employed strategic intimidation tactics, or brutal force to impose fear in them. Deon was a devious person, but a true leader. He had the ability to persuade others and to make them feel they were vital components to his team. Deon ruled with an iron fist, and I was his loyal servant, doing whatever he asked without a rebuttal. I knew those who rose up against Deon paid a mental and a physical price, and I had no desire to be a recipient of any of his verbal or physical assaults. I knew firsthand Deon's volatile rage. Deon made an example out of me one day at Outreach, and this incident had a profound impact on my youthful perspective.

Deon and I were engaged in a closely contested foosball game against two other kids when I decided to laugh and relax in my play, no longer spinning the handrails with aggression and fervor. My lack of desire and effort caused us to lose the game, but I thought nothing of my dismal performance. Deon was drunk with fury, and I quickly realized that he meant business when he decided to strike me in the face with a closed fist for laughing after losing the foosball game. I never unfurled my lips to smile or to laugh during a foosball game again. Mack and I served as Deon's loyal hit men, so we exchanged blows with whomever he recommended because we feared the consequences of saying no to him more than being reprimanded by program instructors.

Deon ruled Outreach, and I learned survival tactics that made me a formidable fighter throughout the projects. My constant fighting, TV influences, Deon's intimidation, misguided observations, and my father's words to "fear no man but God" drove me to be a prolific fighter, both in the "hood" and at school. Many people in our society take the easy road and choose the wrong path because it is easier to wear a mask rather than fight to do the godly thing and be a service to others. In my case, being a "bad boy" or a fighter rather than taking the chance to be laughed at among my peers for making the right decision became my dilemma.

Despite my tough and aggressive outer shell, I had an underlying peaceful resolve that I fought to keep hidden. I did not want to be perceived as meek because I was too afraid of being bullied or mocked by other classmates. I wanted an E-ZPass in school and in the ghetto. This ignorant philosophy followed me in and out of the classroom for the majority of my school-aged years, so instead of focusing on posting high marks or impressing teachers with my reading and math abilities, I focused on trying to be the class clown or to be the kid not to be messed with.

When I focused solely on being a quality student, students taunted me or failed to recognize me as a student of importance. I hated that feeling of being viewed as nobody among my peers. I did not achieve the respect of my peers until I won a fight and exhibited consistent disruptive behavior within the confines of my classroom. Their respect was satisfying, and my observations taught me that fighting was the ticket to respect and to acceptance; nice boys finish last was my adopted theme. My disruptive behavior and negative attitude overshadowed my productive classwork, prompting my teacher to suggest special education courses and medication to control my impulsive outbursts and lack of self-control in her classroom.

I was a headache and a problem, so even though I was, academically, one of the more astute students, she desired to position me with mentally and physically challenged students. I had a loving mother who possessed some positive fight because she saw through my teacher's smokescreen. My mother was not trying to hear that foolish talk from my teacher, counselor, or principal, so she recommended an aptitude test to demonstrate my learning and comprehension abilities. It was puzzling to my mom because I had never struggled academically, so she was determined to prove to those teachers that her baby was academically gifted and did not belong in any special needs classes. My mother was fighting to ensure I had an E-ZPass toward academic success, and she channeled her efforts in a positive manner, contrary to the ghetto E-ZPass I sought. My mother prayed and motivated me with affirmative words before I took my scheduled aptitude test, so I was determined to showcase my intelligence for her and to prove those teachers wrong.

I understood the ramifications that would result if I failed the test, and I was committed to excelling on that particular assessment, taking my time to analyze my responses before color-coding my answers. I whizzed through the test, and I remembered thinking about the easiness of that aptitude test. I cannot recollect my score, but I remember scoring extremely high and making my mother very proud. The principal intervened and decided to switch me to a more challenging classroom rather than accepting the recommendation of special education from his respected teacher. I guess I was challenged a little more because my disruptive behavior in the classroom dissipated throughout the remainder of the school year. Yet, my classroom change did not deter my fighting prowess in the schoolyard or in my neighborhood. Earning an E-Z Pass was crucial to success within my subculture, so I shunned appropriate behavior.

Routinely, I made the honor roll during my elementary school years, but I still managed to get into fights. I started to develop an interest in girls as well, adding another distracting factor to my confused and unstable identity. In kindergarten, I developed my first in-school crush, and I remember Deon asking me if I had kissed her yet. After his question, I made it my mission to earn a kiss from this girl I had a crush on and any future girlfriends. I was strong-willed, and I wanted to be like Deon or appease Deon by informing him that I had finally kissed a girl; it might make me earn my brother's honor.

I thought my kissing in-school crush would also validate me as a bad boy. I pecked my dream girl casually on the cheek one day during mega block time in our classroom. The images I had seen on television and the adult conversations I had overheard, at which were inappropriate for children's ears, kept me intrigued about the excitement people seemed to get from touching, caressing, and more illicit kissing. I wanted to feel the satisfaction. I thought I was seeing and hearing about, though I did not understand the true nature of those images and conversations. Those unmanaged thoughts would eventually drive me to more risky sexual behavior at 12 years of age. Wanting to impress girls and having an opportunity to try inappropriate acts with girls heightened my desire to fight and break rules.

I remained an advocate for resolving schoolyard disagreements with my fists. I did not believe in backing down from a fight because those who backed down became branded as cowards or punks. Conversely, I believed in pursuing a fight with fervor and determination to win the contest and to win respect from the popular students. My determination and my desire to win forced me to develop an effective way to communicate to gain leverage over my opponent. I also learned to utilize nonverbal and verbal communication skills to win favor with others because I realized that it is not feasible to try to fight everybody. I studied the rules of life, and the rules of the ghetto, and in that way I continued to learn how to play America's simplistic educational game, while maintaining an E-ZPass within my tiny world.

Lessons Learned

Most kids want an E-ZPass to escape difficult challenges in life, but there is a very serious problem with this poor and misguided philosophy. The problem is that there is no easy pass in life, and difficult challenges must be confronted with a proactive plan and a backup contingency plan. Our neighborhoods, peers, parents, and beliefs play a significant role in our personal development, and there were many variables that led me to embrace fighting and bad behavior in the classroom as my E-ZPass to survive in school and in my impoverished environment. Implementing a godly foundation is great, but it is not the panacea or universal key to confused kids' survival in unique learning environments (schools and neighborhoods) that reject those religious settings or teachings.

I fully acknowledged God's existence, but I did not agree with some of the religious ways of attempting to survive and comprehend this life. My parents served God and struggled financially; my parents were committed to following God, but people viewed them as weak in our poverty-stricken environment. I came to understand that blessings would follow their faith and good deeds, but I never saw them gain any tangible rewards for their faithfulness that appealed to my young mind. I desired immediate acceptance more than the long-term success that they spoke about because my eyes could not see beyond today's struggle and hardscrabble surroundings. I lived in the moment; the future does not exist for kids living in the projects. I believe it is imperative for parents and educators to focus on all factors when they are attempting to encourage and to build a child's self-confidence. Most children want easy, and we must demonstrate the effort and hard work behind success. Once again, there are no E-ZPasses in life, but education is an E-ZPass to a more productive life.

Chapter 4

The Power of Visual Images

What We See Can Speak Volumes
within a Confused Mind

*"Humanly speaking, it is impossible. But not with
God. Everything is possible with God"*
~ *(NIV) Mark 10:27*

Visual images appealed to my visual learning style, and I felt it
was impossible to deny what my eyes witnessed. I saw a way to
what I perceived as success and world recognition that challenged
my humble beginnings and it led me to embrace fighting as a
survival tactic and an E-ZPass to triumph in my important worlds
(school and impoverished ghetto). My success in school was
mainly predicated on my bad boy image, but I did find minimal
happiness in obtaining good grades; I just lacked trust in the
grading system. I believed grades painted half of the picture
because some students did well on tests but would fail severely in
everyday life; high grades cannot buy common sense. The pursuit
of high grades created a world of cheaters, though.

First and second grades brought cheaters to the forefront, at a
time when it is imperative for students to learn the basics in reading

and math. I observed students who earned high marks through diligent cheating tactics, not from their own merit or intelligence. Conversely, I focused on ways to understand information without studying in order to retain the information. Comprehending information benefitted me later on in life because I knew how to make that data applicable to my life. I sought to know "why," and my inquisitive mindset gave me an advantage in the classroom.

I learned how to think in the first and second grades, which serves as a vital skill for processing new information and developing new brain cells. I asked detailed questions about selected solutions or issues to keep me thinking outside the box. This approach gave me the ability to retain vital information being shared in the classroom, and as a result, I gained a more in-depth level of understanding. As my thinking evolved, my communication skills evolved and provided me with power needed to persuade others. I learned how to use charisma in my dialect to win favor with students and some of my teachers. I understood that teachers are human beings, and most human beings love it when someone strokes their ego; my goal was to stroke their egos. I visualized Deon and my cousin Ced's use of charisma to charm family members, females, and other people with whom they were trying to win favor.

I studied Deon and Ced, and I adopted their nonverbal mannerisms and verbal tones when interacting with people. I worked strenuously to win over my female teachers I thought were beautiful; their beauty made me trust them and feel safe. I felt more relaxed around female teachers when compared to male teachers. I would say, with confidence, to my female teachers, "You look very nice today," or "How is my favorite teacher doing on this lovely day?" When teachers smiled back and spoke with polite words, I was reassured that my approach had worked, and my success ultimately enhanced my confidence to speak to older adults and to people in general.

Wixon Elementary School, the only school I attended in Fall River was my beloved school where I used every opportunity to develop a charismatic approach with people, and I—learned a lot about the unique traits of various types of people. At Wixon, people were pleasant, and they spoke with a distinct accent. My family members down south, primarily in North Carolina, enjoyed the way I pronounced words because I had that distinct Falls River accent as well.

I never really noticed a difference in my pronunciation of words and mannerisms until we moved back to NC. I was nine years old when my father was honorably discharged from the United States Navy. My parents decided to relocate to Stantonsburg, NC, a small town about five miles away from the city of Wilson, when my father fulfilled his four-year obligation to Uncle Sam's Navy.

I was torn about the relocation. I wanted to be near my family in NC, but at the same time, I was comfortable in Fall River. Some may wonder about this statement when given my numerous fights and our impoverished situation; but, this was the life to which I had become accustomed, this was my comfort zone, and I never viewed the fights as a bad thing, just a casual sport. We were moving to a city where blacks outnumbered whites, so the notion of moving to NC brought about some trepidation. I was not used to being around a large number of blacks. I assumed that fights would be more frequent in NC because I heard horror stories about the escalating violence in Wilson County from family members.

I also thought black boys were more dangerous and could fight better than white boys due to the negative media coverage of black males. Media images have a great way of causing blacks to stereotype one another and hate one another; I feared being around them and developed a sense of paranoia when around some black boys. Ced discussed the violence in Wilson; he elaborated on the shootings, stabbings, and fights that occurred throughout the city. His words had me thinking that it would be an extremely difficult adjustment living in NC.

I visualized how I would communicate with other black boys and build my image in NC. I was determined not to be viewed as weak there, so I prepared myself mentally before ever departing Fall River. I thought I would have to mask myself as an even more robust bad boy. I had to transition from having all white friends and listening to rock-and-roll music to having mostly black friends and listening to hip-hop/gangster rap music. The one positive change was that our living conditions improved in NC, but I was becoming more intrigued with violence and sex. I associated violence and sex with a thug mentality that had been introduced to me through gangsta rap and gangster movies in the complex world of my young mind.

There were many factors in NC that would feed my undeveloped but negative mindset. Neighborhoods and churches were segregated in Wilson and Stantonsburg, unlike Fall River; this would be the first time I worshipped my loving God with one race or a particular group of people. Up to this point, I always lived in predominately white low-income neighborhoods, vastly different from the neighborhoods I observed in NC. We no longer lived in the projects, but my mind and soul were still connected and tied to the individuals living in the projects and their perpetual way of thinking.

I noticed that my peers in NC cared and focused more on materialistic items compared to my Fall River associates. Teachers also reinforced, unintentionally, the habit of bragging about materialistic items by encouraging students to bring items to school to display during "show-and-tell" sessions. During show-and-tell, my peers brought shoes, jewelry, and expensive toys to school to show off, while explaining to other students how and why they got these items. The riches I saw during this activity left me awestruck; I wondered how I could get my hands on similar items. I watched students attempt to one up each other repeatedly. I could not compete, so I did not try. Due to my experiences in Fall River, I never completely became a materialistic individual, but I was impressed by some of those items kids showed off, both during those sessions and throughout the school day.

I remember bringing my brand new Mr. Potato Head to school

during show-and-tell and being exhilarated as I discussed my toy. My excitement was short lived when some student brought a large Transformers toy to class; this student had all of the parts, and I soon realized my Mr. Potato Head could not compete. I was amazed at some of the kids who had better clothes or toys than me because those same kids lived in horrific locales in run-down houses or dilapidated apartments. At that time, we were living in a decently sized house, but our apparel was never as fancy as our peers, some of whom lived in impoverished neighborhoods.

As I look back now, I realize that it was a cultural issue in Wilson because some blacks struggled financially but utilized their small income to establish an identity by purchasing what they regarded as the best materialistic items. Some people of all races still use materialistic gains to exhibit a measure of success within our capitalistic society. For some, materialistic gains demonstrate some measure of success when compared to other people in this competitive society, and they mask themselves with expensive costumes — jewelry, clothing apparel, and wads of money. Life for them becomes an everyday costume party, with no true authenticity.

I wore exterior costumes by trying to exhibit a tough demeanor, and I used this to build my self-worth; I wanted the popular students to embrace me with open warms and wide smiles. My parents tried to build my self-esteem with positive comments, but I believed those comments came out of obligation rather than truthful speaking on their part. My paranoia rejected their warm feelings and unconditional love. My mind convinced me that my inner need for their nurture was deceptive and could not be trusted. I convinced myself that I needed positive comments to come from my peers because their admiration was more critical to my overall happiness.

This point of view was damaging to my development because I chose to measure my success by peers' thoughts about me rather than by seeking to measure success by how I felt about myself—it is my life, but many of us need to feel embraced by others. Masks are formulated when we compete for the love and recognition of others for personal happiness; the problem is my young eyes focused on the visual—fake high fives and praise from others when I exhibited negative behavior. I trusted my eyes more than my heart, and this misplaced faith caused me to doubt my morals and spiritual upbringing. I felt compelled to don a mask that hid my true identity because my true identity did not give me a friendship with the world.

"The mind governed by the flesh is hostile to God; it does not submit to God's law, nor can it do so."

~ *Romans 8:7*

I valued some of these materialistic images from my classmates and celebrities on television. Rap videos and movies changed my auspicious outlook toward a productive life because I no longer focused on the necessities but thought more often about the wants. I became consumed with the wants . . . not necessarily materialistic items, but the ability to acquire what I wanted when I wanted it. I looked forward to listening to the constant MTV messages from our television set: "MTV, you hear it first!" My interest did not revolve around their miniature news segments; it was all about the derogatory words and sexual images in music videos, and violence portrayed in music videos.

Ironically, I also loved watching some of the positive afterschool break specials, which included positive messages about drugs, alcohol, anorexia, etc., but I would transition back to more negative messages soon after viewing those positive messages. I would change the channel to "Yo MTV Raps!" immediately after the conclusion of an uplifting show, while eating a bowl of Captain Crunch Berry cereal, with extra sugar to make me feel more hyperactive. In those days, the majority of hip-hop music appeared to be fairly positive or non-violent in the early 90's, even though I preferred the more violent rap music to inflame my bad boy persona.

I preferred the hardcore rap artists, particularly NWA, Ice-T, Tupac, Wu-Tang, Naughty by Nature, and Snoop Doggy Dogg. My parents had no idea how bad some of their lyrics were, even as I listened to them on a daily basis. As my parents continued to feed me positive and uplifting messages, MTV was flooding my young and impressionable mind with messages glorifying the power of satisfying sexual encounters, drugs, fighting, and shooting, all the while helping me fine-tune a f*** the world mindset.

All of this added to the negative foundation that developed during my elementary school experiences. Prior to our family relocating to Wilson, NC from Fall River, my father, Mack, and I moved to Stantonsburg to my Great Grandma Lillie's house, while my mother and Deon finished their respective academic school years. My mom was finishing her associate's degree, and Deon was finishing middle school. Mack and I were a package deal, so my parents probably figured we would be safe transitioning to NC as long as we were together.

Unexpectedly, I was nervous and somewhat intimidated about relocating to Stantonsburg. Ced's words were haunting me, and they had me thinking about the potential bad boys I might face in NC. This notion charged me to devise my approach to a new predominately black school, so I had to study and learn the mannerisms of blacks in NC—I had to fit in. I decided to amplify my Massachusetts accent and Fall River's proximity to Boston, so I told students I was from Boston, better known as Bean Town.

The New England accent had some students spreading rumors that Mack and I were from New York, and my quiet approach had me labeled as mysterious among some students. Ced's assumptions about NC being more violent were wrong because I had no problems in Stantonsburg. I received a lot of respect and a lot of attention from female students, which, in turn, won me favor with the popular male students. My erratic classroom behavior brought me honor in school, but it also won me the harsh reward of the application of an unyielding yardstick to the insides of my palms and paddles with holes in them to the upper part of my buttocks. Teacher punishment was swift when I violated rules in class, and my father reinforced their school policies with some leather belt action of his own.

I weighed the rewards and consequences on my unique mental scale. The reward was positive acceptance from classmates and the lure of pretty girls in the school, and the consequences were disciplinary action received from teachers and my dad. Classmates' attention seemed to outweigh the consequences, and I found myself in trouble throughout my first school year in NC. I had to establish a name there because words travel fast in small cities; I needed my name to spread as a bad boy.

My observation of bad boys having respect among others and the strong influence to dress and act like popular rappers shifted my focus to value the "James is hard or James is cool" more than possible suspensions from school or spankings from parents. However, outside of school, there were no activities for kids in Stantonsburg, so Mack and I were often bored and trapped with our inner thoughts of what to do. We would try to escape Stantonsburg mentally by playing the "if I had a million dollars" game, and I would travel thousands of miles away with my creative thoughts until Grandma Lillie would bring me back to reality.

Grandma Lillie made my life very difficult, but God bless her soul; she is no longer here to defend herself so I will not offer details about her behavior. However, I can attest to the egregious behavior that I utilized to taunt her and to provoke negative responses from her. Mack and I were victims of boredom, so we used our compressed energy to dance naked around her and to jump over her furniture, while we acted out explosion scenes from war movies as she watched soap operas or other random game shows. My father worked a lot of hours and relied on our grandmother to watch over us. However, my grandmother was an elderly woman, and she did not have the energy to keep up with us. Mack and I were left with a lot of idle time, and used that time to play around in the devil's workshop. I thought inappropriately about girls and sexual acts in ways that were far too advanced for my nine-year-old mind.

My father tried to keep us entertained and happy when he was not working, but his work schedule was merciless; he had to work a lot of overtime because he was trying to purchase a home in Wilson before my mom and Deon joined us in NC. Grandma Lillie's neighborhood was segregated, so we didn't see any white children until school hours or until we ventured to the other side of the railroad tracks into a completely different world. The town reminded me of scenes from the movies *Mississippi Burning or In the Heat of the Night,* and the mood of the town was very depressing to me. I went from fellowshipping with white people in church, playing with them in my neighborhood, and talking to them on a daily basis in Fall River to rarely seeing them outside of school hours.

My apprehension about my new home, along with what I was hearing from my mother and my cousin, taught me to be anxious about interacting with whites in the South. My mom warned us to watch what we say around white people in NC. My mom had experienced racism in the South because she had lived during a vastly different time, and understandably, she feared the worst for us based on her experiences in NC. I was too young to comprehend racism, but my mom's warnings made me a little skeptical of whites in the South. I never fully embraced this fear though, nor did I exhibit any apprehension when I was in the company of white people. My mom's words made me feel like life was unfair, so I favored and supported criminals or people who had to rise up against this preconceived unfair system. I viewed life from a warped perspective, and I embraced a victim's mentality, as if the world owed me something. I wanted to blame others for my negative outlook.

We lived in poverty for a short span of time, but I had a family who loved me unconditionally. It was unfair that we were poor, but I had an abundance of love. There are some rich kids with a lot of material wealth, but their parents fail to display that unconditional love. Is this situation fair to the rich kids? There are a lot of unfair situations that individuals face. We still have the choice to alter our dismal situations; we can change proactively or complain reactively. Life experiences have taught me that life is not fair for blacks, whites, or any other ethnic groups, but God still requires us to strive for righteousness and fairness in all circumstances. God creates a balance, and everything happens for a reason, whether good or bad. My life's philosophy was vastly different during my elementary, middle, and high school years though. I do not remember a great deal about that first elementary school year of my life in Stantonsburg. I remembered excelling academically and getting paddled almost every other week.

I also remember the hatred I felt toward my father when he spanked me, but I hated even more to hear his words during those spankings: "This hurts me more than it will hurt you" or "Are you going to do it again?" Those phrases drove me crazy along with the pain from the leather belt that was embroidered with the name "Jimmy." My parents were dedicated to being our constant teachers. They used moral reasoning and spiritual teachings to develop positive behavior and to transform us into young Christians and productive citizens. My father often informed me that his discipline and purpose for disciplining us came from the Bible.

> *"Spare the rod, spoil the child"*
> ~ *Proverbs 13:24*

My father would say, with calm resolve, "I am not trying to raise some little hoodlums," and I joked with Mack that I am a "thug, not some old school hoodlum." A hoodlum sounded like a 1970s term, and I did not want to be associated with that. In my young, naïve mind, a "thug" sounds better. Mack and I were very creative, and we used that creativity to act out fighting scenes, recreating movies like Die Hard. I made a point to play the bad guys who attempted to kill John McClane.

We also became frontline soldiers in our make-believe war

stories by jumping over booby-trapped ditches, by shooting at each other using broomsticks as A-Ks, and by throwing pine combs to serve as hand grenades. We painted our faces with mud, taking our minds far from our mundane lives in Stantonsburg. We wrote scripts for our movies, and we acted out our dying scenes with heart-felt words like, "save yourself brother, I love you" while grimacing as if we were in real death throes. Mack and I were inseparable, and we used acting as our escape. Acting would continue to be my escape as I started to wear masks in the future. We would walk the long, dark railroad tracks at night to see who got scared first, while telling each other phony ghost stories. Imagination is more powerful than experience in some situations.

Nightmare on Elm Street and *Poltergeist* had me fascinated about ghosts. I watched so much television during that school year that my creativity originated from images on TV, the demon tube. Television introduced me to sex, and the way boys and girls made each other feel great through touching and kissing. At nine years old, I wanted to have a girlfriend rather than spend time reading scholastic books and solving the math problems in our workbooks. The problem was that Mack and I found ourselves liking the same girls, but I guess that indicates that we both had great taste in girls. I was a charismatic trickster to win favor with girls because my goal was to beat Mack and to woo the same girl he liked. This persuasive use of words helped me immensely as I evolved personally and professionally throughout my existence. Lessons can be learned from any negative situations and poor behaviors from our past, so I constantly explored past experiences to extract positive lessons and tips.

I was fairly innocent in those days, besides occasional outbursts or talking in class. Life was relatively peaceful and simple in Stantonsburg. Classmates seemed to love me because I won favor with my athletic ability, bad boy demeanor, and northern accent. Life is so unpredictable because blessings sometimes can be the start of many storms and future darkness. The school year concluded, and my dad, Mack, and I traveled up north to Fall River to celebrate my mother's graduation from Bristol Community College and to reconnect with our charismatic leader, Deon.

To my surprise, Deon was in no hurry to move down to NC. In hindsight, Deon understood the mental trappings of people living in Wilson; some people in Wilson dream no bigger than Wilson and settle for conformity even though they have many options. In my opinion, some people living in Wilson fail to raise their thinking above their small city successes and fame that they acquired; but people thinking in Wilson is synonymous to conformed thinkers throughout our world—masked to a world of fear—never pursuing their inner dreams. We should all raise our thinking above our current state and strive for an unimaginable goal to rise us above our temporary situation. My mother was the first person who taught me any realistic academic success when she graduated with her associate's degree, so she gave me some insight into a world of higher education—witnessing the smiling faces and stimulating conversations failed to be interpreted by my young ears and undeveloped mind.

My mom rejected our impoverished situation and the ghetto-minded perspective of some neighbors by committing to college and graduating with honors; she bolstered an impressive 3.8 GPA while dealing with financial pressure and brief separation from her husband and two handsome sons. I was so proud of her because I viewed degrees as an impossible feat among African Americans, even though I did not understand the difference of an associate, a bachelor, a master, or a doctorate degree. I did not observe many blacks within her graduating class, so I was left feeling that it must be very difficult to obtain a college degree. My mother was the only person whom I knew with a college degree, and most of the people I interacted with spoke about sports and getting paper or money. People were so excited at my mom's graduation, and this excitement made me even more fearful of the graduation process from high school and college.

I felt special knowing that my mother had graduated from

college, but I also felt afraid that I might never accomplish the same feat, thus becoming a failure in my parents' eyes. My mom wanted me to be a medical doctor, so college was always a topic of discussion in our household; we were all expected to attend and to graduate from college. My mother was proud of her accomplishment, and she vowed to pursue a bachelor's degree when she moved back to NC.

However, my mom decided to adopt the famous break from school line: "I will get a job and work for a while and go back to college next year." Next year turned into next year, and next year eventually turned into never, and to this day, she never returned to college—life happened. Her decision impacted me in a positive manner because I decided never to put things off until later; I do not believe in waiting to next year so I start working on goals as soon as they enter my mind—thanks mom. My mom used her associate's degree to face the demanding healthcare field because my mom was driven to assist people in need.

My mom and Deon traveled back to NC, so we could continue to build together as a robust family unit. We were all excited because my dad had a high-paying job at Bridgestone/Firestone, and we were in the process of closing on our first home in Wilson, NC, in the same neighborhood of our cousins, Ced, Torey, and Regina. We were beginning to live the so-called "American dream," not knowing what the American dream truly means to a young, middle-class, and an uneducated black family in a city vastly different than Fall River.

Lessons Learned

There are three known learning styles: visual, kinesthetic, and auditory. Visual learning is the ability to comprehend concepts or ideas through imaginary. Kinesthetic learning requires an individual to grasp concepts and principles by physical activity or actions rather than viewing or listening. Auditory learning depends on hearing and speaking as a way of learning. I feel to a degree that I embody all three, but visual learning appeared to be the most effective learning style for me. During my elementary school years, I observed my impoverished environment, observed behaviors and words from power players within my convoluted school setting, observed ways to manipulate teachers and girls, and observed sexual images; and thug behavior in music videos, movies, and television shows. I believed my eyes would not deceive me—I could not trust the heart because I did not trust my hidden self.

I felt my eyes were more reliable than words spoken by others. My eyes never lied to me or taunted me about my character, so I formed my perspectives through observation. My parents did not realize the impact my environment and my experiences had on my young development. It is imperative for parents and teachers to understand the learning styles of others and to teach to those learning styles rather than teaching from a one-dimensional perspective. We must be willing to implement effectual and positive strategies when we recognize situations that impact our kids negatively; they are, after all, the future leaders of our society. If we invest in our youth, we are investing in a more productive future culture. My visual learning taught me to value acceptance, and I saw pleasurable images that led me to sex, drugs, crime, and other perverse behaviors before 13 years of age. A shaky foundation can cause young people to grow up too fast and pursue adult lives, while exhibiting the maturity of a child.

Chapter 5

The Chapel

The Birth of My Crew

"Age is an issue of mind over matter. If you don't mind, it doesn't matter"

> *~ Mark Twain*

As we reunited and adjusted as a single unit family, my parents purchased their first home at 2104 Shamrock Drive in Wilson, NC. I thought we were the Flintstones, and I planned on having a "Yabba Dabba Doo" time in our new home—no more living in petite apartments. I was in a middle-class neighborhood, and I planned on readjusting my thinking to a more positive perspective. When you have a poor mental foundation, your thinking will always be skewed in a more negative fashion, seeking poor situations or the wrong people to build your exterior rather than to renovate the interior. I still yearned for acceptance among my peers, and I could not escape that uncontrollable addiction for school fame. The infamous Wilson Chapel apartment projects were located in the heart of our new middle-class environment, and most of the middle-class children in that neighborhood claimed "The Chapel" as their home rather than being proud of their middle-class locale.

"The Chapel" received more respect in the streets and the claim gave individuals more street credibility. I did not care that it associated me with living in low-income apartments; I preferred to be respected by my peers—I lived impoverished for years anyway. What you claimed and where you were from was very significant to gaining respect from classmates and other individuals whom I respected throughout Wilson. I was new to this environment: a predominately African American neighborhood and school system, where it appeared that peers cared more about your fighting skills rather than your scholastic knowledge and achievement.

Regina, Torey, and Ced lived up the street from our new residence, and Ced was extremely popular in and outside of the neighborhood. The females loved his swag, and the males relished over his athletic abilities in basketball and his overall charisma with beautiful girls. Ced was extremely gifted on the basketball court; he was making two-handed slams in middle school while standing at 5'11 (height). He also had a high arching jump shot that gave opponents difficulty when he flicked the ball off his hands with his quick release, making his game unstoppable over competitors.

Everybody seemed to flock toward him, and he brought life to family gatherings with his silky walk and his confident talk, making him conspicuous around various circles. I aspired to be like Ced because I wanted people to love me, as they appeared to love him. I was singing, "If I can be like Ced, the way he moved, the way he grooved, if I can be like Ced" because in my mind, Ced was going to be better than Michael Jordan; we had the best basketball player in our family. That was my young mind's perspective, but life happened and Ced was deterred from that dream—never finishing school and not living past 38. Some kids were interested in knowing me due to Ced being my cousin.

This relationship gave me instant respect throughout this new neighborhood. I made friends fairly easy, but it brought unwelcomed drama at times as well. I was approached by Johnnie B (JB), one of the more popular kids within this location during my first month living on Shamrock Drive. He asked me, "Do you really know that Judo (grappling form of martial arts) crap?" JB was witty and very clever, and he was the kid to know in the neighborhood. It appeared that everybody loved JB, so I did not want to get on his bad side or become his enemy. So, I was startled by his question, and I reluctantly said, "yeah." He swiftly responded with, "Show me a move then."

Without thinking clearly about my actions, I grabbed his arm and performed a hip toss that sent him crashing violently to the ground. I stunned him because I noticed the increase size of his pupils and a brief grimace on his face. I was thinking that I messed up by performing this move, but apparently, JB thought it was cool because he asked me to show him the move again. Instantly, we became friends, and I admired JB's personality and funny sense of humor. He was impressed by my fighting prowess, and he appeared to be genuine—I embraced him as a brother. JB told people I could fight, and the word spread throughout our neighborhood; and I was revered as a cool kid—fighting was my ticket in the hood and eventually to a crew.

When I met other peers throughout the neighborhood, the story was embellished and made me appear even tougher. They were saying that, "I heard you could perform flying kicks like Karate Kid" or "You got moves like Bruce Lee," all exaggeration, but germane to my reception among peers. This gave me some instant street credibility because everyone perceived me as a great fighter without witnessing me in an actual brawl. This experience introduced me to the power of information, and the power information provides an individual when it is spread in a positive manner through gossip or grapevine communication. Gossip is extremely beneficial to the dissemination of information to a target population, and it was advantageous toward trying to establish a name in school. Some classmates respected me through grapevine messages, and I became known as someone not afraid to fight—no fear makes you famous.

I learned that perceived toughness has its pros and cons because this phenomenon brought me some unwanted enemies. I learned at a young age to stay on top of rumors that involve me because rumors can be crucial to one's rep (reputation), positively and negatively. I was always conscious of my rep or how I was perceived in the streets and among other classmates. I had a way with persuasive words and impressionable mannerisms, so I was dedicated to the art of rhetorical power. Persuasion is influential power, and this power had a way of benefiting me in multiple relationships (i.e. friends, parents, or girls) or confrontational situations. I made a point to associate with students whom I thought were popular among other students or perceived as tough guys. I learned to be cool and cordial with many, but I was very selective with the people I chose to associate with—proper networking is huge even as a minor.

I acted as if I was too mature or too grown to associate with some people on a regular basis. On the contrary, I needed attention and needed to feel accepted so I was the immature individual among my classmates. I formed young and unstructured crews with no real sense of direction; crews typical formulated by similar interest and peer status (popularity). The best-dressed students hung together, bullies together, so-called pretty girls together, and etc. All of these informal groups were called "crews." Some crews spilled over to other unstructured crews, for instance, I was an athlete, part-time bad boy, and had an uncanny ability to woo the girls as well; so I associated with multiple alliances. My crew had a lot of characteristics, but we were about the girls, fighting, and being cool . . . whatever that means.

I learned that all crews have unspoken rules, and we were observant of each other to make sure that we all conformed to these undisclosed rules. The requirements for our crew were simple: we must be able to pull chicks (get females to like us), we must be able to fight or be unafraid to fight for anyone in the crew, and we must be able to stay true (loyal) to the crew. Our crew consisted of other young boys from "The Chapel" when we are at odds with other neighborhoods, but JB, Mack, Kelsie, BJ, Kedron,

Tony, Deon, and Ramon were whom I trusted within my small "Chapel crew." Derrick, AJ, and Trevlan were an extension to my Chapel crew; they came from Snowden Drive, and I trusted them as much as I did my Chapel crew. We were all extended brothers.

We were devious, destroying unfinished homes in our locale with reacted war scenes. We would jump in and out of uncompleted windows, like we were modern day GI Joes. I threw dirt bombs and kicked in doors as if I was a CIA agent. My mind got lost at times, and I thought I was really acting out a drug war or a militaristic style war. We also played battle of the courts (e.g., challenging people on their basketball courts to a game) over the weekend, traveling with a ball and bottles of water to challenge other young boys on their home turf. We would play basketball for hours (i.e., 3-10 pm) with minimal food and small water breaks.

Survival skills learned from Fall River helped me adjust to life in "The Chapel," and I felt mentally older than some of my peers. I felt that I had been exposed to more grown up behavior than those in my crew; Deon's goal was to make me strong and to educate me about students my age—he trusted nobody. At night, I shifted my mind from a young crew to a much older crew that consisted of Deon, Tony (brother from another mother), and Kedron; they were all older than me. Deon called this crew, "Midnight Society."

In the calm of the night, we snuck out of our Christian household to egg houses and to ring doorbells of sleeping neighbors that we considered evil or stupid. I developed close friendships with random circles of friends during my elementary and middle school years, but we never really discussed any positive academic or career possibilities about our futures. We were more focused on the present trappings and temptations rather than future possibilities of going to college and being productive citizens.

We explored the idea of sex early and often, and we associated being a rapper, an athlete, or a thug with the ability to seduce and to sex beautiful girls. No one spoke about grades, and the possibility of going to college to earn a bachelor's degree, majority of us came from homes of hardworking parents who possessed minimal or no secondary education. My parents encouraged me to pursue college, but a picture is worth a thousand words; and I saw hard work, drugs, and street guys as temporary success, not individuals with college degrees.

I had no sample pool of college-educated individuals against whom I could compare my theory, so I accepted my hypothesis—college degrees are for the birds. I viewed college as a stepping-stone to the NBA or NFL, and if that plan failed I would work at the local Firestone plant like my father. My dreams were limited, so my thinking became limited. Firestone paid up to $25 an hour at that time, and a lot of citizens in Wilson were trying hard to obtain employment at that plant. Families lived nicely from the wages earned at Firestone, so I was not opposed to making that type of money. My father worked out there and generated a handsome income, but he was required to work swing shifts (e.g., 8-4, 4-12, and 12-8). His crazy schedule gave me ample opportunity to get into trouble when he was at work designing tires for SUVs and compact cars. My mom got off work at five or six o'clock at times, so Deon was left to supervise Mack and me with little success.

Deon was busy chasing girls or beating us for not complying to his set rules. This small window of time provided me with the unfortunate opportunity to explore sex in middle school, hone my fighting skills, and learn about drugs. "The Chapel" and Wilson introduced me to a world that my parents were not ready for. They had no idea what we were exposed to because my young friends and I were trying to be adults. My parents trusted me because I knew how and when to charm my parents and other adults. I was always respectful to adults, so a lot of adults perceived me as a well-mannered kid—looks can be deceiving. Overall, I think I had a loving heart, but my actions contradicted that heart by committing crimes, violent acts, and other devious behaviors to mirror and fit in with my crew.

I was obsessed with my neighborhood, and the small world around me. If I could be known in Wilson, I would feel as if I accomplished something great. I made the honor roll several times in Wilson during elementary and middle school, but that excitement was not enough to sustain and to reinforce favorable academic behavior. I loved pleasing my parents by making high grades; however, the desire to appease my peers was much stronger than the appeal of satisfying my parents.

Honor students were recognized as nerds, and I had no desire to be grouped in that class of students. I felt ashamed when I made the honor roll. I became self-effacing about my grades because I did not want the attention from others. I was too cool for the honor roll, and bad boys did not care about grades or make excellent grades, for that manner. This slow-witted perspective prompted me to settle for mediocrity, so I stopped trying to make the honor roll. I failed some tests on purpose, so I could receive less than an "A;" the acceptance of my classmates meant that much to me.

I was revered for my lack of fear to fight, being able to win a fight, or being superior in sports rather than excelling academically within the classroom—their recognition and homage mattered that much to me. My father introduced Mack and me to the aggressive and violent game of football when we entered the fourth grade. Some students correlated aggressive football players to exceptional brawlers, and aggression became my style of play in all sports—power, speed, and quickness were my advantageous skills—not height and not size. My skills gave me a superior advantage when fighting and playing competitive sports; I functioned with no fear, which granted me a psychological advantage—much more important than a physiological leverage.

The mind is stronger than the body, so the focus should lie in the thinking not the abilities. My father constantly reiterated this statement, "Fear no man, but God." I turned those spiritual words into a livable mantra that fed my negative and positive actions as I maneuvered throughout life's experiences. On the football field, my pint-size body was fearless, and I averaged about two touchdowns a game the second year of midget league football. My success got the attention of some adults who praised my performance, and it drew seductive looks from the team cheerleaders. I don't know if they liked me due to my performance or dazzling looks, but either way, I did not care—I adored the attention and recognition. This love for attention or deadly sin of pride became a significant contributor to poor future decisions.

Past observations from television, projects, and crew conversations had me curious about kissing and touching girls. I transformed that lustful thought into sexual behaviors; I practiced kissing and rubbing curious cheerleaders after several football games. I would sneak off with girls to solitary settings while my parents were preoccupied in conversations with other adults . . . sometimes as they were engulfed in conversations with the girls' parents. The scary thing is that some parents viewed kissing as no big deal, but kissing can create a sexual attitude and mindset that influence more serious sexual conduct. Most sexual liaisons precluded from passionate kisses and aggressive touches. I learned that it is vital to protect the mind, and small sexual encounters can assist in the development of more risky sexual thoughts and behavior. Everything starts small, a little flirting and a little kissing, eventually transforms to sex and sex without condoms.

I am overemphasizing this point because I want readers, especially young readers to understand the seriousness of feeding your mind with negative material. Eventually, I started making more self-destructive sexual decisions when I entered middle school. In "The Chapel," it was important to lose your virginity because my cohort would attack my masculinity, suggesting that I was "queer" or "gay" because I was still a virgin; ironically, I felt less than a man by not following the in-crowd and losing my virginity. Growing up there were no badges of honor or medals being passed out for remaining a virgin, so I was trying to lose my virginity as soon as possible. Still, fear deterred me for a while.

I could not seem to repudiate my parents' biblical teachings that "Sex is a sin before marriage." My parents' rhetoric worked early on in my life, but my crew's words and thoughts carried more weight than theirs, and I wanted to appease my crew. My sexual thoughts and indiscretions started with images and words that I fed my mind with on a daily basis. Eventually, all those formalized images and words transformed into uncontrollable and disastrous sexual passions within my heart. When we feed our minds with negative thoughts, negative desires build in our hearts. I adopted the vernacular of my crew and my environment, so I incorporated swear words and derogatory terms into my speech patterns.

I dumbed down my vocabulary with those offensive words because it took no thought to say such ugly words—those words are fillers and require no critical and creative thought patterns. I displayed ignorance in my speech as well as some of my mannerisms. I studied and analyzed the pulse and behavior of the streets, and I was dedicated to mimicking serious players throughout my neighborhood and my city. I changed my walk, my talk, and my attitude to fit my idea of a "thug" or perceived thug behavior. I fell in love with the hip-hop culture, BET, MTV, gangster movies, and local drug dealers who wore eight ball jackets. I dreamed about purchasing an eight ball leather jacket and a dookie chain, so I could have people stand in awe of me like I stood in awe of those dope dealers at high school basketball games. The mind is a sponge, and it soaks up whatever information correlates to some fashion of success, negative or positive . . . I wanted to be someone adored by many.

During the late elementary to middle school stages of life, individuals might adopt behaviors and masks that guide them in a positive or negative direction, so this stage of development was critical to my discovery of identity. At this stage of my life, I was committed to being like some of the famous rap groups and rappers of the late 80s and early 90s era, NWA, Wu-Tang Clan, and Tupac Shakur to name a few. Mack and I would act out the scenes from the popular gangster movie "Colors." We always picked a gang member to portray; I was "Rocket," a murderous

Crip from the highly acclaimed movie that depicted known gangs in Los Angeles, California.

This mindset perpetuated a mentally that lead me to associate with the "BLOODS," while attending Methodist College to play football. My parents had no idea how music videos and movies were impacting my impressionable young mind, in a negative manner, and they probably were unaware of the programs being watched behind their backs and under their roof. Sometimes my brothers and I would watch HBO and Showtime when our parents were sound asleep to educate ourselves about sex, knives, guns, and street life—street lessons were learned at night—a time when our minds should have been at rest. I learned how to imitate gangsters, while my parents were in their rooms on their knees praying for our safety and future success.

My parents tried their best to warn me about the dangers of sex, but they were oblivious to the changes in my behavior, in regards to sex and other street life decisions. They taught me that sex was a sin and to refrain from sex until marriage. However, TV, crew, and some family members made sex seem very exciting and enchanting to me. My interest toward sex grew in the fourth grade when I witnessed Rosie Perez breasts in the movie *Do the Right Thing* as my mom attempted to cover my eyes during the scene that Mookie rubbed ice cubes on her stiffened nipples.

Once again, those images resonated in my psyche, and I wanted to be Mookie for that particular scene. In "The Chapel," I became vulnerable to these images because my parents' work life provided me with free time away from their constant supervision and teachings. The so-called "American Dream" provided me with too much unsheltered idle time. Images from my past television experiences were ingrained in my mind, and the lovemaking and violent scenes appeared real to me, coming to life within my poorly developed mind. Those actors and actresses appeared happy before and after the physical act of having sex, so I became more convinced than ever that sex is a great encounter rather than this deadly sin my parents warned me to avoid.

My personal experiences with sex altered the way I would communicate with my future children about sex. My parents taught from a spiritual perspective without combating the visual images on TV and the influences of my crew, so I make it my business to manage my children's limited television time, They are allowed five hours of viewing time out of the 168 hours in the week. We are very selective about their television programs, and we do not allow televisions in their bedrooms. My wife and I limit their television viewing, and I explain questionable scenes to my children. We make it a point to watch television with them, trying to make it a positive learning experience. I also will not allow them to roam the neighborhood without supervision due to the temptations that arise when children have idle time and are without proper supervision.

I was still very young when I started thinking about sex; I was two years shy of entering middle school. I was attending Vinson-Bynum elementary school, and Vinson-Bynum was a school of firsts for me: first kiss, first in-school and out-of-school suspensions, first time I did not make the honor roll, first time I thought of selling drugs, and the first time my pride was shaken in a fistfight.

Lessons Learned

An environment does not make an individual, but one's environment can be a strong contributing factor to that individual's behavior. I cared about adapting and fitting into my environment, so I quickly embraced the ideals of my crew rather than rejecting negative situations or behaviors. Pictures are painted all around us, and we tend to gravitate to the pictures viewed on a daily basis. My locale presented pictures of bad boys and athletes prospering, and this notion of prospering mirrored the growing gangster rap and drug culture I was emerged in. These images matched my observation from Fall River and television due to my visual learning abilities—trusting my eyes more than my parents' spiritual rhetoric and guidance.

My parents thought the "American Dream" would provide our family with some solace and deter their kids from the street life. Their version of the "American Dream," rewarded them with a new home, more money, and the ability to purchase nicer items, but it provided me with more free time and more temptations. This new life forced my mother to work long hours and created opportunities for me to have lots of unsupervised idle time. When we were living in an impoverished environment in Fall River, my mom watched us more closely.

We were more protected then from the temptations that arose during idle time in that environment than we were in the seemingly secure environment of our new neighborhood. The lesson to be learned is that more money does not substitute for quality time as a family. This is not a shot at my parents, but a reality. We must always focus on what our children are being exposed to and limit their interactions with negative individuals and circumstances. Because my interactions with unsavory characters and potentially dangerous situations were not limited, I decided to raise the stakes and take more uncalculated risks.

Chapter 6

First Puppy Love Had Me Trying New Things

A Willingness to Take Uncalculated Risks

"Living at risk is jumping off the cliff and building your wings on the way down"

~ Ray Bradbury

The first time I experienced a new situation or a new thing, it had a profound influence on me—becoming a momentous image in my mind. My most memorable first moments as a child were surrounded by poor decision-making that would assist in the molding of my mask in future stages of my life. Fourth grade was the first year that I went to school and cared about how my attire looked in front of classmates—not about name-brand apparel but about wearing acceptable attire for my subculture—I had to be fresh. The night before school, I would neatly layout my pants on the bed, shirt laid slightly above my pants, and sneakers meshed below the outfit on the floor, to visualize the outfit on my wiry body—it all starts in the mind.

I envisioned the outfit on my body as I galloped proudly

through the school hallways. Sometimes, Mack and I would model our outfits for each other, while we tried to perfect our pimp walk (slow stroll with supreme confidence); I tried to model Rocket's walk from *Colors*, walking extra slow to appease the girls and force the boys to mean mug (stare with envy or ill intent). I felt the most charismatic boys walked extra slow, and I was striving to be the first boy in school to date the so-called prettiest girl—instant recognition comes from that feat. This attitude perpetuated more damaging behavior, and this attitude failed to mesh well with this honor student persona—my grades begin to suffer.

The negative behavior heightened in my personality and demeanor, and my quality grades quickly diminished during my fourth and fifth grade school years. I was beginning to displease my parents, but on the flipside, I was beginning to gain more respect among my fellow classmates. Some girls thought I was sexy, and some boys thought I was tough in their fantasy world of bad boys. I spoke tough, and I was very quick to support my words with physical actions when prompted to react in that volatile fashion. Vinson-Bynum elementary was a combination of low-income and middle-income families, and some low-income students from known projects bullied other students from middle-income neighborhoods or better living conditions if they came off as soft. I claimed "The Chapel," so I could be, once again, a part of that low-income world and project worldview. The Chapel was a rough segment of Wilson, so we were perceived as rugged for claiming to reside in that neighborhood.

I was small in stature, a lean individual with quick hands and a fearless approach toward life, and I used these attributes to win favor with other bad boys in my environment. My brothers and I trained for years in Judo, and we always sparred and grappled within the comfort of our modest home, attempting to hone our fighting skills on a daily basis. Deon and I did not want to be perceived as weak, so we implemented push-ups, weighted-curls, and sit-ups to our homemade strength-training regimen. I clung to my father's words of fearing no man, but I used them for negative actions. I never backed down from an individual who attempted to challenge me in any way. Whether the challenge was verbal or physical, I was determined that no one would be able to shut me up or beat me up. I learned throughout life that every man or woman has a weakness. There is no possibility for growth or success without an awareness of one's weaknesses.

My weakness was the desire to fit in and be accepted into the popular circles; I did not comprehend that to be a weakness— it was a way to street fame. I took my father's advice to fear no man and walked around school with a chip on my shoulder. I made dumb and irrational choices as if I had something to prove to my classmates. I never felt adequate enough to associate with them, so I needed to become someone who fits into their perfect circles—frankly, I assumed that I was just too square and needed to become a circle to fit in their circle and stay crew.

Frequently, I attended church and respected adults in that holy environment, but at times, I disrespected and failed to listen to my teachers throughout the school day. I repeatedly got counseled for speaking out of turn during class or passing notes to other credulous classmates. My big mouth created a lot of problems for me during my school years, especially as a child because I was very loquacious and always gossiping with random people about other random people—I was a walking soap opera.

My mom instructed me to read the book of James in the *Holy Bible* because she thought I needed to tame my tongue—she would say, "Your mouth is going to be the death of you, and you gossip more than a girl." The book of *James* speaks of the power of the tongue, but that book taught me that no man has the individual power to tame the tongue—I am man, and I lacked that power. However, God has the power to tame the tongue, and God provides us with abilities to use self-control and sound judgment prior to speaking. I learned that words were extremely powerful, and words have the power to speak life or to speak death into a person or a situation—law of attraction (i.e., love rewards love). I strongly believe words can generate positive or negative energy in our lives, so we should focus on delivering favorable tones and positive rhetoric on a daily basis. One day at Vinson-Bynum during the fourth grade, my tongue got me into an altercation with Tim. Tim was an instigator, and had some local street credibility among his Park Avenue classmates.

Park Avenue breeds tough and robust individuals who lack fear and possess an uncaring attitude. Nowadays, Park Avenue is a segment of Wilson that can become a very sinister locale at night. During my Vinson-Bynum days, we were more concerned about getting jumped rather than any dangerous use of weapons. Gunplay never entered the equation until my high school years.

Tim was a white boy, and it was rare to envision tough little white boys not afraid of little black boys at Vinson-Bynum during my school era. Fall River had a city filled with tough little white boys, but in Wilson, I was engrossed in an environment filled with tough little black boys. Tim was an outlier to this preconceived norm because he actually intimidated some black boys at Vinson-Bynum—not to make it a race thing, but to demonstrate the difference is in the culture not the color.

I admired Tim prior to our unexpected conflict, and I had no personal issues with him. However, Tim was trying to impress some girl one day at lunch, and I must have said something that provoked him to call me a "little punk." I was shocked and felt perplexed by his comment; it caught me off guard. My little world started to spin, and I was caught in an unfamiliar and very unique situation—I might have to fight and to prove myself, and he did not fear me.

Blatantly, Tim ridiculed me in front of our classroom cohort who proceeded to laugh and to instigate me to fight in this unfamiliar situation. Surprised, I did not know what to do—I attempted to laugh off his comments, and said, "You can't beat this little punk," not realizing those words would soon initiate a fight between us. Tim apparently was out for blood, and I was unaware of his bad intentions. Tim smiled, and said, "alright." I thought that was the end of the conversation, and I quietly sat at my designated lunchroom table smiling and flirting in the company of some random girls until the teacher told us to line up for our return to class.

I calmly gathered my belongings and proceeded to the front of the line as we headed back to class, not knowing that Tim was plotting on me the whole time. He was devising an intricate plot in the back of the line, while I was galloping through the hallway with no care in the world—conceptualizing that I stunted him in the lunchroom and thinking I am the man, forget Tim. Tim was out to make an example out of me and to test my ability to brawl.

At this time, I was still living off my Judo myths and hype that lingered from my brief encounter with JB in his backyard. This incident gave me a pass until I met a motivated Tim in Mrs. Sharpe's classroom, who informed classmates of his plans. I find it funny how nobody ever told me that Tim was planning to hit me when I entered the classroom, and these so-called friends were also encouraging him to hit me. A warning would have definitely prepared me for the hard hit that would shake my face and test my confidence to fight and to overcome this unexpected challenge.

Mrs. Sharpe was lagging behind the class, so she could monitor the slackers coming from lunch and needing a bathroom break. I found out that Tim told Mrs. Sharpe that some boys were clowning around in the bathroom to gain an extra jump on her back to our class. I walked in the class, laughing and playing around with Tyneisha and some other classroom peers when Tim sailed a right haymaker to my jaw and shook my foundation, and this punch took me completely out of my comfort zone or mental element. This was the first time somebody hit me without warning. I braced and clinched as I saw him out of my peripheral vision, so the punch failed to land flush on my jaw.

However, the power generated from the punch slid me backwards on a poster tucked underneath my feet, and I was fighting violently to maintain my balance and my composure. Once I gathered my thoughts and understood what was going on, I fired off a quick left and right hand cross to create space and distance in this awkward and intimidating situation; this surprised Tim. He stumbled back, and I clamped down on him with two solid uppercuts. Tim grasped me after I released several more punches, and the fight transitioned from a boxing to a wrestling affair.

I had fast hands, but I lacked any knockout power to drop him or most of my peers at that age. I lacked the ability and motivation to break away from his grasps because my heart was beating inside my chest from the overwhelming excitement and anxiety that came from this situation. Eventually, students broke up the fight as Mrs. Sharpe arrived to class with no resistance from me. I was ready for this shocking ordeal to be over with, not realizing this incidence awarded me three days in after-school suspension and a leather belt lashing from my father. I learned two things that day: people who like you will be quick to say you won the fight, and people who do not like you will be quick to say you lost the fight. This experience meshes well with the notion that it is impossible to please everyone and encourage everyone to like you.

In business and in life, respect is more valuable than someone liking you, and respect stems from being true to yourself and being true to your God-given purpose; we should use that purpose to continue working toward fairness and equality. My self-esteem was predicated upon the in-crowd, so it bothered me when some students suggested that I lost the fight. It made me question my performance in the brawl, and I was worried about maintaining my small city popularity. There comments had me questioning myself on a daily and nightly footing. I should have evaluated and tried to learn what got me in this situation rather than trying to figure out how to keep students praising and liking me. I cared more about how classmates viewed me as a fighter rather than being intellectual or different (e.g., walking away from fights). I became determined to make students view me as a bad boy or thug, and suspensions from the bus and school shortly followed and piled up.

The suspensions forced my parents to adjust their busy

work schedules, placing them at an inconvenience. And, it truly bothered me that I was getting into trouble, but I cared and focused more about fitting in and gelling with my peers—my parents' feelings became an afterthought. I was bothered by the idea that I might be perceived as uncool or unpopular among my cohort. As crazy as it sounds, I would rather upset my parents at that juncture of my life because school was my existence and being respected by friends was all that mattered in my short life span. School years felt like an eternity, and it was the only world that was of importance to me at that time. It was imperative that I fit in with the popular students or individuals I judged to be relevant to my popularity and street fame.

I was willing to hide my true identity and conform to the in-crowd by emulating their attitudes and behaviors to fit their poorly sculpted molds. The donning of a thug life mask became too easy to acquire, and the mask started feeling authentic and enjoyable to me. I had my first girlfriend (Monica) in the fourth grade. She had a black father and a white mother, so classmates labeled her as the "mixed girl." I thought she was pretty, and I took a liking to her and developed thoughts beyond the innocence of normal 10-year olds. My parents perceived it as a harmless relationship; we were just kids my parents thought—nothing bad could come of the relationship. We were young kids, but some of our conversations were far from rated G.

Majority of our actions were innocent in nature, but our conversations, and my thoughts were as raw promiscuous adults; I thought about having sex with her and what it might feel like to lay naked with her—nothing positive can come from thoughts like this, nothing. I had no idea what sex was about or how to perform the act, but I was sure that it would be a great feeling to share with my girlfriend. I believed as long as you could connect love with the sexual act, then sex would be okay in God's eyes. Now, it is my belief that love does not make wrong situations or what we feel as love to be okay—love is powerful, but we cannot place love on situations and accept it as right. Love does not cover sin because I could commit a multitude of sins and use love to support it.

My girlfriend and I would profess the words, "I love you," mimicking what adults would say to each other or to how people acted on TV. My relationship with my wife eventually taught me what real love is, and it did not have anything to do with sex—sex is just an added plus—a gift to a married couple. However, I did feel special dating my girlfriend during my Vinson-Bynum school days. Monica gave me my first kiss on the lips, and I felt the little flurries churning in my stomach; but no music played and no sparkles ignited around us like the depictions and renditions in romantic movies and songs. As the school year came to a close, Monica and I broke up due to a false rumor that put us at odds.

Some of our classmates told her that I was speaking ill words about her mother. She became rightly enraged, and her brothers wanted to cause my body some physical harm. Her brothers were a few years older than me, so I decided to involve my older brother and cousins in this situation. It is funny how rumors can create uncontrollable anger in some individuals, and ultimately cost some individuals their life or freedom. It reminded me of an activity my teacher administered in class when she started with a simple sentence and had students pass the message on to other students quietly in their ears—the message always circles back around in an incorrect manner. I tried to tell her over the phone that the rumor was false, but the conversation quickly turned into a swearing contest between Deon and her brothers as they intercepted our phone call.

Deon formalized a plan for our crew to ride our bikes to Starmount Circle where she and her brothers resided, and it seemed like a great idea as the influential words left Deon's mouth—not realizing, it is suicide to fight on someone's turf. We had no idea what feat lay ahead of us and looking back it was not a very bright idea at all. The crew that was venturing out on this journey to fight consisted of Torey, Deon, Tony, and me. Deon served as the unspoken leader of our crew. He had all the confidence and his forceful personality that commanded our respect. We decided to mount some basic K-Mart bikes as the modern day "Black Posse" and ride 5 miles to fight her brothers in one of the roughest projects in Wilson.

We laughed and played out fight scenarios in our minds, and I felt invincible as we approached the intended destination. I truly felt indestructible and thought we would go there and strike fear in her brothers' hearts by beating them up and laying this matter to rest. When we arrived at their residence, we saw two of her brothers on the porch and a third brother ardently exiting their apartment. I got anxious and nervous as the scene began to unfold. Deon started to smile and to ask, "Let the punk ass nigga on the phone with all the mouth enter the street and try to whoop my ass." When Deon finished his bold spill and tough guy talk, it seemed like the whole neighborhood came alive by the hundreds—maybe an exaggeration, but people came out from everywhere—trepidation halted my brain from thinking straight.

About 5 people came from inside their apartment, and about 15 came from behind their apartment. Her older brother stood on the porch grasping a long and shiny machete that he shielded behind his hamstring. At the time, I was unaware of the long blade he was clutching behind his leg. Deon proceeded with a smile and a bold statement, "I am not afraid, so let's rock," while retrieving a small pocketknife from his jacket for assistance in this endeavor. Her brother sprinted into the street and pulled the machete from behind his baggy pants, and Deon backed away with an uneasy smile and said, "Let's put the knives away nigga."

It is comical as I reflect back now, but it was very frightening during that encounter. I was very quiet and nervous during this ordeal. I started silently praying to myself, attempting to make deals with God: "Please God get us out of this situation, and I will never sin or fight again." This was an unrealistic prayer and deal to make with God, the knower of all things and the ruler of the universe. Deon and her older brother started exchanging inappropriate and unpleasant words in the middle of the street, and I froze up; my attention shifted toward the large crowd starting to besiege us.

Thoughts of death slowly penetrated my young mind, but just minutes before this confrontation I was confidently claiming victory in my mind. Life is so unpredictable, and we have no control of how poor decisions or destructive behaviors will play out. Our poor choices and thug mentalities got me in a situation, where I contemplated death for the first time. I wonder how many people boldly and ignorantly walk into fighting situations, not realizing death is silently and quickly around the corner—paraphrasing the words of the late great rapper, Tupac Shakur.

This was also the first time, I realized that I was no longer invincible, and I sought God for the first time out of desperation in silent prayer. I never let Deon, Tony, or Torey know how scared I was in that moment of despair because I wanted to appear hard and robust in front of my much older crew. I was a fourth grader, associating with middle school and high school subjects for a project brawl. My heart was pounding on the internal structure of my chest. I knew that the end of my life was near, and I was terrified, imagining in my mind how those boys would take turns stomping the life out of my miniature frame with little resistance from me.

Then, right on time, God sent an angel, because some young man took it upon himself to break up the confrontation between both parties and dispersed the hostile crowd. I wonder how many people today would intervene in a brawl rather than use their cell phones to record the incident and then post it to YouTube in hopes of it going viral? The angel God sent was apparently respected among our opponents because they backed away without neither resistance and nor argument as he reasoned with them. I gave no resistance as well. I was overjoyed that we did not have to fight, but Deon did not appear to be afraid during this volatile ordeal.

This was the first time that I realized my older brother might be a little crazy—his faced displayed no fear and left me wondering if this guy believed he was a modern day Greek god—Zeus among us. I stared at Deon as he brandished a smirk on his face, and

I believe a little part of him wanted to know what would have happened in that situation; but not me, I wanted no parts of that situation. I could not figure out if he was happy that that young man came to breakup this potentially dangerous altercation or proud that he showed no fear. Once this young man influenced the crowd of young boys to allow us to retreat from their presence, I mounted my Huffy bike excitedly with the rest of my crew, and high-tailed it out of there.

As we were riding away and changing gears on our special bikes, Deon displayed unpredictable behavior as he smiled and looked back at the crowd getting farther and farther away. Deon uncharacteristically stopped his bike in the middle of the street and positioned himself toward the fleeting crowd. I was getting a little irritated at the smile on his face and his defiant actions because I knew he was up to something sinister. I tried to focus on pedaling my bike faster and faster out of that intimidating project environment.

However, without warning, Deon yelled out, "I smell pussies" to emulate a famous line from a popular movie among our subculture, *House Party*. Next thing I witnessed was a mass of individuals forming as a mob and sprinting with fury toward us like the movie *The Warriors*, and I pedaled my bike even faster and harder, fearing for my ultimate demise as Deon continued to laugh uncontrollably like the "Joker" from *Batman*—this crazy guy had no fear and a small part of me wanted to be like him.

That was the first time I felt a multitude of emotions: fear, excitement, pride, and anger as I pedaled my bike out of that impoverished setting toward the busy Ward Boulevard intersection, which was adjacent to the Wilson mall. As we approached the road, I thought that the immediate danger was behind us, believing wholeheartedly that we made it out of the neighborhood safely. As I was beginning to relax and fight desperately to force oxygen into my young lungs, a black car swerved onto the sidewalk and knocked me off my bike. I was scrambling on the ground in agitated desperation, knowing in the back of my mind that my ex-girlfriend's brothers and fellow project thugs were in that vehicle. Some enormous and demented looking man got out of this bent and battered black car and swung violently at my brother's small head.

I was stunned and did not know what to do, so I ran to a nearby bowling alley to get some help. I went into fight or flight mode, and my body decided to accept the flight fashion. I was terror-stricken about the idea that my brother might be killed; but ignorantly, I arrived to this situation with a hardcore masked persona and ended up feeling like a scared fourth grade little boy who desperately wanted to be at home with his parents and in the midst of their safety and comfort, irony.

> *"Our realities are authentic to us until we are awakened to the world's version of authenticity; sometimes the world's version has a way of smacking us in the mouth with an abundance of truth"*
> ~ *Dr. James Williams*

Lessons Learned

We all gravitate toward specific people or situations in this complex life. As a small child, I drifted toward peers who were perceived as cool or relevant among my peers. I adopted a follower mentality, which prompted me to try new social circles that encouraged bad behavior and which led me to mask myself with a thug persona. From what I had seen in videos, movies, and, to a lesser extent, in real life, thugs sauntered around with good-looking girls, so I was determined to date a beautiful girl for the first time.

The problem is that dating forces young individuals to try to get involved in relationships that are focused mostly around sexual behavior or adult behavior, so I am not a fan of young people dating and claiming titles as boyfriend and girlfriend—speaking from personal ramifications of this mindset. I firmly believe people should not date until they are absolutely comfortable with themselves, and most kids are unsure of themselves until after college—divorce rates and unhappy homes might serve to support my belief. My first girlfriend experience put me on cloud nine and had me indulging in grown up behavior and extremely sexual conversations—creating the desire or thought in my immature mind. The revolving circle of life has a funny way of humbling people who are masked with false identities.

My first girlfriend and kiss lead me to fear death and make unrealistic promises to God. This first time contemplating death had me silently questioning my bad boy demeanor and thug perspective on life. Traumatic events can temporarily alter bad behavior, but one's mind must alter in order to eliminate or minimize that bad behavior permanently. Reflecting back, I learned from my fight encounter that God always provides us a way out, but we must seek out the appropriate route from the intricate conflicts or general situations in our life. We must pay attention to our firsts.

I should have never been allowed to have a girlfriend in the fourth grade, and I should have been the first to apologize on the telephone with her, even though I said nothing wrong—love cools anger. Tension can be calmed with pleasantries in a lot of situations, but evil attracts more evil. Fighting does not solve problems, fighting may temporarily manage problems; but those problems still exist. I never should have ridden my bike to their neighborhood—nothing hardcore about that decision . . . pure stupidity. Many black brothers from my past have died and long been buried from similar ignorant decisions; we must take more time to proactively think before impulsively reacting to others. Proactive thinking eliminates a perpetual thug mindset, but it took me many years and a lot of traumatic events to grasp this logical and profound concept.

Chapter 7

Adopting Criminal Behavior

Trying to Validate my Name

*"A man may wear a thousand faces before he looks
in the mirror and identify the authentic face was
there all the time, hidden in his world of darkness"*
~ *Dr. James Williams*

As I began my fifth grade year, my last year of elementary school before trucking off to Darden-Vick middle school with the anticipated big boys, I was determined to be the top dog (most popular and one of the toughest in the school) during my final year at Vinson-Bynum. However, some geniuses decided to redistrict our schools to move more impoverished students away from wealthier schools in the district, altering my strategic vision of running this subculture of thugs with my crew. Some students from very harsh and economically challenging environments were integrated into our school culture.

Some of these new students were more driven to validate their street cred throughout Wilson than the current students at Vinson-Bynum. Note that nothing related to schoolwork challenged my thinking or the thinking of my peers; our minds were focused on the wrong things. Majority of the new male students were older and already street validated. I heard about some of their legendary fights prior to interacting with them at our school. I convinced myself that I would validate my name and have no fear. Names do not make a person credible in my eyes because I focus more on their actions. I adopted this leadership lesson throughout life, and I still make a conscience effort to authenticate my rhetoric with actions.

However, those students definitely earned my respect, and the respect of many of classmates. CoJack and Dennis were noticeable brothers and two major players in our school environment, both were skilled amateur boxers, known for knockouts in and outside of the boxing ring. For some reason, both of them favored me, so they were never a realistic threat in my eyes. They became a formidable ally during my last year in elementary school; this taught me the power of networking with the power players or appropriate people because knowing street endorsed people, as they were gives one a ghetto pass (access to certain underground cultures) in a dangerous environment—knowing the right people in life gives one a pass with professional credentials.

I remained in survival mode, so I strategized most friendships, fights, and poor decisions in a way that improved my status among current and new classmates. All actions were done with a calculated purpose of fitting in and being popular. All masked individuals expend tremendous effort trying to hide their true identity. What if we utilized all those efforts and energies for positive thinking? We all could be innovators and owners of profitable companies or our lives—many fail to lead their life according to their plans and true potential.

My life was great in the fifth grade, but a kid named Chris remained a true threat to me; he could not stand me for some reason. He was about six-feet tall with a more physically developed frame at the older age of 14 when compared to my customary 11-year old miniature body structure. I knew he was older, bigger, and stronger, but I had a big mouth and talked a lot of jive. I implemented a tactic of avoidance with more physically intimidating foes, not out of fear, but out of strategic brilliance in my opinion. I shifted focus toward appeasing girls and being a crafty class-clown rather than being the boy so quick to fight. I managed my temper throughout the school year, and this plan of action benefited me later on in life in more serious situations. Challenges will force us to adapt or succumb to changes. My father would always say, "You cannot beat everybody, so learn to think with your head not your fists." Even though I tried to exhibit a tough exterior and thug persona, I always listened to sound advice . . . always.

My fear was never in the opponents, only in the outcome. I invested my time into winnable battles that strengthen to validate my name. I placed no stock or value in situations that positioned me to fight someone irrelevant among my peers or to fight someone in solitude. Fighting in seclusion posed too many risks because no one would be there to break up the fight and no one would be there to spread the word about the fight—this is a lose-lose situation. I focused my attention on disrupting classroom teachers rather than fighting bullies. I was being more and more troublesome to my teachers because I assumed that the more unmanageable I appeared in the classroom, the more masculine I was viewed among classmates. Classmates would laugh when I cracked jokes, and it made me feel significant, like I was an in-class standup comedian.

I was no longer seeing my name on the condensed school's honor roll list, and I would not see quality grades until my return to college in 2001. My last year at Vinson-Bynum elementary school was a blur, but three major circumstances stood out: my fight with Sam, my assault on Mrs. Parker, and my lies about having sex to my circle of friends. Sam was one of the neighborhood bullies from "The Chapel" not a charlatan like me, Sam was known for picking on smaller boys; I thought I had a pass because I was no "punk." Sam decided it was wise to disrespect me on the bus one day by thumping my head and talking slick as we traveled home from school—school buses can be a dangerous place for some kids. I had a lot of respect for his fighting prowess, but I did not fear him and trusted that my hand speed could overwhelm his massive size and slow body movements. Deon sharpened my skills daily by boxing and wrestling with me, so he helped to solidify my confidence in brawling with older and bigger individuals.

Deon did not want me to become prey in school, so he was determined to turn me into a predator and a survivor within the school food chain. The toil spent with Deon in our tan-walled bedrooms developed my confidence in critical fighting situations. Deon wanted me to be resilient, and he wanted me to standout when it came to being fearless. It was his twisted way of attempting to make me exceptional, and his way of bestowing valuable knowledge on me. Most of my classmates feared Deon because they perceived him as crazy, and I think he liked it that way; I perceived Deon as crazy and as an innovative genius—he created paper football games and all of our fun activities, but that is another story for another time. Sam would occasionally joke that I needed Deon to fight my battles. Sam's sly innuendos irritated me, but I would smile and say, "whatever" to belittle his sarcasm. However, this particular spring day on our hot and stinky school bus, Sam began to taunt and to physically assault me as peers encouraged him with laughter. I felt utterly disrespected and ridiculed, so I jumped up and yelled out, "I bet I can whoop your ass."

The laughter silenced and seriousness drove the movement of this conversation. He said, "Alright, we will see when we get off the bus" with an imperious attitude and arrogant grin on his face, and at that brief moment, I had every intention of knocking that smirk off his round face. I soon realized the seriousness of this confrontation as students placed bets on the fight and egged us on with their deceptive speech (e.g., "He said something about your momma James")—it was no turning back now . . . man up or be perceived as weak, and I was willing to die before I come off as soft—a somewhat ignorant philosophy. I state somewhat because it is okay to be willing to die for something positive but not anything of ignorance.

I was not about to let my peers know that I was nervous and having second thoughts about this potential fight, so I proceeded to boast about what I would do to Sam as I confidently spoke whatever words entered my mind. I became more relaxed and optimistic in my athletic abilities, the more I spoke. I was trying to speak my outcome into existence. I was spewing rhetoric and putting on a show as if I was Muhammad Ali or the more contemporary boxer, Floyd Mayweather. I learned that words were extremely powerful, dispelling the dumb notion that, "Sticks and stones can break my bones, but words will never hurt me." We had seven bus stops within the circular radius of our neighborhood, and I used this time to continue instilling credence that I could beat him within my mind. Reminiscing on this situation, I learned that negative behavior could be employed to create self-assurance, so I communicated in a loud fashion to build poise in my attitude and actions—speaking in an obnoxious tone.

My bus ride concluded at the third bus stop, so I assumed that Sam was getting off at my stop if we were really going to fight. To my surprise, Sam stayed on the bus and planned to get off at his scheduled stop. I was relieved that I might not have to fight him and might not have to put my credibility as a bad boy on the line. As I walked home, I joked with my crew and other neighborhood students about breaking Sam's jaw if he stepped one foot off that bus, attempting to hide my trepidation about a possible fight with him. My father was asleep when Mack and I arrived home from school because he was working 12-8, the graveyard shift. Mack and I shelved doing our homework and turned on the TV to watch an afterschool special, while eating our customary bowl of Captain Crunch Berries. About 20 minutes into our cereal ordeal and after the after school special concluded; we heard a disturbing knock at our front door. I wore a puzzled look on my face as I soon realized that Sam and others were convening outside and in my front yard.

I quickly proceeded to warm-up by shadowboxing and

stretching throughout the house to calm my nerves and to loosen my tense muscles. I attempted to expel the anxiety through a routine of boxing combinations as I calmly galloped inside my house as a professional boxer on the HBO boxing circuit. Proactively, I began to visualize my opponents' strengths and weaknesses, while visualizing my opportunities to mentally counter any potential preconceived threats—I utilized the SWOT analysis long before attending businesses courses in college. I knew Sam was taller and heavier than me, making it impossible for me to grapple with him in the fight. I focused on utilizing my hand speed efficiently and effectively to win this perceived lopsided battle.

I became convinced that I could win, but Mack feared my demise and fall from grace if I left the house. Mack told them from the inside of our door that I could not come outside. Even though his words made me appear weak or afraid, a more rational side of me supported Mack's rhetoric. Sam said, "If he does not come outside, I am going to piss on your flowers." Sam was a man of his word because he pulled out his penis and commenced to urinate on my parents' colorful array of flowers. I said, "Mack I cannot let him disrespect me and our family like that," so I unlocked the door and ran outside to escape the safety of our secured door.

I opened the door and said, "I am going to knock you out for pissing on my dad flowers," and he said, "Well, what's up then." I said, "Let's take this to the back of the house" with a casual smile. As I walked to the back of my house, thoughts began to flood my mind. While organizing these thoughts, I realized I was fighting Sam to validate my name among my peers who could probably careless about me. Ignorantly, I thought that Sam was a big boy and beating him might give me the respect of classmates. I bounced and galloped around to loosen up my arms and legs before engaging in combat and to minimize my nervousness while attempting to find the perfect fighting rhythm. I had much practice fighting from my Fall River days, so I knew the importance of being in rhythm and feeling relaxed. Sam initiated the fight by saying, "what's up now," and before he finished his sentence I unloaded a vicious assault with multiple punches toward his face. My hand speed was convincing and overwhelming to him, but I lacked the power to drive him down to the ground.

Sam was no match for my quickness, so he rushed me in an attempt to smother my punches and to clutch my small physique. I realized that I was no match for his size and strength, so I pushed back to avoid his clutches. He maneuvered effortlessly to my legs to scoop me off the ground as if I was a light piece of paper, and his grappling move startled me. Somehow, I broke away from his grasps and begin to pound his face again with some more boxing combinations. This went on for another 30-60 seconds until he managed to gain the advantage and the power to drive me to the ground. Then, he mounted me with his smelly green sweatpants placed over my face. Once he positioned himself on my chest, he sailed punches at my face nonstop and every punch brought stars and faint darkness to my eyes. I was dazed and in trouble because he was too heavy for me to lift him off of my chest and to stop his barrage of punches.

At that moment, I knew I made the wrong decision to chase my ego outside of my safe house, but it was too late now. I could hear the crowd that I desired to impress encouraging him on as he continued to pound my face. I went from winning to losing the fight in a matter of seconds, and I wondered what my face was going to look like. Life is so unpredictable, and real life does not play by the rules within our mind at times. I sit here and ponder about how many kids lost their lives thinking that they would beat somebody up and casually laugh about it the next day, not realizing that bullets would later play a role in their demise.

I did not know what to do in this dazed and confused state, so I sunk my teeth into Sam's thigh, biting with tremendous force; he went from punching me to trying to pry my mouth off his leg. During this ordeal, Mack ran in the house to wake my father from his pre-work nap, and he angrily came outside and tossed Sam off of me like a ragdoll. I jumped to my feet in a daze, and I tried to sail two more punches at Sam's face to no avail. I was happy with my standup fighting performance, but I knew some people would assume that I lost the fight due to his mount and punch tactic. I decided to lie to family members and people about the fight because mentally, I could not handle the fact that I lost a fistfight. Prompting me to tell everyone Sam's older brother, Toby tripped me and helped Sam beat me in our altercation. Toby was a great kid, and he grew to be an even better young Christian believer. Toby would become victim to an assault from Deon due to my consistent and malicious lies about Sam and Toby.

I wanted revenge and did not care who got hurt, and I knew that lie would motivate and inspire Deon to fight Sam and Toby. I guess Sam was right about me using Deon to fight my battles because Deon was the first person I thought of when the fight did not end in my favor—many people die in our subculture because they cannot handle bruises to their ego. Cowards involve other people into their affairs when they lack the ability to resolve their issues; I donned the crown of a coward because I selfishly involved my brother. Deon became extremely enraged by my lies on Sam and Toby, and he quickly made some phone calls to Torey and Tony without my parents' knowledge.

My parents were persistent to involve the police, but I wanted street justice to gain a little of my lost respect among my peers. Calling the cops would make me appear desperate and weak, and my parents failed to acknowledge that I was just as guilty as Sam in this situation—there unconditional love overlooked this fact. From Deon's account, he met up with Torey and Tony about two blocks from the Chapel apartment complex before taking the journey into Sam and Toby's impoverished turf. Deon angrily and aggressively approached anyone protecting Sam and Toby.

Deon smacked around some kid trying to protect Sam until Sam decided to come drag himself outside. When Sam bravely entered the fray, Deon smacked him repeatedly to embarrass him and to honor my name. Then, he set his sights on Toby, while Sam stood at attention crying in utter disbelief. Toby was caught off guard, and Deon beat him mercilessly for no true involvement in my fight. Toby was beat due to a lie that I told to protect my misguided ego. Selfishly, I hurt two innocent individuals from my altercation: Toby and Deon. Deon fractured his left hand during the assault on Toby, and he was forced to miss his high school football season.

He had high promise for that season, and his coaches expected big things from him as a defensive back. It bothered me that he would miss the entire season due to my lie, but I was ecstatic about his vengeance on my behalf. Sam never gloated about his win over me when I was around; his win was overshadowed by his own bruised ego by getting smacked. I also think Deon's anger placed a little of fear in his heart, so he strayed away from that conversation in my presence. However, I still expected my classmates to tease me about the fight, but a lot of students respected my heart and revered my will to fight someone much bigger than me.

I should have learned that fighting never solves problems, but I was donning a mask that was separating me farther and farther away from this rational truth. From time-to-time, I would allow my physical appearance and size to negatively impact my self-esteem, and I would act out of character to demonstrate to others that I was bigger and tougher than my actual body—in words and in action. My lack of self-confidence prompted me to constantly ask my mom and dad, "Do I look handsome?" and "Do you think I am smart?" I needed people words and actions about me to validate my existence because my self-assurance was tied to others' recognition. I did all this to fit in and to appear cool, but most of my classmates probably still viewed me in the same fashion or laughed at me behind my back. However, in my small and weak mind, I thought that I was proving something to people who lacked the power to positively improve my life. My fifth grade teacher, Mrs. Parker wanted me to succeed, and she believed in my academic aptitude. I know God had to touch her because I never really gave her much to witness or work with—I talked excessively in her class and belittled her instruction.

Mrs. Parker raved about how smart and sweet I could be during conferences with my parents. I loved her complimentary words, but at that time, I cared a little more about my reputation among fellow classmates. Reflecting back, I recognized that God always sent angels to inspire hope in me, but it was my responsibility to identify that positive hope—hope was always there in my life, but I overlooked it. One day, Mrs. Parker was chastising me about speaking out of turn in class, and I said, "I will say what I want to say" in a very disrespectful fashion. Mrs. Parker told me stay inside with her, while she dismissed the remaining students for recess.

I became agitated and vexed about staying inside for a teacher conference. I had an impulsive temper, and my body language displayed my frustration as my head drooped and my words correlated with despondent behavior. Mrs. Parker continued to scold me and as she drew closer, I grabbed and pushed her away from me. Immediately, I began to weep and to apologize, knowing the seriousness of my actions and the pain that I caused her—not physically but mentally—I witnessed the hurt and pain in her eyes. Mrs. Parker called my parents and summoned them to school for another conference. I was afraid because I knew the seriousness of my infraction. Mrs. Parker never reported the incident to the school officials because she did not want the situation to be blown out of proportion; she had witnessed students receive assault charges and short-term incarcerations in Dobbs reformatory school for similar infractions. I was grateful to her love and kindness.

I was shocked to find out that students served time in reformatory school for similar assaults on their teachers. The reformatory school that house students or kids from Wilson was in Kinston, NC. I heard stories about the bad boys in Dobbs, and I had no desire to press my luck with those individuals within those solitary walls. Eventually, I spent some time at Dobbs as a motivational speaker, and I am still honored by that invitation to this day. Mrs. Parker taught me that love does not belong to one ethnic group or gender because she was white and loved this little black boy. There were droves of people with different ethnic backgrounds who tried to reach out to me throughout my existence.

I was confused and trapped behind a mask that desired to fit in with so-called friends. I am thankful that Mrs. Parker had the ability to visualize how my actions or behaviors in the present could impact me negatively in the future. I never disrespected Mrs. Parker or disturbed her classroom again; I actually became her consistent student helper. I still cared about my bad boy reputation, but I was no dummy, and had no desire to hone my survival skills in Dobbs Reformatory School. I was determined to remain on Mrs. Parker's good side, so I spent my time in her class being a quality student. I shifted my attention away from being disruptive and more toward appeasing my teacher and occasionally female students for the remainder of my fifth grade school year.

I always had a girlfriend, and I always tried to claim the title of being a "boyfriend" with girls whom I perceived as being the best looking within school. As young boys, we were always comparing and competing when it came to girls, sports, or any other dumb endeavors (i.e. who can urinate the farthest, who can fight the best, or who can spit the farthest . . . dumb stuff). We discussed girls' facial features, body structures, accents, and attires to determine their informal beauty class rankings. However, the girls created and implemented a more formal and sophisticated male ranking system. They had the names of the boys at the top of their notebooks, and all the popular girls would comment, sign, and rate the boys by percentage points (0-100) on an individual page. The points were combined and averaged for an overall percentage rating. I found out that my score was around 94 percent, not the highest, but it was close to the best among the group of male classmates. Kelsie had the highest rating; I think his hazel eyes placed him over the top. He was a smooth young brother though.

During this time era, I frequently chatted with my friends

about sex, and we traded sex stories like some old chaps by toasting our cartons of chocolate milks while sitting stationary at our circle lunchroom tables. Even though I was still a virgin, I listened to their detailed stories and stole pieces of their stories or scenes to fabricate sexual encounter lies when it was my turn to share sex episodes. I lied to those smiling faces that drew close to me like I was telling them how to earn a million dollars—never letting on that I was still a virgin. I went from being proud around my parents to be a virgin to being embarrassed about my virginity when I sat with these young boys.

I wanted to be perceived as being cool and virgins were bottom feeders, so I created scripts of sexual encounters to maintain that cool image. If I was a gambler, I would bet that majority of those young boys were fabricating their sex stories as well because I refuse to believe that that many young boys were sexually active in the fifth grade. I practiced closed-mouth kissing at that age, but nothing else—I was scared to go farther—sin talk had me terrified in that regard. These innocent kisses might appear to be no big deal, but they were planting seeds of lust and sexual desires in my mind and heart, developing a pattern that would lead me to engage in risky sexual behavior in middle school and high school.

Parents, there is nothing innocent about puppy love or kissing among elementary and middle school students, and please do not think your child will be able to handle the emotions that will surface during these youthful relationships. My idle mind was definitely the devil's workshop because I found myself being defiant with too much time on my hands and too little supervision in my life, both at school and at home. I was losing myself to the desire to remain popular with and validated by my peers. My parents provided sound spiritual guidance, but their admonitions were unrealistic weapons against the temptations and pressures I faced. My parents were great leaders, but they were a little naïve about dating; they did not comprehend the dangers children of my generation confronted. They perceived dating as harmless during my school days because they instilled too much trust in me. They learned and shifted gears when my baby brother, Ajay came along, and the adjustments they made to their attitudes and philosophies have served Ajay quite well. He is a top scholar and athlete at Beddingfield High School in Wilson, NC, with scholarship offers dangling in front of him.

When I was growing up, my parents assumed that their righteous teachings would suffice and shelter us not only from making poor decisions, but also from the temptations of this world. My girlfriend and I had explicit and X-rated conversations about sex on my parents' house phone, but they were completely oblivious to our inappropriate dialogue.

Lessons Learned

"Slothfulness casts into a deep sleep, and an idle person will suffer hunger"
~ **Proverbs 19:15**

My rhetoric fit the situation or company because I was searching for validation in an extremely complex world of elementary thinking and positioning. Classmates respected street cred, and I worked to build my name and validation among my peers by taking negative risks in and out of school. I took risk in fights, deceived and schemed in relationships, and fabricated sexual encounters to gain recognition and instant credibility. I masked my identity and positive upbringing to be accepted in a subculture that emulated destructive behaviors and poor decision-making. At that time, I still developed an apprehension toward having sex, but overtime and constant exposure to friends who lacked fear toward engaging in sex; I was willing to conform to my subculture's poor choices.

It is vital that parents keep their children active and as close as possible to their productive and positive family structure to minimize poor choices. Millions of kids have lost or altered their lives due to the lack of proper supervision. Unsupervised kids are like stranded fish caught flopping on the ground outside of water—no hope and no realistic chance for survival. I am afraid that I would have lost my virginity or tried to lose my virginity in the fifth grade if an opportune time presented itself—that is a scary notion to conceive, but many kids act on this notion or embrace this notion . . . supervise and educate your kids. Elementary school was the start of my mental warfare, but middle school was the time I became a criminal-minded thug. Middle school would change my life forever and set the course for negative and unchangeable outcomes for my unpredictable future.

Chapter 8

Finding My Mask

The Definition of Thug Life

"If you can't find something' to live for, you best find something to die for"

~ Tupac Shakur

My early mission was to dominate in sports and to hook up with a multitude of girls during my formidable middle school years. I fell in love with football and basketball, but I also ran summer track that took me out of state for track meets. My father coached Mack and me in football and basketball, and he made me believe that I could be the best in both sports and eventually play professionally in the future. I was determined to perform at a mastery level in both sports. I was blessed with God-given speed and quickness, and I was strong-willed, benefiting me significantly in competitive sporting events—I don't like to lose in anything.

I was never fearful of sacrificing my body or health for a basket, a touchdown, or even a hustle play in any sport. Bo Jackson and Barry Sanders were my favorite running backs, so I supported the Oakland Raiders and Detroit Lions in the early 90s. I always followed professional players rather than following a professional sport's franchise. Personally, I do not have the energy or the time to cheer for a losing organization that lacks quality or talented players on their team. Sports became my life because I regarded sports as another avenue to win favor in peer relationships—I masked half of my identity with sports, and the other half with thug behavior.

My father was the head football coach for the Beddingfield Cubs (midget football league), the second year that Mack and I played contact football. Throughout my fifth grade year, I failed to play a critical role to my team because I played behind some really talented football players who were a little older and more experienced than me—I was learning the ins-and-outs of the game. In the fifth grade, I struggled on the basketball court as well, but my intense work ethic was synonymous in all sports.

My father was excited to coach Mack and me, but he was fair and never played favorites with us on his teams. It was obvious as I road the bench majority of the year when he coached our basketball team at the Boys/Girls club. When I got in the game, my job was to rebound the ball and to pass the basketball to our team superstar, Julius. Julius averaged well over 20 points per game, and he was the reason our team excelled on the basketball court. Everybody loved Julius, and his appeal to people taught me the power and value of being great in sports—I wanted his prestige because he was the closest thing to Michael Jordan in our respective age group.

My dad sacrificed his precious free time to coach us and to share his sport's wisdom with us. His love for us exceeded his own self-interest. He was the epitome of a real-man by loving us unconditionally and going above and beyond as a father—much more than a financial provider. I was blinded by my small world and overlooked his commitment to my personal growth and success. As the head coach of the Beddingfield Cubs football team, my dad positioned Mack as the starting quarterback and me as the starting running; all this occurred during my sixth grade year, and first year at Darden-Vick middle school. Our team was beating everyone in our football league, and I averaged over 150 yards and 2 touchdowns per game—people noticed, and my popularity swelled in my minuscule city. My confidence on the football field was at an all-time high, and I was sure that this success would continue throughout middle school and high school. Newspaper clippings had me convinced that I was destined for greatness. I gained a lot of attention from classmates due to my on field football prowess, and it meshed well with my smooth and semi-bad boy persona. I was proud to witness my popularity increase in the school and throughout the city.

All of this self-confidence fed my ego, and my ego supported my gift for gab. This unique ability to communicate in small circles of peers boosted my status in school. Effective oral communication skills can provide individuals with influential power over others; I had this power, and I was aware of it. This power gave me the confidence needed to persuade girls that I was someone worth dating and walking hand-in-hand with in the populated hallways. My mother set forced conditions to develop my oral communication skills at a young age, making me give Easter speeches at church, read scriptures at church, and perform in professional stage plays. All of this practice gave me the confidence to speak in front of small and large groups of people, so I was never afraid to rely on my communication prowess to coerce people to accept my beliefs. I generated the fortitude I needed to approach a sixth-grade girl named Rhonda, whom I perceived as a "dime piece," our term for any girl whose face and physique were of the highest quality.

I was mesmerized by her beauty and aggressive personality with others, so I sent her a note that said do you like me; please circle "no", "yes", or "maybe." I was practicing hospitality as a kid because "please" was embedded in my thug-style communication. Most boys employed a similar dating worksheet to woo girls. This courting strategy appears extremely corny and whack as I reluctantly reflect back on it; but young girls adored this method, so I embraced it. Rhonda wrote back and implied that I was cute with some poorly drawn smiley face and a wet lip-gloss imprint to validate her interest in me. Lip-gloss was popping in those days to mimic the song from Lil Mama, and girls carried two and three tubes of lip-gloss in their knockoff high-end designer purses.

I focused on kissing, so girls glossed over lips drove me crazy,—lustful thoughts created a desire to kiss those glossed lips. I wanted to crossover to manhood and to embrace this thug culture; so sex remained on my mind. I concluded that engaging in sex would add more credibility to my mock thug persona. I decided to send another message about how I thought Rhonda was my soul mate by writing some romantic lines to her that I had memorized from some old blaxploitation flicks with characters named "Huggy Bear" or "Dolomite."

I never understood the notion of having a "soul mate" until God blessed me with a true soul mate later in life. I was dedicated to being accepted by my peers, so I was in search of a mask that could get them to pay more attention to me. I wanted everyone to love and respect me. I operated as a grownup, so I maneuvered as if I had all the answers. I began speaking what I thought was adult language by adding lots of profane and sexually explicit words to my speech, but I was still a young boy adrift.

Nonetheless, Rhonda eventually wrote me a letter back that implied "yes" to my surprise, and she became my girlfriend for the next three to four months; but as an 11-year old kid, it felt more like three years. It is amazing how kids view months as years, and the clever and crafty young boys utilize that short span of time to influence naïve girls to have sex with them. Some young minds tend to believe kissing and sex is the natural course of a school dating relationship from my perspective and experiences.

This is why I strongly believe immature kids and definitely kids at elementary and middle school ages are too young to date; dating force unrealistic rules (i.e. kissing, touching, and sex) on young undeveloped minds—that breed trouble and unwanted pregnancies or STI's. My young relationship experiences taught me that most girls are searching for love, while most boys are searching for instant gratification through sexual interactions.

Rhonda and I were inseparable my first year at Darden-Vick; she consumed all of my time and my attention—mentally and physically. Her popularity and tough girl attitude gave me even more thug appeal and respect from classmates. I snuck many notes to her during class, so we could set a time to ask our teacher to use the bathroom and meet each other out in the hallway. This somewhat harmless behavior taught me to minimize the importance of school and absorbing vital information while attending some classes. My excitement for school hinged on my ability to impress and please my cohort—all the wrong reasons.

My mind was consumed with thoughts of "what is she doing," "what is she thinking about," and "does she really like me?" Once again, from my experience, elementary school, middle school, and most students in high school are too young to be in relationships; it consumed majority of my thinking, thinking that should be used for absorbing crucial information in and out of the classroom for personal development. I cannot find any experiences to support some beneficial reasons to be in a relationship during those school years of my life. I think the larger issue is that most people fail to find their true identity until their adult years, so it is impossible to be true to someone when you are wearing a mask or unsure of your own identity.

Rhonda was the first girl that I ever French kissed or tongued as they say in the South, and it inspired me to think about sex often, not the actual kiss between us, just the notion of moving from first base to home plate as some boys suggested. Kissing was rather disgusting as I thought about the trading of spit between me and my girlfriend, but I did not waste too much time dwelling on that emotion—I was busy rejoicing in the high fives and celebratory rhetoric from male classmates who would repeatedly ask, "When are you going to hit that man (have sex with her)?" The more interaction from students who attempted to convince us to engage in sex, the more Rhonda and I discussed engaging in sex with one another. Our conversations had the propensity to shift toward a discussion about sex, and the possible pleasure received from a sexual encounter; but honestly, we knew absolutely nothing about the throes of sexual passion, just lust, and probably some made up stories from other classmates.

We were both virgins, so we formulated assumptions from other students' experiences, older family members, or overly dramatized sex scenes from popular movies like *Jason's Lyric* or *Fatal Attraction*—we never should have seen those movies at that age. This relationship consumed so much of my vital and productive time. I should have used that time to improve my relationship with God, to read books, to enhance my academic success, and to hone my athletic skills in chosen sports. My parents were naïve about the negative consequences from me dating at that age by allowing me to converse with girls on our rotary telephone for long periods of time—too immature and too much time on futile conversations lead to trouble.

Dating consumes so much time, and as a child, time is so precious and critical to our psychological development. I should have been focused on identifying my true voice as a leader of my life rather than a follower of popular trends or advice of mindless peers. Leadership starts as a child, and it is contingent upon our life experiences—leadership is truly everywhere and is in many situations. The fashion in which we react when faced with challenges can determine future leadership patterns and behaviors. People cannot lead and inspire others until they first learn to lead and inspire themselves, but I wore a mask and lacked the ability to see through the smog and lead my life in a positive manner.

Thoughts of sex and popularity preoccupied my mind, and I adopted any actions or behaviors that made me seem special or important among other school classmates who exhibited those same behaviors. I had a stronger desire to be loyal to my friends than to seek the love and favor of God. It was a very foolish decision on my part, but it seemed to be the best path for me during those difficult years. Middle school was the time that our neighborhood cliques grew more resilient and merged with high school cliques. There were no known gangs in Wilson during those years, but our neighborhood cliques adopted similar characteristics of structured gangs. We fought together, chased girls together, smoked weed together, and occasionally, traveled together throughout the city to present a presence or connection to one another.

People stayed loyal to their neighborhoods, but some neighborhoods worked together to formalize even larger cliques throughout the city. The main cliques I associated with hailed from these adopted neighborhood names: Five Points, Snowden drive, Atlantic street, and the Chapel, all hoods within our impoverished school district. I adopted the mantra that "there is strength in numbers," so I made it a point to never be caught sauntering or venturing out in other people neighborhoods solo—get caught alone by people with bad intentions, and it might be a bad day in certain segments of Wilson.

In the sixth grade, there were not a lot of issues among other neighborhoods that involved me. I was focused on chasing pretty girls and increasing my popularity with the in-crowd—fighting was never planned, it was something I did to improve my reputation—I had love for most people, but I also had a quick temper. From my small-minded perspective, most sixth grade students seemed to mesh well together at the start of the school year, maybe our unfamiliarity with one another created a drama free period. I spent my time trying to form alliances and to minimize conflicts with potential foes, and I thought I did a great job of strategically structuring my crew and adding beneficial outside associates to the crew as extended members.

I learned that substantial numbers looked intimidating, but it is hard to generate loyalty among big groups of immature kids or immature adults for that manner. Small groups can be more effective than large groups when individuals are trying to establish trust and authentic relationships. I preferred large numbers to curtail my number of potential enemies, but small numbers to build loyalty and minimize too many voices communicating in our group. I had no real issues with too many people in the sixth grade, but some kid named Tron decided to make me his mark for no apparent reason during lunch in the cafeteria line one day. Tron was a small and a gregarious individual from Five Points.

He was very creative, artistic, and wore expensive apparel, but some people wrote him off as arrogant and obnoxious; however, at that time, I respected him and viewed him as a cool kid with a lot of style—I did not really know him. Yet, I was chatting with some classmates in line when Tron hauled off and smacked the spit from my lips for laughing. I guess he thought I was laughing at him. Whatever the reason, he caught me completely off guard. I paused as the assault made the entire lunchroom mute, and it sent my world in slow motion and a brief panic.

I vividly watched his hand retreat back to his side while still feeling the warmth and sting from his open-handed smack to my right cheek. I witnessed students jumping out of their seats and grabbing their faces in disbelief out of my peripheral vision. Students were pointing and laughing at me, and instantly, I became enraged and sought immediate revenge for his blatant disrespect. I wanted to embarrass him, so he could feel the embarrassment that I wore on my face—all the respect and admiration that I possessed for him dissipated in a matter of seconds.

I violently grabbed him by his shirt to draw him close, while I tried to gather my thoughts and to gain my composure in this unfamiliar situation. I thought about how people might perceive me as a punk if I did not retaliate and fight back. My anger fueled and sparked my adrenaline, so I proceeded to lift him off the ground and sailed him over the nearest lunchroom table. Lunch trays, an assortment of food, and Tron crashed to the cold and sticky lunchroom floor. I pursued him as he attempted to collect himself from the floor, maneuvering through the congested crowd to finish him off like the finishing moves of the popular video game *Mortal Kombat*.

I saw the fear and shock in his eyes as I was closing in on

him, but I had no regard for his concern; I became impulsive and lost all control—my temper drove me, and there was no room for compromise—I felt as if I wanted to kill him. I sought revenge, and I was game to do him physical harm. By this time, teachers were dispersing the crowd and retrieving Tron from the confrontation; shortly after, a teacher clutched my collar and escorted me to the front office.

I was baffled by this situation, but as I was escorted out of the lunchroom, I heard students applauding and cheering me in the fight. This response from the students inspired me to smirk and become stoic, and I developed a desire to be escorted away from more trouble if I could achieve a similar response from my peers. I knew this experience would be beneficial toward building a thug reputation. With that being evident in me, I still had no desire to get suspended from school and risk the wrath of my father's leather belt. I realized that a suspension might warrant a stern form of discipline from my father, so I had to find a way out of this situation and save face with my peers. I was shook and terrified about the potential ramifications from this altercation, so I quietly recited

Psalm 23:

1   *The Lord is my shepherd; I shall not want.*
2   *He maketh me to lie down in green pastures: he leadeth me beside the still waters.*
3   *He restoreth my soul: he leadeth me in the paths of righteousness for his name's sake.*
4   *Yea, though I walk through the valley of the shadow of death, I will fear no evil: for thou art with me; thy rod and thy staff they comfort me. mine enemies: thou anointest my head with oil; my cup runneth over.*
6   *Surely goodness and mercy shall follow me all the days of my life: and I will dwell in the house of the Lord forever.*

My father made me learn this spiritual psalm when I was in elementary school, so I continued to quote this scripture in troubling circumstances. I thought that God came to King David's rescue, so he would understand my heart and come to my rescue in my time of need. To my surprise, students and teachers told the principal that I did not start the fight, so I was not suspended for the altercation with Tron.

I believe that God intervened on my behalf and spared me from out-of-school suspension and a lashing from my pops. Instead, I was sentenced to serve some days in in-school suspension for my part in the brawl. In-school suspension was hard, long, and boring. Students were separated by partitions, and my homeroom teacher provided me with massive assignments that had to be completed prior to returning to class. Students were not allowed to leave for bathroom breaks; we had to form lines and leave as a class to go to the bathroom and lunch—no elective classes could be attended.

We were not allowed to talk to other students or sleep in the silent room, so I had to rely on the exchange of notes for communication and to stay alert. This isolation was confinement from my classrooms and hallways were I yearned to be somebody important. I felt like everyday in this isolated hell made me more and more insignificant in my middle school world. In there, it felt like the wall clock never moved, and I wanted out and back in my masked world. It was extremely difficult for me because I love to converse with other students, to follow the school drama, and to flirt with girls throughout the typical school day.

This experience gave me a lot of time to think about school experiences, but most of the thoughts did not pertain to being a better student or to being a productive citizen. My thoughts were about grabbing girls' buttocks and sprinting down the halls as they followed chase or rolling dice against the walls in stinky bathrooms or under dark gym bleachers. This was my middle school-minded perspective, and it was the perspective of majority of the students whom I associated with. My mind was being conquered by thoughts far from my parents' religious and moral teachings, and I was consumed with this notion of being a ladies man and a thug. My mother always told me to pick my friends wisely, but I had no inkling of what that truly meant. I recognized that my friends had negative desires that fed the appetite of my masked persona. It was not cool to sit around and discuss grades or dreams of being engineers, doctors, or lawyers—that talked got you laughed at within my small-minded crew.

Friends who made the honor roll were self-effacing and never bragged or debated about their exceptional grades. It was an underlying norm that we never discussed or associated coolness with grades. We bragged about who was the best in a particular sport or fastest runner, who dated the prettiest girl, who had sex, who sold drugs, or who possessed the best fighting skills. But now as I mull over those past discussions, those discussions were meaningless and destructive as I attempt to paraphrase King Solomon out of *Ecclesiastes* from the Holy Bible. When I grasped that concept later on in life, I finally traveled the road not normally taken by many of my African American male contemporaries from Wilson, NC. Yet, in middle school, I decided to follow the most traveled road (i.e., being popular and feeling important among peers).

I realized that most romantic relationships ended prematurely, and most sport careers ended in high school; but girls treated us as husbands, and we believed that professional careers were in our futures. A large pool of my friends contributed to procreating children out-of-wedlock, which resulted in the creation of unstable families for future generations—I would add to this statistic. Another vast majority lived sporadically in various prisons due to their aggressive personalities and defiant attitudes toward the law.

We all claimed to be down for the crew (i.e., loyal without fear), but I realized all of us were fake and unrealistic to some degree. We were only kids imitating what we saw from neighborhood superstars (i.e., dope dealers) or television tough guys. The sad situation is that the cycle continued with majority of our children born out-of-wedlock—kids having kids are incapable of providing profound knowledge to their children because they are still maturing themselves.

People who are true to themselves seek out noteworthy ways to find their true passion and purpose in life rather than following the masses as I did. I realized over years of obstacles and challenging life experiences that most people try to emulate the lives of phony characters from television shows or movies rather than find their true self-worth—source is self and God; this formula developed unstoppable and undeniable belief in me. I grew up not knowing the face reflecting back from the bathroom mirror; I was masked with a false perspective toward my existence. Sometimes we chase the media's definition of a dream life by acquiring materialistic items.

This concept can incite us to attempt to impress our friends, parents, or random individuals rather than attempting to be different and find our individualized dream that works for our pertinent life. We mask ourselves with these fake lifestyles or personas as we progress to different stages in our lives, and middle school was the time that I was donning the mask of an unknown individual pursuing a "thug life" perspective. I adapted to this troubled subculture and adopted small negative behaviors that led to bigger and more egregious behavior in the future. Tupac Shakur revolutionized "thug life," and I had no idea what "thug life" was or represented; but I, like many wanting to imitate many rappers and movie bad guys like Tony Montana in *Scarface*. Tupac made the idea of "thug life" among my school peers and me alluring, and I developed a strong desire to be a thug and adopt this gangster persona. As I fine-tuned my image, I gained respect among my peers and began to be noticed by sex-driven girls.

I was fascinated with the young dope dealers in middle school—the way they dressed, and the way they appeared to not care about anything germane to school and life. These students worked some of the local drug infested street corners at night and posed as middle school students during the day, normally to chase girls and be admired by young and impressionable students like me. I lost my positive perspective on life because I was drawn to school drug dealers' fashionable attire and carefree demeanor. I was very observant, and I noticed that students gave street hustlers (drug dealers) esteem and most of the gorgeous female students appeared to be attracted to them.

I wanted what they had or what I thought they had. It appeared as if they had it all figured out, and I wanted their perceived happiness. They had money, girls, honor, and were unfazed by school policies and procedures; they never went out of their way to oblige teachers or their classroom commands. I desired that negative attitude toward administrators and teachers, and I wanted their easy money and the temporary benefits that surrounded their fast money: beautiful girls, esteem, and materialistic items. I always dreamed of making a lot of currency with a laidback lifestyle—I wanted an easy life, a life less stressful than my parents toiling jobs. They worked hard as middle-class citizens, and they worked to gain leverage on annoying creditors and bill collectors. Eventually, I learned that nothing substantial comes without hard work in life, but I did not support this viewpoint or stance during my middle school stage of life.

Periodically, I would daze off and envision myself living in a fancy house with a few luxury cars, but I had no realistic plan of how to obtain those splendors in middle school. I thought that playing professional sports or an occupation, as a skilled physician would provide me with the means needed to acquire those luxuries—all about the money, but no realistic thought about serving people—thousands of doctors probably receive their licenses every year with this notion and a minimal desire toward serving mankind. People would get excited when I said I wanted to be a medical doctor, so I would always say it to inquiring minds about my future goals.

I had a split focus that clashed with each other, a negative and a positive: how to be a successful citizen and how to be perceived as popular among my peers. I was paranoid and felt friends were phony; I did not know how to embrace their friendships. I was never satisfied with my dating and peer relationships because I thought people lied about their feelings toward me (e.g., you look good or you are the man J)—I was not the first to trust, so it was no possible way to generate trust in our relationships. I never believed their comments the minute those words rambled off their perceived deceiving lips. My mind was diluted because I wanted their recognition; but I failed to trust their words and actions—my mind was playing tricks on me.

My brain ran crazy with random thoughts of people snickering behind my back, and these thoughts made me feel uncomfortable as I walked gingerly through the school halls. My thinking was always preoccupied with do they really like me and do I look like the so-called cool kids. I did not think people genuinely liked me, and I would assume that they spoke ill of me when they laughed or conversed with other people within my vicinity. I was very paranoid, and it would drive me crazy to hear people chattering if I was unable to decipher their viewed deceptive speech. This paranoid state of mind made me more willing to don the mask of a thug if the mask would bring me the respect and acceptance I sought desperately. I surmised that being a thug might eliminate those crazy thoughts because I believed people would surely accept me as a thug.

I was not born to be a thug because deep down inside I was an individual who loved people and wanted to display an empathetic side toward others. However, I started committing crimes and acts of violence to appease the in-crowd or individuals whom I considered as my boys. This was an ignorant mindset, and it is a mindset that sets in without notice. Many people in today's society develop this mindset by pacifying their parents' wishes with unfulfilling careers and disregarding the stress this unhappy decision may cause them—stress kills as often as violence, so both choices are harmful to these masked individuals.

The more I watched television, the more I fantasized about being a successful athlete and a neighborhood kingpin, but once again, a negative and a positive do not create positive results according to life's experiences and logical mathematics. Both consumed majority of my thoughts because I focused all my attention on athletes, rappers, and personified gangsters (fiction and nonfiction). I wanted to be the black version of Tony Montana, and the alarming phenomenon was that many of other young black boys in my subculture wanted to assume his identity as well.

The media has a manipulative way of tricking troubled and demented individuals into chasing false dreams of how to acquire fast riches and fame, even if it is street fame. Most of the individuals whom I portrayed, thought they were above the law, and they had no respect for the law, viewing cops as pigs or the bad guys. In the big picture, the so-called bad guys (cops) were the ones attempting to uphold the law, but I never thought of cops as the good guys when I was younger—I embraced their fallacy.

This is one of the most ignorant assumptions that I adopted during my school age stages, but I embraced the dope dealers and street thugs as the more reliable source of information rather than the police who daily sacrificed their lives for random citizens throughout our city. My circle of friends and me believed that luxury cars, expensive sneakers or apparel, and gold jewelry indicated high-level success. My parents had more money than some of the street thugs whom I chose to follow, but I perceived the street thugs as having more loot due to the perception of their fancy clothes and high-priced trinkets. This outlook on life is a grave injustice to these brainwashed individuals, and I was one of those misguided fools. The life I lived always felt uncomfortable and fictitious to me, but I sheltered those emotions with aggressive actions and a nonchalant demeanor toward loving people and societal laws.

Lessons Learned

Self-discovery is a never-ending process, and it is a very daunting task for any individual. However, self-discovery can seem impossible for young boys trying to fit in unfamiliar circles, attempting to date girls, and participating in disruptive behaviors to gain popularity. Everybody wants to feel special or relevant in some way, and this need to feel important can drive an individual to change, and, in some cases, that change is not positive. Sometimes people embrace different attitudes and behaviors that are contrary to their true identity or inner beliefs. Majority of the time this change is fake because it contradicts with their true identity or inner potential.

I have a friend, who spent 14 years of his life becoming a dentist to satisfy his father's desires, but he detests his career choice—his dream was to be a journalist—far from the medical field, but less prestigious. He chased the distinguished reputation and money that surrounded his title of D.D.S., but he is no different from the millions of people on earth chasing things opposed to their true identity. I was in pursuit of school fame and recognition, and I rejected my inner self to appease people whom I valued within my small and insignificant world. We must remain conscious and aware of our goals, and we need to search deep to make sure those goals align with our true identities and inner potentials. We must never sell our souls or identities for people, money, prestige, fame, or acceptance. When we reject our inner self for others, it leads us down dark sinful paths chosen by many and that has pernicious consequences.

Chapter 9

The Wages of Sin is Death

An Ignorant Mind brings about a Life of Crime

"The only true wisdom is in knowing you know nothing"

~ Socrates

Anger can serve as an anchor to a multitude of criminal-minded behaviors, and anger is an emotion that can spread like cancer to impact a slew of other negative actions. The bible taught me that Jesus was without sin, and God, the father detests sin. The more a person sins without a sound relationship with God, the more that human is separated from God's love. I had no relationship with God, and I did not desire one at that time. I felt distant from God, and I was secretly rejecting the spiritual teachings of the church and my parents as well. Those spiritual teachings failed to coincide with my objective of desiring acceptance from my school-aged peers.

Anger is closely related to wrath which is one of the seven deadly sins, and anger was a sin that I became accustomed to. Anger would play a pivotal role in my poor decision-making throughout my teenage years, and my anger transformed me from a calm boy to a raging bull—no self-control. I had a quick-temper that showed up in all aspects of my life, in sports, in classrooms, and in personal relationships. In the seventh and eighth grades, I displayed a unique prowess in football and in basketball, but I also exhibited an array of street skills, in fighting and in hustling. Like most young and dumb boys, I thought I could differentiate from the norm and become an outlier who never got caught or in trouble with the authorities for breaking set rules and laws.

Sports served as an advantageous vehicle in my life because sports helped me focus on the management of decent grades. Sports galvanized my passion toward school at times because I knew that I needed to comply with school policies to maintain my eligibility for middle school athletics. My parents sacrificed time and money, so Mack and I could attend basketball camps and three-on-three basketball tournaments, locally and nationally.

I matured to be an exceptional basketball and football player. Also, I was fairly decent and competitive in track-and-field, but I never established a sound and reliable work ethic in this sport. I traveled out of state for track-and-field meets during the summertime because track helped me enhance and maintain my top end speed in basketball and in football. I even participated in gymnastics for one year to strengthen my core and improve my overall flexibility, and I concluded that this experience refined my overall balance during explosive football maneuvers on the field.

I worked hard to become viewed as a great athlete, but I failed to work as hard as I could to be a productive student within the structured walls of my middle school classrooms. I did the bare minimum in school; I went to school and passed tests to remain eligible in middle school sports. School and classwork came easy to me, and at times, I had a desire to make excellent grades. Sometimes, I demonstrated my intelligence on tests and discussion topics, to dispel the rumor of being a dumb athlete or thug—I wish I used this competitive attitude to compel me in academics on a daily basis but I chose not to. I did not have the best grades in class, but I did not want to be perceived as an idiot—I wanted teachers and students to know that I could compete if I chose to. My interest and focus shifted toward gelling with the in-crowd because I had no drive toward finding my inner voice or my true identity.

I had too many self-inflicted distractions and too much pressure as a confused middle school student; those distractions derailed me from taking the road less traveled as in the Robert Frost poem, *The Road Not Taken*. Pressure was being generated from my lies of sexual encounters, image of being a thug, and poor decision-making that I adopted to protect my masked identity from the real James Williams—whoever that boy was—I lost him.

I lied to my parents who attempted to pry off my masked identity of this counterfeit thug and fake ladies man as an undiscovered virgin. At that time, I had no desire to hurt an individual or engage in violence, and I was a virgin who was scared to become involved with sex—no one was privy to that knowledge though. I was the epitome of a charlatan, but I claimed to be real; the real me wanted to be an innocent teenager and someone who aspired to be an academically gifted student.

I was confused and lost because I no longer recognized that individual hiding behind the mask and honestly, I did not know how to bring that innocent teenager back. Being an honor student and disassociating with this masked identity felt artificial and left me even more discombobulated. I became a chameleon by adapting and adjusting my attitude and my mindset to present situations or locations for survival. As I evolved much later in life, I acted as a chameleon to successfully lead and inspire others in a productive fashion because I transformed my mannerisms, rhetoric, personality, and demeanor to match situations or individuals. However, when I was in middle school, I acted in a similar manner but for deceptive reasoning. I exhibited respectable and pleasant mannerisms when conversing with adults, so they witnessed the sweet and innocent James who hid the masked individual that emerged around his peers.

Sex was a constant thought in the forefront of my mind, but I always reflected on my mom and dad's didactic teachings that sex was a sin and a detestable act before marriage. I compared and contrasted the pleasure witnessed from the moans and groans on television, and my friends depicted and detailed satisfactory sexual encounters to my parents' sinful biblical theory. Then, remembered that Deon always reiterated that, "We are not held accountable for our sins if we do not see it for ourselves in biblical text."

It was not hard for me to accept and embrace Deon's philosophy; I used my deductive reasoning and concluded that his words sounded logical to me. As I grew older, I believed wholeheartedly into Deon's doctrine because I wanted to believe his credo as the gospel truth. My friends were also illustrating stories that demonstrated how great sex felt, and how easy it was to ask God for forgiveness as any other sin (i.e., lying or overeating), so why not have sex and enjoy the beautiful bodies of these girls, in so many influential words.

Either way, I never heard much conversation about condoms and diseases from my friends or parents, and any valid reasons to dissuade me from participating in risky sexual behavior. My parents briefly mentioned the possibility of getting girls pregnant from unprotected sex, but I am sure my parents assumed their biblical teachings would prevent me from engaging in sex—I love them, but they were very naïve on this subject matter. In their minds, they thought that speaking about preventive pregnancy or STI measures (i.e., condoms) was contrary to their spiritual conviction that sex was a sin before marriage; and realistically, they were products of a time when their parents avoided the sex talk. I never believed it was possible for me to have a child or to contract a sexually transmitted disease as a teenager and none of my peers thought it was a probability for them as well. Sexually transmitted diseases were never spoken of, so I had no inkling of STI's in middle school; questions: what does it feel like and why is it never discussed among my parents with me? I observed boys whom I thought were thugs and popular around girls who actively engaged in sex prior to marriage, and they appeared jovial by constantly bragging about how great it felt to ejaculate inside a girl; and secretly, I wanted that experience and craved for similar factual stories—no more fictitious stories or make believe sex episodes. Deon, Tony, and Ced seemed happy, and beautiful girls flocked toward them. Most of the guys I knew who had sex appeared ecstatic and confident in their manhood.

Sex appeared to be tied to maturation and masculinity, and thugs exhibited those characteristics. In the sixth grade, Mack and I tried to have sex unsuccessfully with the same girl, but we left the house scared to death with our virginities still intact. We both stated that we could not get aroused, but we both walked away with our shorts poking out about three inches or so from the normal position—being aroused was not the issue and knowing that I had trepidation about engaging in sex bothered me. Our virginities were still protected, but in hindsight, I started the process of losing my virginity within that moment—actions begin in the mind.

I ventured to have sex with a random girl in the sixth grade with no protection, so I created an attitude that would prompt me to explore risky sexual behavior off and on throughout my teenage years. This situation was wrong from so many angles because a young girl should never be left alone with boys of any age. This young girl could easily have been raped, or she could have easily yelled rape, which would have led to disastrous consequences for us. A 30-second decision can affect our lives, but most kids react in the moment and fail to realize how present actions can impact their futures—the present remains relevant while the future is perceived as unimaginable. I focused solely on pleasure, and that pleasure pleasing perspective is what shortens the lives of many individuals in our society.

When sex is committed at a young age, I truly believe participating individuals tend to devalue sex and fail to connect sex with an experience between two individuals in love—a gift from God within a marriage. I think that most young fornicators view sex as an act solely for pleasure, and this can create problems later on in relationships; some individuals will have a hard time visualizing sex as a special experience between someone whom they love after engaging in so many teenage promiscuous sexual encounters.

Society does an excellent job promoting casual sex in our society, but society fails to accept accountability for the millions of children born out of wedlock and contracting STIs. Now, we have a society filled with split households and struggling mothers who try desperately to raise their children as the mother and father. God bless those mothers, but it is impossible to assume the role of a father because they lack the ability to think as a man and vice versa for fathers assuming roles as mothers. Sex plays a significant role in the thug life culture; it was impossible to be perceived as a thug without having sex with multiple girls in my subculture.

Even though, I was shaken and scared off for a span a time from having sex, I continued unsuccessfully several times to have sex with random girls during my sixth and seventh grade school years of middle school. I was on a desperate mission to lose my virginity as if it would validate me as a thug and dispel the teasing taunts of being a homosexual—nobody wanted that labeled in my neighborhood within the early 90s. It brought unwanted attention from bullies that I worked diligently to convince of my thug persona. I was exasperated by the comments, so I wanted to prove my machismo. I was mocked and ridiculed by friends for running out the house of one potential sexual encounter in the seventh grade.

This girl was gorgeous and a lot of boys desired to be with her, but Mrs. Battle, a teacher I respected shared some vital information with me on this subject. Mrs. Battle warned me that this girl slept with older men, and it was rumored that this a HIV-positive man picked her up from school. Her words frightened me, and it inspired me to embrace my mothers' words to "run when tempted by sex." When I got alone with this girl, I felt blood flow to my penis; and I transformed that blood flow to my legs and sprinted out of that house and to the serenity of my home.

I paid dearly for that decision when I arrived at school the next day. Many students throughout the school day taunted me. I could not escape their negative words, and the words pounded and echoed in my mind, damaging my self-confidence. This experience motivated me to have sex so I could stop those merciless taunts. The masked identity served as my true identity because my thoughts were consumed with pleasing students I regarded as popular. Eventually, I succumbed to self-imposed pressure and peer pressure from classmates, and I lost my virginity in the eight-grade to a friend within a solitary laser tag room at the skating rink, while my cousin Shaun stood guard at the doorway entrance. The room was not conducive for a romantic setting, and it was not a place that someone should lose their virginity.

I also hated the little respect I exhibited for the young lady who participated in this sexual act because no girl should be subjected to engage in sex in a smelly and dirty laser tag room. However, I did not consider any of these rational judgments because I was so driven to show people that I was a man by having sex; this sentence is filled with irony, and it demonstrates that random sex fails to make an individual a man or a woman. My hormones worked to impede the discernment for inappropriate behavior that day. Another scary issue about this sexual act was that I failed to use a condom, and I never thought about using a condom prior to that sexual encounter. I noticed a heightened sensation during sex, but my naivety about sex had me unaware of the magnitude of this situation or what was happening. When I realized what happened, common sense and panic entered my mind along with a barrage of internal questions: "Why didn't I use a condom, what if she is pregnant, why did I give away my virginity, and what if she has AIDS?"

Magic Johnson made AIDS a well-known topic in the black community, but STI's was foreign to me. I was losing myself and giving up my soul for a mask opposed to my true identity, and I bought into this fictitious persona to paint this picture of a stoic individual who has sex with random girls for fun and bragging rights. Inside, I despised this person, and my heart wanted to spread genuine love rather than love covered up with meaningless sex and fake high fives and smiles in the presence of classmates.

I went through spells of resisting and rejecting sexual liaisons, but I continued to engage in risky sexual behavior until an incident during the 10th grade, changing my life and altering my thinking forever. I can honestly say that I always felt guilty about having sex prior to marriage, lying, fighting, committing crimes, and some other various sins committed throughout my life, but I still found myself committing the same sins over and over again and falling to my knees in guilt over and over again—a frustrating cycle of remorse and internalized pain that repeated like a broken record.

I was failing as a leader because I was failing to lead and control my own life. I strongly believe you cannot lead others until you have the ability to successfully lead your own life. I was engaging in bad behaviors and taking impulsive risks to fit in with peers who failed to have my best interest at heart. My mind was constantly attempting to rationalize and to justify my sins, and I started categorizing my sins to minimize the seriousness. I would lust over girls, but I would convince myself I have not done anything wrong by looking, or I formulated lies about selling drugs, not realizing I was creating destructive thoughts that led to future actions.

Everything starts small, and bad behavior springs from bad thoughts or so-called small sins. Sinful behavior always leads to more sinful behavior, as a snowball affect, and ignorance without applied knowledge leads to stupidity. I found myself becoming the epitome of stupidity. Sex had me smelling myself as my elders tended to say because my attention quickly shifted toward making fast and easy money to appear as an authentic thug among my contemporaries.

I utilized my creative thinking to promote innovative ways to make currency, and I realized that those who possessed money generated respect in school. Mack and I bought a jug of *Now and*

Later candy from Sam's Club at bulk, and we decided to sell the candy to our classmates for a quick profit. We formalized a plan to sell the candy at different prices at various locations around our school, so we could decide on a proper set price for our school demographic.

I instructed Mack to sell some packs for 30 cents, and I sold some packs for 50 cents to determine how each price would sell in our target market. Mack's packs sold much faster than my packs, so we agreed to sell the rest of the packs at a set price of 40 cents to maximize our profits. I learned at a young age, the importance of supply and demand, and the advantage of surveying a market segment before introducing a new product. I gained valuable information from my qualitative research approach toward life, but I utilized that knowledge for criminal purposes rather a positive outlook on life.

We used positive instances to employ criminal mischief in school, in personal relationships, and in our unique life situations. Sports were the one constant positive endeavor that Mack and I participated in during our challenging teenage years. My father thought that Mack and I possessed elite athletic skills and abilities, so he began to invest in football and in basketball camps. My cousin, Coach Maye was a charismatic sports reporter for the Boston Celtics and WILD radio station, so he was well known in Boston, MA; his popularity earned him a contract with Reebok, and they still sell some of his products till this day.

He has a close relationship with one a Boston Celtic's legend, Robert "Chief " Parrish, so Mack and I were invited to attend the famous Robert Parrish and Dee Brown (Slam Dunk Champion) basketball camp of the early 90s at half price and eventually the camp became free to us; our likability and exceptional basketball skills benefited us in this particular camp. Mack and I became popular figures at the camp. Some of the campers valued our presence and looked up to us as camp superstars. I had exceptional speed, lateral quickness, above average ball handling skills, and an unmatched drive toward the basket, giving me an advantage at getting to the paint—this skill gave me the ability to score layups in bunches. Mack had a killer crossover, excellent ball handling skills, and a consistent mid-range jump shot that made him difficult to guard from multiple distances on the court; he developed an array of basketball mastery.

Our skills on the basketball court won us favor with other campers, and this combination of skills earned us instant credibility and fame throughout the campsite. Some campers would form small lines and ask us for autographs . . . I know this is laughable, but these episodes were very real for my camp friends and happened quite often. It made me feel like a low-budget superstar, and it fed my basketball ego—I felt as though I arrived in the basketball world.

When successes happen to you at a young age, the experience can sometimes make you feel larger than life and above societal rules, which can create a detrimental philosophy toward a productive life. Strong admiration and love from others had a negative affect on me because this unsolicited attention made me a little egotistic; I craved this attention more and more—like a drug—this experience fed my masked identity even more. This miniature fame that Mack and I accumulated actually inspired some campers to bring us breakfast and lunch during mealtimes, to serve as our in-camp waiters.

At first their unexpected actions felt uncomfortable, but I started to expect this service and felt a little dejected when this behavior subsided toward the end of basketball camp. I failed to capitalize on this precious moment, and I never showed much appreciation for this kind behavior, but instead, I displayed an expectant attitude and failed to connect on a more personal-level with those individuals. True leaders value followers, and true leaders make sure that their actions do not jeopardize their standing with their followers. There were a large demographic of foreigners who attended this camp, and I observed their body language toward Americans and their passion toward NBA players and NBA apparel. They were fascinated with NBA jerseys that other campers donned at camp, and they were ardent about obtaining an autographed jersey—speaking in their native tongues with avidity.

Mack and I were not in awe of NBA players or other random entertainers because Coach Maye introduced us to so many professional athletes and entertainers at a very young age; their presence never wowed us. We attended a variety of Boston Celtics games when Reggie Lewis and Larry Bird played, and we utilized backstage passes to converse and interact with a multitude of NBA players. I viewed entertainers as regular people with wads of money, and I was convinced that I would be an entertainer or professional athlete sometime in the near future.

I only recall asking for one autograph when I was younger, from Da Brat, a popular rap artist in the early 90s. I loved her hit song "Funkdafied," and at that time, I thought she was a very attractive woman. She reciprocated that love toward me because she stated that I was cute and inserted a similar comment above her autographed picture to me. This warranted me some bragging rights when I started school in the fall. I shared that summer experience for months until her song lost some popularity among the masses.

However, foreigners were highly impressed by NBA players from my detailed observation of their body language. Deductive reasoning provided me with the conclusion that I could make a lot of money from their impulsive behavior about obtaining basketball jerseys. Mack and I devised a plan to enter next year's camp with about five NBA jerseys. We only had three jerseys from previous purchases, so my sins of deceit and sins of greed grew to larceny. Mack and I seized the initiative to steal two NBA jerseys from Sam's Club, while our parents were congregating on an adjacent aisle and mulling over some potential purchase—I was focused on theft—no desire to purchase anything. I nervously took my jacket and t-shirt off while pacing franticly down the aisle to generate enough confidence to slide the tagged jersey over my head. I remained nervous until I could re-clothe myself with my t-shirt and jacket that I entered the store in.

The irony is that I felt nervous and unnatural committing this larceny crime with my masked identity, but I was willing to feel uncomfortable to solidify my plan of swindling foreigners out of their money during basketball camp. The sad part is the only reason I wanted a wad of money was to flash money in front of my friends at school; it would put me on the level of a baller or a legitimate dope dealer and boost my status as a thug. I sat quietly in the car as my parents drove home. They had no inkling of the larceny that had occurred while they shopped. I never thought about the embarrassment that I could have subjected my parents to had I been arrested for my crime. I was focused selfishly on my personal gain of making money. I was determined to fit in, so I closed my mind to logical decision-making.

I decided to use my professional looking signature to forge NBA players' signatures on replicas of their jerseys with a black sharpie. I knew foreigners would not know the difference—their overexcitement about having an NBA jersey clouded their logical judgment. Once the signatures were perfected, and we (Mack and I) formulated stories of where and how we obtained the signed jerseys; we sold the jerseys for about $65 a piece. These jerseys moved rapidly, and the quick money motivated us to sneak into other campers' rooms and steal some of their jerseys for resale as they unknowingly slept in the silent nights to re-energize their bodies for the strenuous workouts the next day.

Mack and I grossed over $500 from selling stolen jerseys, and I was not proud of stealing; but I loved the quick and easy money— sin was growing out of control in my life—decision-making was altered and skewed toward negativity. Stealing was never my forte, but the love for what money could offer my street fame drove me to take criminal-minded risk. This is a prime example of how sin and inappropriate behavior leads to more sin and more destructive behaviors in our lives.

My larceny endeavors softened my attitude toward committing crimes and fed my criminal minded perspective. Majority of my illegally made money was stuck deep down in my pocket with $20 bills on top of a stack of $1 bills. I was too frugal to spend all of my money. Frugality benefited me in a positive fashion throughout my life, so I am grateful for my thought process of spending money. I did not like having empty pockets, so I made a point to never spend all of my money. It is wise to utilize extra money for sound investments rather than using majority of our money on depreciating items. I used a portion of my illegally earned money to buy jugs of candy from Sam's Club to continue my in-school candy selling business until school administrators decided to shutdown my untaxed business venture.

Those experiences taught me how to survey a target market, to appropriately set product prices, and to understand the basic logistics for restocking our stolen and non-stolen products— some simple business rules. The pursuit of money drew my interest toward some of my friends who sold crack cocaine on Atlantic Street not too far from our school. I witnessed older classmates who sold drugs in my early years of middle school, and I admired their expensive attire, their defiant personalities, and their wads of cash from shiny money clips.

I observed them closely, but I had no friendship or trusting relationship with them; so I did not aspire to sell drugs with them. However, in the eighth grade, I was focused on trying to hustle with my friends who put in work on Atlantic and Freeman Street— in my mind, I was no longer a virgin and became an official thug when I committed larceny at basketball camp. I wrestled with this decision as I thought about the D.A.R.E anthem *Dare to keep a kid off drugs* that I learned in the fifth grade from our local police enforcement officers, and I thought about my parents' desires for my life and my hidden desires to accomplish positive endeavors. At this time, my mask and my desire to appease peers overrode any sound judgment and rational-thinking needed to honor my parents' spiritual wishes. I promised to never use or touch drugs during my positive experience with the D.A.R.E. program, and I signed a promise card to validate my oral response.

I learned later on in life that the words: "never" and "promise" are empty words that hold no barring with individuals that lack integrity; I lacked integrity and character. I was a very flawed individual, and I replaced my flawed characteristics with a masked thug persona that matched a perspective opposed to what my parents tried to instill in me. I made it a point to venture out into sketchy low-income neighborhoods because I revered the life of individuals in that underground complex subculture.

Today, Wilson is a city that graduates about 50 percent of its high school students, and there is an abundance of citizens living at or below poverty level—remaining invisible to citizens thriving throughout the city. I had been a part of this intricate subculture that productive citizens fail to see, so they will never be invisible to me. My masked identity did not want this life that my parents sought out for me because I preferred to embrace a thug nature of negativity. I was curious and anxious to find out why my parents wanted us to stay away from those low-income and drug infested neighborhoods.

I was intrigued by the negative activity in those crime-ridden sectors of our city. I found myself never being content with the normalcy in my parents' world because I thought I was destined for something unique and out of their norm which I considered boring. This is a proactive approach toward change, but I sought negative ways to escape the norm and implement change. This perspective has proven to be destructive to many confused lives throughout America, and I was unknowingly headed down the road traveled by many. I sought desperately to be a part of that forbidden world and to grasp the temptation of that forbidden fruit. I thought my parents were holding me back from being a man or someone special in this difficult world.

Everything contrary to my parents' religious and righteous didactic teachings appeared to be the forbidden fruit that I sought. I found myself hanging in and around Five Points, Trade and Amoco area (Atlantic St.), Snowden Drive, and the Chapel; all areas that brought about potential trouble and negative consequences. I lived in a middle-class family with blue-collar working parents, but I was more fascinated with low-income neighborhoods and the drug life that my parents vehemently warned me about.

I felt more connected to that crime syndicate world, and I wanted to prove that I belonged in that world by any means necessary, even if I had to violate my D.A.R.E. oath. My parents worked diligently to isolate and to take us away from that impoverished world, and ultimately, it was a world where I felt I truly belonged. My mask correlated with those individuals and rejected the productive and positive citizens whom I interacted with—viewing positive and productive citizens as fake. What's real and what's fake; you cannot ask that question when you are wearing a mask.

Lessons Learned

Ignorance is a lack of information and knowledge, and stupidity is the lack of intelligence and common sense. I displayed ignorance and stupidity at different phases in my life, and both served as a source to my sins and crimes. I accumulated small sins that led to a more destructive and more sinful way of thinking. Small sins or small destructive behaviors should not be ignored because those sins or behaviors lead to more risks and detrimental life styles. I started lying about sex and committing crimes, and then my actions followed suit by having sex and committing acts of larceny. Everything starts small, and the more those small things compile, the more the small things can rob us of our identities. I evolved into a thug, and someone who wanted to appease others. Millions of Americans suffer from this faulty thinking, and they struggle to overcome bad relationships, addictions, and careers from this adopted philosophy to conciliate others.

Parents and caretakers should address any negative changes in their children and confront those small destructive behaviors before they expand to major issues. We must maintain control of our true identities and behaviors associated with our true identities; failure to do so might make us stray from our inner beliefs. I was a masked thug and losing control from my true identity, so I was driven to take more risks in the eighth grade. Risks have always been a part of my life, but negative behavioral risks normally equate to negative consequences. Stemming from small sins, I tested the waters for the remaining portion of my teenage school years.

Chapter 10

Yearning for Fame

Sports to Selling Crack Cocaine

"Life is a dream for the wise, a game for the fool, a comedy for the rich, a tragedy for the poor"
~ Sholom Aleichem

In the eighth grade, I was viewed as a talented tailback and shooting guard for the Darden-Vick Trojans (middle school team). I viewed football as an aggressive sport that meshed well with my aggressive and masked disposition. I quickly fell in love with this sport as well as the local fame that followed. I was a very elusive and aggressive football player in practice, so I earned a starting tailback position for our middle school team. I studied all of the great NFL running backs, and I tried to tailor my running style to Barry Sanders and Bo Jackson. We ran a Wing-T, which incorporated a three-tailback set. Corey and my cousin Brian shared the backfield with me, and they were both perceived as street thugs. We all got along, and we shared similar traits with our desire to pursue girls, to be popular, and to appear as street thugs.

Corey was a great friend of mine. My mom and dad allowed

him to live with us for a short span of time when he ran a way from home. He was tied in with the Trade and Amoco crew, so I sought to sell drugs with him and his crew. The more I hung around them, the more curious I became about standing on the block to distribute crack cocaine. I witnessed Corey, Trell, and Jack practice football and walk home to move cut pieces of crack at $20 a pop. I believe that they were pitching crack to provide financial support for their families. They lived in poverty, and they were immersed in that world of illicit drug sales and usage. I walked into that world, wanting to be like them.

I was there because I found their world exciting and yearned to be known as a drug dealer—pure stupidity. It was imperative to me to be able to inform my classmates that I was a legit drug dealer, and I thought it would be exciting to have actual stories to share with them at school—no more room for fairy tales; I had to keep it real. I never had to stand on that corner or any other corner and sell drugs because my needs — shelter, food, and safety — were always met by my honest and hardworking parents, but I wanted to prove that I was a thug and could survive in the intimidating streets of "Wide Awake" Wilson. To this day, I have no idea what I was attempting to prove, but I was in search of something, like the millions of lost middle school souls trotting through their overcrowded hallways striving to fit into some group they deem as pertinent.

After gaining Corey's confidence and the confidence of his crew, they allowed me to enter their intricate drug world, providing me with about (3) $20 pieces to sell from a freshly cut 8-ball that was retrieved from a semi-boarded up trap house. Instantaneously, in my immature mind, I became one of them—I was an official dope boy. This made me feel like a real man, and I valued their realness more than the honest citizens waking up at the crack of dawn to work factory jobs—street fame was more addictive than the reality of my situational ignorance.

I became the streets by dressing like them (e.g., sagging my pants, wearing white t-shirts, and sporting timberland boots), by speaking in street vernacular, and by developing a willingness to fight at the drop of a dime. "No fear" was my mantra. I stashed the crack in a used lip balm container and would pace back and forth while shaking the container as if I had no fear and was a natural in the streets. On the inside, my chest was pounding fiercely out of fear. I was nervous and exhilarated from this experience; I never realized this incident would haunt me for the rest of my life. As I paced back and forth at the corner of Atlantic St., I was paranoid about being in the presence of some of the shady characters within my vicinity and amazed by how many people were addicted to crack whom I never suspected. The volume of people was paralyzing at times; the streets came alive at night with walking zombies.

People were "geeking out" (e.g., exhibiting obnoxious behavior from a high off drugs or desire to have drugs) for another hit of some crack, and I instantly realized the power that this chemical component had over these crack zombies. As a 13-year old boy, I was shook by this unfamiliar drug culture, and I found myself quickly retreating to the clutches of darkness when vehicles emerged on the block; I did not know whom I needed to sell to or needed to run from. I knew about jump out (narcotics task force) in black vans and in black SUV's, and I was terrified by the thought of being arrested and exposed as a drug dealer to the world my parents lived in—I wanted to remain innocent in their eyes and the eyes of their counterparts.

I never took the time to process the impact that this drug epidemic had on the drug addicts and their families until crack invaded and devastated my family—two of my favorite cousins succumbed to this merciless addiction. I tried to gain illegal profits from local street drug abusers while those drug abusers took on a slow death process from their drug addiction. I observed drugs rob individuals of their ambition, health, and overall zest for life, to create a slow and conspicuous fall from societal grace. I spent my time bragging to Mack about what I had seen and what I was doing on the streets, but he was never impressed and constantly worried about an untimely demise—my negative mindset and continuous desire for fame scared him.

I focused on making money and ignorantly told peers at school that I was selling crack. I spoke as if it made me powerful and significant in middle school. I deliberately sought to bring attention to myself because even though it was stupidity, I wanted classmates to recognize and acknowledge me as a thug—I needed their approval as those crack addicts needed those pieces of crack I held in the palm of my hand. I wanted people to know I was about that street life, and I wanted people to adore me as I adored previous drug dealers in school.

I had dreams and visions of being a drug kingpin and driving fancy cars throughout local neighborhoods so people would view me as a superstar or somebody who had large stacks of money. I thought a vast amount of money validated my success in this world, and I wanted everybody to look at me as a success. I pursued success and had no idea of what real success looked like. I never really obtained the attention that I desired, and it fueled me with anger and made me desire to commit more violence in the streets. My mind was crying out for acceptance and attention.

Some people probably never assumed that I would sell crack, and I can easily identify with their thinking because I never thought I would partake in that undercover world, even when it intrigued me. Other people probably did not care, and some probably thought I was a charlatan who posed as a thug; and maybe, they were right because deep down I was far from a thug. I was a fake thug masked from my positivity. Internally, I wanted to pursue positive endeavors and spread love but my subculture surrounded me with callous individuals that I desired desperately to please.

I was drawn to street fame, and I sought that street fame through criminal activity or recognition through sport's teams. I had the mask on tight, but nobody who cared about me was really buying it. I tried my very best to be one of them and buy into their drug world, but my parents' didactic teachings and spiritual guidance consumed me with guilt as I stood and interacted with drug addicts and dope boys. One night stood out in my mind, and it changed my perspective on selling crack cocaine forever. I remember vividly selling crack to a man in his late 30s who approached me with two small and timid children. Those small children were hiding behind his legs as if they knew instinctively that their father was participating in something wrong and potentially dangerous.

My intuition kicked in, and I felt sorry for those kids—it made me think of the pain drugs was causing my family. However, I could not exhibit any signs of weakness or emotion in my disposition. I leaned back and pensively stood for a couple of seconds, and then I sternly said, "Take your f**king kids home," motioning him away with a disrespectful hand gesture. At 13 years of age, drugs gave me the authority to speak to this 30-year old man in that manner, and his craving for crack brought him into submission—sad but this is a depiction of the power of drugs. The power frightened me, and I silently prayed that he would not come back.

I felt bad for those kids and hated the way I spoke to their father. Some of the other young boys on the block smiled as if my disrespect to this man validated me, and I flashed an undeveloped smile; but I was hurting and held strong remorse on the inside—feeling nervous lumps in my throat and a heightened sense of pressure in my chest. While I was venturing to manage my emotions, he came back overjoyed for this lifeless minor piece of crack like a child on Christmas or a dog panting for doggy treats for displaying good behavior. It took him about five minutes to return, and my eyes connected with his eyes as I handed him a $10 piece of crack—the underlying pain in his eyes resonated with my upbringing, and this association nagged at my conscience.

I never sold crack again because I regretted my participation in a world that sells death to people as if I was so-called keeping it real by selling crack to other African Americans and impoverished people. I had no desire to get locked up, but fear of incarceration was not strong enough to stop me from selling crack; my conscience was the source of my desire to quit distributing crack. I would later find out that my cousin was buying crack from the same block, and this news, along with memories of my hustling days, taught me how powerful drug addiction is and how damaging crack is to all segments and races in our society—not just the poor and disenfranchised. Knowing that my cousin was on drugs —crack, specifically—hurt me to the core. I felt that I had unwittingly contributed to his addiction by glorifying selling crack by supporting this lifestyle with my callous actions in the streets and my solidarity and loyalty to known dope dealers. I witnessed first hand the power of crack, and its early intrusion into local neighborhoods around Wilson.

I no longer participated in the distribution of crack, but I continued to hang around with boys who sold crack. I was drawn to boys who broke the law, and I would not hesitate to break the law if it won me street fame and favor with these individuals. I hung with JB., and JB. was the kid who established my reputation among peers by bragging about my martial arts abilities when I moved on Shamrock drive and in our unique neighborhood. He came from a typical middle-class family, but he was attracted to the street life as well, creating a mutual partnership and friendship between us. I would walk with him to the Chapel while he made his daily crack sells.

We walked through the neighborhood in search of trouble (e.g. looking for girls looking to hookup). On occasion, he would give this woman a 20-piece of crack to rent her run down Ford Escort for hours, so as middle school students, we drove her car with no licenses throughout the city to appear cool and generate some random fun. I did not realize until later that she was the mom of a student that we shared classes with in school. We were young kids in middle school who were cruising through neighborhoods with no regard for the law. Our unspoken rule was to bail on the car if we were ever pulled over by law enforcement. I had no intention of surrendering or being subjected to any parts of the justice system.

I was aware that it was wrong to drive cars without a license, but I never rationalized juvenile prison time with this criminal offense or the shame that it could bring to my immediate family. I stated immediate because honestly, some of my family members would have been happy for my failure, no different from any other family though—blood is not always thicker than water. I realized later that it was a felony to ride in stolen vehicles, and I thank God that I never had that blemish on my record. God spared me from this illegal infraction. Both of our fathers made great money compared to the socio-economic demographics in Wilson, but JB and I were more attracted to the crime elements rather than hard work that our parents were accustomed to.

During this span of time, my life was filled with poor decision-making and regrets. I was tormented daily by thoughts of being viewed as a failure and ways that I could mask myself to be accepted by others. Drugs and alcohol were not viable options for me because I was very mindful of what I allowed to enter my body at that time. However, I do understand how inner turmoil could cause someone to indulge in substance abuse. I was paranoid, and I was scared that substance abuse would add to my paranoid state of mind.

I managed my daily stress with sex or the attention received from sports or criminal behaviors, street and sport's fame. Sometimes, I retreated to a small closet in the bedroom I shared with Mack, and I cried out in desperation for God to help me with sex and this desire to impress other people many times; but I could not escape this internalized pain and guilt, causing me to grow angry with God, religious leaders, and other people who loved me. I attempted to beg and to make promises to God: "If you help me got me out of this situation, I will never do it again." I negotiated to escape any consequences that followed my destructive lifestyle and dismal behavior, never seeking to make any true change; I desired no harsh penalties.

I did not know how to seek God. I tried to establish a relationship by attending church and by trying to understand the pastor's persuasive rhetoric to no avail—I was drove to the brink of despair and frustration. I went through the formalities of church, but my mind retained nothing and left me wondering often about God's love for me—there was a void in my life and a complete disconnect. I was not too fond of church as a teenager because we practically lived at church—feeling judged throughout the tedious process of church services. Some ushers ridiculed and judged me for chewing gum or attempting to get an extra piece of chicken at quarterly meeting services (food was also served at these services).

We attended vacation bible school, Sunday school, regular church services, choir rehearsal, usher practice, and church dinners. Honestly, I was churched out by the time I reached middle school and high school, and I connected church to a business or something to do rather than to serve God almighty. I firmly believe as King Solomon that too much of anything can be challenging to the human flesh, especially if the passion is not in it.

> *"So don't be too good or too wise! Why destroy yourself?"*
>
> ~ *(Ecclesiastes 7:16 NLT)*

I believed that everyone sitting in the pews clapping their hands, stomping their feet, shouting sounds of praise, and singing hymns was without sin; and I assumed that I was bound for hell because I was not engaged in the service like them—there was no passion coming from me. I felt like my pastor preached in a manner that made me afraid of sinning rather than focusing on the abundant love and joy that comes from serving God and striving for renewed righteousness. I focused more on not trying to sin rather than trying to seek and establish a relationship with God.

I believe when we seek to establish an intimate relationship with God, He will align our thinking to His purpose and will for our lives. This relationship and an understanding that Jesus died on the cross for our sins will trigger a desire within us to pursue righteous living and not be judgmental of others. Yet, change does not occur over night, so do not expect to completely walk away from habitual sinful behaviors and negativity. I was far from change because even though I decided to walk away from selling crack, I had no desire to walk away from street fame. I was masked to being a thug, and I was willing to portray this persona in different criminal endeavors. Church failed to correlate with my plight of acceptance among my peers.

I never thought I was worthy of God's grace or love, but I learned later none of us are worthy of God's grace or love. Today, I firmly believe God desires us to serve him out of love rather than fear—I was confused in middle and high school. This confusion within church added to my attraction of thug life and a masked identity. Wisdom from life experiences taught me that a lot of people are masked to please people whom they regard as important in their circles. For instance, there are a lot of sinners who play church (i.e., attend service every Sunday or follow religious practices and customs), but they lack a true relationship with God and an understanding of God—they act religious to impress their respective denomination or religion. Most people want to feel important or be embraced by their specific interest group.

I was angry and searching to be a part of something that would bring me love and respect from the masses because I was confident that with this approval I would gain citywide fame and success. I pursued everything aggressively and competitively, in both positive and negative situations. I was driven to prove people wrong, and this drive helped me in sports, fights, and troubled situations. I strategically sought out ways to win, and I developed this belief that I could accomplish anything or like rapper 50 cent stated, "die trying."

My will to win and to prove others wrong superseded my talent and miniature body at times. One time, Deon told me that

I could not lift a car, and I sweated for hours trying to lift that car until I was satisfied with the back-and-forth movement of my dad's old-beat up Cutlass Supreme—I was driven to win, even over logic. I made a lot of bad decisions in middle school, but sometimes I tried to avoid problematic situations. I wanted to be James, but the masked identity won by default when my desire to appease my peers outdueled my will to be authentic.

I vividly remember battling my fleshly desire one time in middle school because I was trying to avoid a fight with Telly. Telly challenged me to a duel over some girl, I guess, I still do not know what the true motive was to this day. Instantly, I became nervous because I was trying to understand the reasoning behind his level of disrespect. At this point, I was receiving information from third party individuals, not Telly, so I hoped that the information was misleading and a mistake. I prayed hard for some kind of positive resolution because I was determined to avoid this fighting situation. I avoided him for days, and I made the extra effort to stay away from common areas where students congregated in school, such as bathrooms and the gym in the morning where students congregated. Kelsie, my neighborhood friend and informal crew member whom I respected as a fighter and as an athlete came to me in the locker room after PE to tell me that Telly was waiting for me in the bathroom—I knew my school cred was on the line, but I had no desire to fight.

I tried to come up with excuses that would make me appear tough while avoiding this potential fight. Kelsie seemed disappointed and stunned by my words and his despondent attitude, and his facial expressions made my mind wonder about what other classmates must be thinking or saying about me "James is scared and James is punk," so I gathered myself and quietly said, "Let's go." I started praying that this fight would be resolved with words because I was still opposed to any physical combat with Telly.

I tried to laugh and belittle this situation when I arrived in the condensed and smelly bathroom, Telly was squared off in the center with his small hands clinched—no compromised appeared to be in sight. As he continued to disrespect me, people began to laugh and probably question my toughness, so I became enraged and wanted to shut his mouth with my shaking fists. Without thinking, I closed the distance between us in the bathroom with ill intentions to gain an intimidation advantage (lessons learned from Deon). When I could tell mentally that he was not going to back down, I unloaded two solid punches to his chin and maneuvered my right arm around his neck to put him in a standing submission chokehold.

I had lost all control, and I locked in on him like a lion to its vulnerable prey. I choked him with so much force that he started to lose consciousness. Bystanders rushed in to extract me from the altercation, but my adrenaline kicked in, and the room went silent to me as they fought to separate us from each other. Eventually, the principal heard about what happened in the bathroom, and we were summoned to his small-spaced office with boxes stacked on top of his desk. Once again, I started murmuring the 23 Psalm while I nervously waited in his office. My prayers appeared to be answered because Telly and I worked together to convince the principal that we were playfully wrestling in the bathroom. I planned to receive a suspension, but I walked away with a warning. I was convinced that God showed me favor for my prayer, but I was still far from submitting to his will.

Lessons Learned

Fame is intoxicating because most people want to be known or appreciated for something, negative or positive; some people want to believe they will be remembered after death. I desired fame by any means necessary, using Malcolm X famous quote but in a negative fashion because I sought fame as a thug; however, I loved stardom from sports as well—any love was great love in my eyes. I witnessed admiration from my peers as my popularity grew, so I worked to enhance my noticeability, leading me to adopt a masked identity. Some Christians who I came in contact with wanted to be perceived as holy, so they spent a lot of their time at church, even when they despised being there. I met other people who worked countless hours for a job that they hated, only to barely make their ends meet. Why do we navigate our lives in this fashion? There are multiple factors that cause us to submit to this form of legalism, but the desire to appease others and conform to their expectations in prison people to their masked identities and masked lives.

We must fight to refrain ourselves from embracing this enslaved way of thinking because it keeps us masked from our true potential and in search of fame that never brings ultimate peace and happiness. I chose the street and sports fame, and I was willing to hide my authentic self for the love of the fame. My last year of middle school and early years of high school brought much promise, but if the inner self is flawed, it is a matter of time before the external image cracks from strained pressure . . . pressure bursts pipes.

Chapter 11

Sunshine Before Rain

No Second Chances with these Choices

"Success is not final, failure is not fatal: It is the courage to continue that counts"
~ *Winston Churchill*

Along with negative recognition, my eighth-grade year was also the year when my name started to get respect from athletes and coaches throughout the city. Darden-Vick middle school was my stage, and that school gave me two main platforms (i.e., the football field and the basketball court) to display my athletic prowess and aptitude. I was short and small in stature, but I had some amazing speed and quickness that enhanced my success in football and in basketball with the bigger boys. I was passionate about sports, so I played with a lot of heart and with a winning mindset.

To my expectations, I concluded a subpar middle school football season with a final game at Beddingfield high school, in front of my future high school coaches and classmates—this game was played at that arena so our future high school coaches could observe their upcoming talent from the two feeder middle schools (Darden and Speight). This contest featured both schools against each other, so I was determined to represent Darden-Vick and put on a show in front of the Beddingfield coaching staff. The game drew in a crowd of about 500 or more spectators, which constitutes as a large crowd for a middle school football game in our locale.

I only carried the ball four times in that particular game, but I scored 3 touchdowns on runs of 30 yards and more on each tot. I left a positive impression on Coach Johnson and most spectators who crammed their bodies in that stadium on that day. I believe the limited number of touches played in my favor because I amassed for over 100 yards rushing in my efforts, inciting the crowd for more. I was determined to show everybody that I had the ability to succeed and to dominate at the high school level, regardless of my small physical frame.

Some people took notice, and my athletic ability enhanced my popularity among girls and classmates; it made me more visible within our city and prone to even more temptations, which is cancerous to a weak-minded individual. I learned that success breathes happiness and an array of sunshine, but success can also generate jealousy amid so-called friends. Some friends down played my performance, and some stated that it was still just a middle school game, not a high school game, making the performance appear as no big deal—but, it was a huge deal to me and that's what mattered most in that moment.

If I cared only about what mattered to me with all actions and behaviors, I would have been an academic standout and athletic triumph. This sunshine obstructed my vision to a cloudy forecast in my near future because I was still masked; I was just enjoying something positive for the time being with sports. The trick is that sports are closely related to the thug culture within the minds of a lot of impoverished black youth. Even though I can state boldly that my victorious performance in the game excited me, I allowed some of those negative comments to bother me. At that time, I failed to truly appreciate my play in that game because I dwelled on some of those negative comments, trying to decipher the underlying meaning (i.e., "Maybe it was not a great performance and maybe I am not that great at running the football as my father stated"). My willingness to be liked and my perpetual way of questioning people's comments or body language made me never feel up-to-par or good enough for others—I adopted this thinking well into adulthood.

Life experiences taught me to stop placing time and energy into negative thinking, negative situations, and negative people because negativity constricts our thinking and limits our true potential. A successful life is predicated upon an individual finding their true voice and leading a life tailored to their God-given purpose. However, I did not think in this manner, and I preferred to continue tweaking my identity to mesh with my friends' desires and strong opinions of me. During those years, I secretly adopted an ignorant mindset and embraced a philosophy of never-ending violence or poverty.

I found myself seeking out like-minded ignorant individuals and frequenting impoverished environments. I never appreciated the life I had at home, or my parents until I got much older and much wiser. My parents always told me that I would be judged for the way I spoke and acted when I was around intellectual people and productive citizens—I saw no importance in their utterance though—I did not know too many so-called intellectual people. I wanted to care, but in my mind, I was in too deep and refused to allow myself to grasp my mom's point of view.

I had parents that wanted to protect me and to guide me to an auspicious future, but at that time, I wanted parents that would allow me to roam the streets and do as I pleased, not realizing that that is poor parenting. I found balance and solace from my participation in sports because sports gave me an opportunity to take off my mask and be the real me for several hours. It was a small span of time that allowed me to be comfortable in my own skin rather than trying to emulate neighborhood gangsters or fictitious characters on TV.

I created one simple and concise prayer that I recited before every football and basketball game: "Please God don't allow anyone to get injured, and allow me to play my hardest and be great out there." As I transitioned from football to basketball, I averaged about 16 points per game for my Darden-Vick Trojans basketball team, and I made majority of my points by utilizing my speed, to beat opposing players to the hoop. I had an extremely quick first-step, an impressive ability to float the ball over taller opponents, and a respectable jump shot, making me fairly dominate at beating my opponent off the dribble; I can still beat most defenders at the age of 32.

My final year of middle school helped me develop a sense of confidence in sports, and I was sure that I could compete and succeed in sports at the high school level. I felt normal while playing sports. I did not have to don a mask while engaging in athletic activities because the sports came natural to me. My ability and my mindset propelled me into stardom and success in football, basketball, and wrestling during my high school years. However, many distractions deterred me from ever reaching my peak in either sport, and worldly temptations and a masked identity would drive me to unchangeable consequences and away from the comfort and safety of my parents' home. Defiance served as a factor to most of my poor choices in high school—the rain was coming, but to me the forecast still appeared fairly clear.

My ninth-grade year, I dated older girls, and it made me appear as a "playa" to juniors and seniors at Beddingfield; but I was determined not to engage in sex—I wanted to be a born again virgin. I wanted to keep this unrealistic goal. I state unrealistic because I had no relationship with God, and I continued to position myself in lustful relationships and sexual situations. However, this goal seemed plausible at the time, but in hindsight, I found it more difficult to stop having sex after losing my virginity due to my immaturity.

I knew what it felt like, and I was willing to compromise on the position that I did it once; so one more time will not be bad— many of us play that one more time game. My freshman year, I held true to that promise because I refrained from sexual contact that entire school year; I would kiss and rub on girls to satisfy my lustful desires, trying to trick myself into thinking this behavior would suffice and keep me from having sex. Lustful desires will eventually lead to sexual intercourse or to inappropriate behavior, and it did not help that I loved the comments received from classmates about me being a "playa" or "the man" because it created an interest from some of the pretty girls in our school.

Some people may be confused about the power of those words or any words for that matter. The implications of those words helped validate my status among the elitist of our high school, and those words were spoken in a fashion of acceptance within our unique vernacular of our subculture. My intentions were never to treat young ladies in a disrespectful manner, but I was always aiming to be someone who fits in with the in-crowd that tended to disrespect naïve and beautiful young ladies. All of these accumulating behaviors served as a contributing factor for the donning of my mask that was far from my true identity of exhibiting kindness and love to everyone in this complex world.

Unresolved poor behaviors or issues can transform into major crises. I learned within two short years of high school that everything reaches a boiling point before circumstances explode and become uncontrollable. I dated throughout my life, so I was never single in high school. I felt like I was a little less of a man if I did not have a girlfriend because thugs paraded around with a beautiful jump-off (girls that they sleep around with) or a girlfriend. My male peers sort of expected me to have a girlfriend or a jump-off, and if not, they would taunt me with questions about my sexual preference or make comments that challenged my manhood. Almost everyday, they would overwhelm me with questions of, "Are you hitting that," and "how many girls have you been with?" If I came off as not having sex, they would tease me relentlessly until I made up lies about girls I was sleeping with—to maintain my lie, the girls came from out of town.

They were very intrusive and felt privy to my life, and I obliged to fit in and to keep this array of deceptive sunshine. Being great at sports shielded me from some of those jibes because my male classmates spoke about sports just as much as sex. The main topics of all of our conversations revolved around sins of being vain and prideful. We discussed girls' looks, sex, sports, money, cars, fighting, or our apparel—it was as if we were little kids bragging during a show-and-tell session. I wore Timberland boots, jewelry, bagging "Champs" sweatpants, and a plain t-shirt majority of the time in high school as if I was a member of Wu-Tang Clan (popular rap group in the 90s). I portrayed the thug life role with my walk, my talk, my mannerisms, and my attitude, so some people embraced me as a thug that happen to be above average in sports.

I played junior varsity (JV) sports my freshman and sopho-more years of high school, in basketball and football. I ran for over 1,000 yards both seasons in football and tallied 14 touchdowns, and realistically, I should of had more yards and touchdowns; but I shared the backfield with two other very talented tailbacks, Brian and Eugene (Rat) my sophomore year. I was also suspended for several games due to my attitude and to team infractions that incurred during school or during football practices. Coach Neal was my JV football coach, and he was legendary to football play-ers at Beddingfield and a great role model; he did not put up with my ignorant or irrational behavior on or off the football field.

He cared more about saving my soul and turning me into a positive young man. He was driven to direct me toward the road not taken—he benched me at times and risked losing games to teach me some life lessons. He was one of those rare people in my life that I viewed as authentic and special, and even if I did not consistently show it, I always respected and valued his opinions. Junior varsity basketball was more challenging than football because basketball was more psychological. I lacked self-assurance on the basketball court and questioned my height and abilities at times, causing me to freeze up and mess up at vital points of the basketball game.

I wondered if I appeared sexy to the ladies on the basketball court—paranoid, thinking that smiles in the crowd indicated that people were quietly laughing and picking at me. My mind was crowded with belittling thoughts that stifled my progression because I cared deeply about what others thought about me— opinions controlled my life and continued to mask my identity. I was not mentally tough enough to handle my coaches' or fans' comments about my basketball abilities, so I wore an unsure mask about the quality of my skill on the court. In football, I felt like my helmet and other football equipment shielded me from the stares of fans, so I was able to focus more on my game rather than on attempting to impress people with my image.

Mentally, football felt more natural than basketball as well. I believed my physical appearance mattered in basketball, so I drove myself crazy thinking that fans would ridicule and critique my body and appearance—my confidence was shot, and I had a hard time believing females when they acted as if they admired my looks. I shielded my paranoia from others with a charismatic smile and sly innuendos about me not caring what no one thinks about me—if only those classmates could read my complex mind, I would have been exposed as a fraud. When I ran up the basketball court, I envisioned everybody in the gym staring and laughing at the way I looked and at the way I dribbled or shot the basketball—this crazy mind imprisoned my abilities and limited my personal maturity.

A successful basketball game was normally predicated from some generated confidence at the start. If I made shots early and often in the game, I felt confident and played well for the rest of the game. I lacked the ability to motivate myself from poor starts because I was too focused on what other people thought about me—their thoughts were more important than my individual thoughts and inner convictions. I was married to popularity and thoughts of sunshine, and it became my ball-in-chain—a crutch from my true potential. I remember constantly asking my parents and my brothers, "Do I really look good," "do you think I am muscular," and "do you think I am really good at basketball or football," and for some peculiar reason, it bothered me when my family members would say "yes" because I did not believe them—I thought they were saying that out of love.

Their responses elicited anger within me, and that anger made me work even harder on my image, to ensure that I was accepted by the school in-crowd. It pains me to think about how many young boys and girls probably appear confident everyday at school, but struggle internally with the fear of not being good enough or accepted by their classmates. Some hide their feelings until they cross a point of no return and take their own precious lives. This mindset makes us prisoners of our own mind by generating stressful thoughts on a daily basis. For some reason, the stress diminished when I wore football equipment, but elevated when I donned those embroidered Bruin tight shorts and muscle man jerseys. The Bruin bear face is the only part of that embedded symbol that gave off the perception of a fierce team; and I lacked the fierceness needed to trot confidently up the court at times.

I received a lot of love from my parents and siblings, but I wanted to feel that same affection from everyone within my intimate social gatherings (i.e., parties, pools, malls, gyms, and lunchrooms). I never could quite acquire that same satisfaction in relationships with classmates and school-aged peers, and it drove me farther and farther away from my true identity. I played basketball because like most kids in the early 90s, I wanted to be like Michael "Air" Jordan. I wanted desperately to score a lot of points like Mike, but I felt insecure in most games, and it limited my abilities on the basketball court. I never played up to my gifted-abilities in most high school basketball games because I fought with psychological fear—fear blocks the mind from those corridors to successful neural pathways. I battled internal thoughts about my image like a 12-year old school girl . . . sad but very true—I was 15 and more confused than ever. I was consumed by thought after thought until my body froze up on the basketball court, causing me to pass the ball to teammates out of fear of making a bad decision rather than attempting to dribble or shoot.

However, I still managed to average about 15 points a game on the JV team during my sophomore season, and it was primarily due to the recognition and to the affirmative feedback that my coaches and my teammates provided me during a memorable game against Tarboro high school. Entering the final quarter of our game, we were losing by 8 points, and somehow, I scored 12 impressive points in a span of about 3 minutes with one circus shot off the backboard to give our team the lead with six seconds remaining in the game.

My teammates went crazy and this favorable energy carried me for the remainder of the season. It is amazing how praises and name recognition can motivate or inspire an individual to perform at a higher-level than usual. I felt like God shined on me during that unforgettable game, but dismal choices afterwards transformed that night into something regrettable. Somebody on our team had a genius idea to smoke weed after the game, and ignorantly, I felt obliged to affirm this request with a subtle response of, "I am down."

Up to this point, I had never smoked weed, but I was willing to go along with everybody involved in this poorly planned decision. I felt special to be a part of this unique cohort. I only smoked weed that day to participate with the in-crowd, so I sold a part of my identity to embrace a behavior that I was opposed to. Sadly, I have known drug addicts and reformed addicts who smoked crack pipes or sniffed lines of cocaine or heroin to fit in with some negative subculture. Even though I engaged in this behavior, it never became habitual due to my inner fear that weed and alcohol could negatively impact my athletic abilities—sports were more important than anything at that stage of my life. For some reason, some of the players who decided not to join us on our weed-smoking venture made it a point to offer unsolicited information to teammates and coaches after encouraging us to smoke weed, so as soon as they saw an opportunity for some cheese; they bit and swallowed the moldy cheese like mice with pleasure. There were a total of five basketball players, and three cheerleaders sauntering to Tarboro's activity bus in the quietness of that night to smoke weed and to possibly score a sexual encounter.

The boys out numbered the girls, so some girls did not find a lust interest in all of the boys. Kelsie and I were the odd boys out, and we happily served as lookout for the three couples engrossed in high-level PDA (public display of affection) as the military refer to it. I became personally invested in this lookout task because Mack was on the bus locked-lip with one of those cheerleaders; I did not want my brother to get caught in this risky ordeal because he just got back on the team after his academic suspension. While Kelsie and I swayed our heads back-and-forth from the sexual action on the bus and the exit door to the gymnasium, we spotted some flashlights aiming toward the vicinity of our bus. We knew that those lights meant trouble, so we yelled out "Police" and bolted from the bus, sprinting with an aimed focus toward a Popeye's restaurant across the street.

We were not running toward that quick-service for their delicious chicken strips and biscuits; we were running from the authorities and foolishly darted into incoming traffic on a busy highway as if it was a life or death situation—doing wrong can cause individuals to cloud their judgment and to make erratic choices. We positioned ourselves in harms way because we had a desire to smoke weed and to engage in lustful behaviors. It brings to mind this scripture: "The wages of sin is death." I was oblivious to the danger of running through car traffic because my mind was fixated on getting away and not getting caught.

Eventually, we dodged our way out of traffic and found ourselves circling back to the front entrance of Tarboro high school gymnasium. My adrenaline was wearing down and transparent thoughts were starting to enter my mind. I understood and thought about the stupidity of this situation, the danger of darting across the highway, and Mack possibly getting caught on the bus.

Once again, I made a dumb decision, but this time my decision involved and impacted my brother; I never wanted Mack to get in trouble. I went from having the best game of my life in high school to smoking weed for the first time and getting in trouble—irony.

When Kelsie and I arrived at the entrance of the gymnasium, we were able to persuade the door attendant to allow us to reenter the gym—charisma blessed me in a lot of troubling situations. We snuck into the stands while the varsity girls were still playing, and comported ourselves like we never left the gym. People were whispering and asking us questions about the incident, but we proceeded to act dumbfounded and to my surprise people bought our fake story of hanging out with some phantom girls from Tarboro. Mack and the two other teammates who remained on the bus were ultimately suspended for five days from school and suspended from the two upcoming basketball games. I hated the fact that Mack got suspended because I felt like I played a significant part in his suspension. I probably influenced him to follow us on the bus, but I never wanted him or my teammates to get in trouble—there is no predicting how ignorance turns out though.

Mack never played high school basketball again after that season due to his constant academic issues. Those factors prevented Wilson basketball fans from witnessing one of the most talented basketball players in our school from showcasing his talents—there are thousands of people like Mack whom I have met around our great country who never showcase their talents due to poor decisions. During my sophomore year, I started to rethink my vow of not having sex because girls were developing and looking more like the provocative video girls from television and music videos—I wanted to be down with O.P.P. (popular sexual song of the 90s by Naughty by Nature). Female students were wearing tighter clothes and filling them out like Jet Beauty's of the Week, and they spoke more aggressively about wanting to have sex. My hormones were raging, and I could tell bad decisions were in my near future. I thought the sun was still shining on me, in more ways than one, and the interest received from girls served as one—in my mind.

I developed this habit of hanging around at school after basketball practice to flirt with cheerleaders or random girls who stayed after school as well. I spent my time thinking about having sex with some girls who stayed after school, and some of the girls hanging around must have thought about similar things because our conversations always led to discussions of sex. There never seemed to be teachers around after school, so it provided us with opportunities to be sneaky and to engage in sexual behaviors.

No adult supervision and no parents equaled ample opportunity to make bad decisions and take dumb risks. I am convinced that as children mature, children need positive guidance to enhance their chance of making wise decisions. One day a group of us were hanging around in the commons area after school, and sex became the topic of our conversation. I began to lie and to brag about random incidents during which I pleased girls sexually. In reality, I was very inexperienced; the biggest boasters are often the biggest deceivers.

Cynthia was trading sexual banter with me, so we discussed what it might feel like to have sex together. Soon, this playful conversation led us to engage in unprotected sex in some dusty and dirty unlocked theater arts room. I utilized the popular ghetto-minded pullout method because it was chosen as a way to prevent pregnancies within my sex uneducated subculture. Not once did I think about sexually transmitted diseases, I only thought about potentially getting her pregnant—I thought about how impressed some of my classmates appeared to be with my ability to woo Cynthia into this sexual encounter.

I felt confident that the pullout method worked until about a month later when she stated that she was possibly pregnant by me. I quickly expressed to her that the baby was not mine, and I demonstrated no interest in the conversation or a future relationship with her. As soon as I hung up the phone with her, I retreated to my shared bathroom with my brothers, and I wept and pleaded with God to make this problem go away.

I had no desire to be a father—my intention was to have sex and to have fun and keep it moving—never to change diapers or to burp a needy baby after their feeding. I pray that teenage girls reading this book focus on this underlying theme; most young boys desire sex, not true commitment and definitely not a baby—baby talk runs immature boys away, speaking from experience. I wanted the sexual encounters to add to my sunshine by bolstering my name as a playa, but I was not ready to be a father and shutdown all talk to her and to anyone else attempting to bring up the uncomfortable situation.

I thought if I refrained from speaking about the baby situation, the situation would go away. This situation had me stressed as a 15-year old boy because I was still trying to figure out my convoluted self as a person . . . how could I possibly raise a baby? I was terrified by this ordeal because my parents still thought I was a virgin; and I had no interest in Cynthia or a baby with her for a lifetime—poor choices do not give us an opportunity to call the shots.

I have never met a boy in high school who had a strong desire to be a young and bare-chest father. My cohort of friends desired sex with minimal commitment, but we did not want babies to ever enter the equations—babies created improper fractions or illogical solutions in our unique circle. I was very stressed the entire nine months of her pregnancy, trying desperately to keep her condition a secret. I tried to live in this state of denial about Cynthia's pregnancy and keep the information from my parents.

Cynthia stopped coming to school, so I tried to disregard the pregnancy. My mantra was "out of sight out of mind" when it came to her condition. She taunted me by telling me several times that she had aborted the fetus. So, I was surprised and a little pissed off when I saw her belly swollen with life six months after she decided to return to school from her voluntary leave. I was afraid of having a child and eventually that fear transformed to anger because I was potentially having a baby with a girl I barely knew and did not particularly like.

Regardless of how I felt, DNA testing concluded that I became a father two months after my 16th birthday, thus contributing to the dismal statistics of young black teen fathers in our society. In one uncomfortable conversation with my parents before the baby's birth, they not only learned that I was no longer a virgin, but that I might have a baby on the way. This floored them and shattered my innocent image in their eyes forever.

Trust was a virtue that I lost in my relationship with my parents. I lied to my parents and wore a mask for all of my teenage years, and now, my parents were being introduced to a James whom they were not familiar with. It is hard for young mothers and young fathers to effectively raise a young baby, but it is even more daunting when they are too immature to properly communicate and to get along. I was mad at myself and mad at Cynthia. I was fatigued by the entire situation, and I wanted no parts of being a teenage father.

During those early years, I was known as a part-time father because I could not allow my immaturity to see past the mother of my child; this ignorant mindset would not allow me to commit to being a father until years after high school. My daughter (Tia) was a beautiful baby, but I had no desire to be around her at times; when I looked at her, I saw irreversible failure and a decision that I despised.

My experiences with my children out-of-wedlock taught me that raising children with genuine love make you a real father. I was there a lot of times in the physical with my daughter, but mentally, my mind would wander off to, "what if she never got pregnant" or "what if I waited till marriage to have sex?" Having kids out of marriage brings many challenges that young boys never think about when they are attempting to raise their sexual numbers with beautiful young girls. The fact is people get older and mentalities change, and parenting philosophies become an issue when one parent has a different perspective and it's impossible to work as a loving team.

Sunshine came in abundance early in my high school years,

but poor options to embody this coward thug persona gave me no second chances. After 16, I would have some great moments, but the sunshine was fleeting fast. Thug life became my father, and I became the obedient son. At that time, I was blinded to my ignorance and crude behaviors; I blamed Cynthia and society for my ills rather than unmasking and looking internally at the source to my problems—me.

Lessons Learned

Life is a continuous process, but sometimes we stay stuck at the start. As I paraphrase Ecclesiastes 9:11, the race is not given to the fastest, but to those who endure. Life is not a sprint, it is a marathon, and all those who finish the marathon are winners. I was stuck at the start because I was so impressed by the sunshine received from athletics at the start and recognition generated from that sunshine. I was masked from my true potential and true self because I chased fame and recognition.

This pursuit of temporary happiness drove me to don the mask of a thug, and the destructive behaviors that came with it. I believe it is impossible to progress when you are stuck chasing things at the start of any cycle and negative distractions (i.e., having a child as a teenager, smoking weed, and blaming others for mistakes) kept me stuck in the beginning stages of life's cycle. Sunshine does not last forever, and we must acknowledge when the sun is gone. When my sun went to set, my world became cold and dark, finding myself lost in a world with more confusion and chaos.

Chapter 12

Which Way is Up? I Can No Longer Recognize My Face

My Mask became the Enemy

"No thyself, no thy enemy, a thousand battles, a thousand victories"

~ Sun-Tzu

With no direction and purpose, I believe people walk aimlessly and unprepared for life's challenges. I was still trying to find myself, while attempting to blame other people for my self-inflicted problems. I started to define myself more and more as a thug—I was about that life. I hung out with classmates who skipped school, so I adopted those same negative behaviors as well—I loaded my parents' vehicles with those friends and traveled to places to smoke weed and to engage in risky sexual behavior. My mother always passionately expressed, people tend to mirror the behavior of the company they keep, or in other words, negative activity attracts negative actions or behaviors when added together.

School was starting to be an after thought because I viewed school as something I was obligated to do, rather than something

I needed to do. I lacked the desire for attending school for educational purposes; sports were my inspiration for sharing the classroom environment with my peers who appeared to have their lives figured out. I spewed false rhetoric around my parents though because I played the daily I going to college game—all I really wanted to do was play football or basketball professionally. I thought the NFL or NBA was the only way to fix my messed up life, and I perceived this endeavor to be more attainable than earning a college degree. Having a baby at 16-years old felt like a death sentence, and I thought I was destined for the streets and some ultimate life's failure.

I decided to revisit the world of street hustling, but I no longer had the heart for distributing hard drugs (i.e., cocaine, crack, and heroin). I sold ounces of marijuana from time-to-time for my cousin Mitch, as he attempted to slowly transition me back into the ins and outs of the street game. I worked at McDonald's with Mack and Mitch, but Mitch and I maintained the side weed hustle—Mitch for the love of money, and I pursued it for money and maintenance of street cred.

I wanted the legal money to shield me from any suspicion of selling drugs, now that I was older, I did not want anyone knowing of this arcane drug dealing life—I was no longer a juvenile, so charges would stick to my record for life—I cared about having a blemish free record; I am not jail material. Mack, Mitch, and I worked the same shift at McDonald's, so we devised strategic ways to smoke weed at work. We took turns acting as if we were taking out the trash, so we could take turns smoking the blunt left behind on a phonebook in the outside trash area.

With eyes red and reeking of marijuana smoke, we internalized the hunger and lethargic emotions to cheat our job with dismal work habits. We used our time gossiping, flirting with girls, and eating chicken nuggets and doubled stacked big macs—it was not long before we all received our termination papers. I was never a huge fan of smoking weed, but I gave in at times, feeling this behavior fit the thug persona mold. I thought weed smoke would restrict my lungs from performing appropriately and impact my production in sports. I was known for stating, "I do not smoke weed, I am an athlete," at times when my friends or some family members asked me to smoke.

I was convinced that I was a thug—I had the girls, semi-street cred, and no fear of the police or breaking the law. I tactfully planned to keep respected street boys and girls in my parents' vehicles for specific reasons: those individuals could vouch for my street cred and those individuals egged me on to feel great about doing things contrary to my beliefs or hidden identity—that is needed when you assume a masked identity. I cruised and hung around with boys from Snowden Drive, Five Points, and the Chapel, smoking tightly-rolled blunts and having sex in my parents' spiritual vehicles that was used to travel to bible studies and church services.

One night, I met a girl named Tammy strolling around Atlantic St. while I was attempting to sell a couple of dime bags. We proceeded to get involved sexually, but eventually that relationship materialized into a more serious relationship; she became my girlfriend. I was drawn to her street demeanor and to her sexual desires. My parents opposed of this relationship from the start and with good reason, but my hormones disagreed with their rational and logical way of viewing relationships; they wanted me with a wholesome girl who walked around totting bibles and pails of holy water—complete exaggeration, but girls I could not be happy with—I was too immature to date anyway though.

Tammy and I were raised in vastly different homes, but lust forced us to compromise and to suppress any sound judgment. She came from an impoverished and more sinister neighborhood, and her parents gave her a lot of freedom (dating and hanging out all times of the night)—I loved the freedom, and she had the life I thought I desired. Dating her made me feel more like a thug because I had a girl with some street credibility. I was 16, and several months shy of 17 when I began to rebel against my parents' rules as a confused junior in high school. In my mind, I was grown, and I was going to make my own rules regardless of my parents' religious philosophies—nothing or no one was going to stop me—not even God in my mind.

I lost respect for my parents, and I was mad that God allowed me to have a baby and sports were not working in my favor. I left with Tammy one night to Fayetteville, NC about an hour south of Wilson, and our car broke down, causing me to return home tired at around 2:00 am. My parents were waiting and met me at the door with a barrage of questions that stemmed from my late arrival, and my night out with Tammy.

The argument reached a boiling point when my parents forbade me from dating her and placed me on punishment—I was determined to stay with her and do what I desired. I still remember looking at the pain in their eyes because they probably saw a child no longer recognizable from their perspective. There disappointment made me feel calm and rational for a brief moment, but negative thoughts attacked my psyche and challenged my manhood and my thug persona.

My temper took me from being calm to ignorance in a matter of seconds, so I stormed off to my shared bedroom with Mack, as he observed me from a distance with sadness in his eyes—from his perspective, his twin has snapped and lost it. I was born strong-willed, and my pride would not allow me to turn back and apologize to my parents. I packed some clothes and arrogantly walked toward the front door with an imperious demeanor; I looked back in my mom's watery and tired looking eyes and said, "I am out." My mom cried uncontrollably, and my dad said, "Let him go Dot," with disappointment and disdain in his voice.

I almost cried as I walked out of that door and had a strong inner desire that told me to go back home, but my ego was stronger than any rationality, taking me far from the safe comfort of 2104 Shamrock Drive—now, I was homeless and embarked on an unknown journey. I walked five miles in the dark while the cold wind whipped my face and pierced my young lungs. I found myself lost and headed to the one place I thought I was welcome—Tammy's parents' trailer. I felt tough as I proceeded to her residence, and I possessed no fear walking those murderous streets as a 16-year old, not realizing God had his arms around me and protected me from any lurking dangers. I had no gun, and I was no threat for the real tough guys that lived those streets on a daily basis—I was trapped behind this mask and could no longer recognize my face. I decided to depart from my warm and safe home to move in with a girl whom I dated for about three months.

I went from a house with my own room to a small singlewide trailer with one toilet that required a bucket full of water to flush, one kerosene heater, and limited space to circumvent throughout this unique environment. This depiction of their living conditions is no slight at them; it is to demonstrate my thought process, and how my masked identity obscured my vision and my rational thinking. It was a limited supply of food, but none of these hardships were strong enough to influence me to return home—in my mind, I was free, and I was a man that did not have to listen to my parents. I did not care that I was hungry, dirty, and subjected to danger on a daily basis; I cared more about proving a point and adopting this so-called thug life that Tupac portrayed.

At the time, I had a modest 2.5 GPA, and I knew that it was sufficient enough to potentially earn me an athletic scholarship in football. School and sports conflicted with my new living condition because I stopped attending school, nobody held me accountable for missing school; but I will admit that Tammy did encourage me to continue attending school—I desired to stay out of school with her and her friends. Her parents were not bad people, and I appreciate how they rushed to my aide in my time of need. But, they did not force me to go to school because they failed to comprehend the importance of a sound education. They did not allow their daughter to sleep in the same room with me, but we snuck off together at night when they were sound asleep— we never used condoms for protection.

I never was too worried about her getting pregnant for some illogical reason. I was certain that it would not happen again to me, God would not allow me to have another child before marriage. I took self-imposed risks and relied on God to bail me out; this was an ignorant way of approaching life. People attempted to persuade me to return home, but I was stubborn and repudiated their coherent thinking. Derrick Liles (RIP), AJ, Aunt Lit, Tony, Mitch, Coach Johnson, and my brothers all tried their best to sway me to return home, to no avail. Eventually, Tammy and I got kicked out of her house for failing to abide by her parents' rules, so we tried our best to survive the winter streets of Wilson.

We exited from the cold streets to a local post office in Five Points because we had no viable options to retreat to at that time. I went from my respective home to trying to remain warm and safe in a local post office with my girlfriend—that's crazy. After staying out our welcome in the post office, we covered all radius of the city scrapping for money to purchase a room in some dirty and smelly motel for the night on highway 301. It was taxing to sleep soundly with no money and no help, but I felt I gone too far to go back. I stopped attending school, and I had no real intentions on going back—college was becoming an afterthought.

When we ran out of money, Tammy was able to convince her friends to allow us to stay at their house since their mom worked the third shift. This was a great arrangement, and in my young mind, I thought this deal would last forever. Deon taught me that nothing last forever, but I wanted to believe this arrangement was the exception to his rule. I soon realized a dead situation could become a live situation in a matter of minutes when I failed to tame my deadly tongue.

> *"The tongue can bring death or life; those who love*
> *to talk will reap the consequences"*
> *~ Proverbs 18:21 NLV*

I had the propensity to brag about fights or people I could

beat to brand myself more as a tough guy. As I congregated with some of Tammy's friends, I found myself bragging about my past confrontation with Monica's brothers, and I joked with them about putting fear in her brothers and made it known that I could beat all of them up—remember, I was the one running to the bowling alley the last time I seen them in the fourth grade.

I never paid any attention to one of the girls sneaking out of the rear door of the house, but I soon learned that she brought some savory looking individuals to Tammy's friend's house. I sat in the house unaware that some of Monica's brothers and friends assembled outside of the house, posing in the street with blunts and 40 bottles. My boasting and big mouth got me in some uncharted trouble. All of a sudden, one of Monica's brothers requested my presence outside, speaking with an aggressive overtone. When I arrived outside, Monica's brother began to question me and some trepidation overcame me.

I was intimidated by the presence of some of those full-bearded adults clutching their 40s bottles and closing in on me with bad intentions written all over their faces—the hair stood up on the back of my neck, I felt danger was near—I had no desire to find out what would happen next. I calmly backed up and separated my face and body from their striking distance, and I stated, "You all want to jump me right," with a slight smile on my face as I turned and sprinted as fast as I could from the scene and toward the oncoming Tarboro Street traffic. I wore Timberland boots and bagging jean pants, but they were the ones who lacked the speed and endurance to pursue me on foot. I ran like Forrest in the 1990s popular movie *Forrest Gump* until I reached a Hardee's on Herring Avenue about 300 feet away. I was desperate for assistance, so I rushed in the establishment and convinced the employees to allow me to use their phone to call my friend Kelsie; there were no cell phones in those days.

I was able to outrun those young adults as some trailed me on bicycles. At that time, I was running a 10.8 in the 100 meters, so I was confident that my speed gave me a decisive advantage over their smoke-infested lungs and poorly managed bodies. Once those guys spotted my terrified 16-year old face, they saw me on a telephone and quickly dispersed—probably thinking I had called the police. Calling the police was far from my mind. I thought about getting even, and I was trying to locate anyone who had a gun.

The more I thought about the setup, the angrier I got, and my paranoia made me think that Tammy was aware of this situation and how these guys wanted to jump me—I thought about them stomping me out and leaving me toothless in the middle of the street. Finally, Kelsie picked me up from Hardee's and took me back to Tammy's parents' house even though I had been kicked out; I preferred their house rather than retreating to my parents' house. I heard whispered accusations that I was a punk for running; and I still laugh at that notion and think what I did was a very smart move—he who runs away live to fight another day.

I lived to witness another day, and I pray people read this and understand that it is okay to run away and walk away from fights—fight in paid competition, not to prove a futile point and to build some meaningless street fame. I have known many people who lost their lives from fighting; they won the fight, but lost their life—they lose to this world and will never play any significant part on earth again . . . remember that. However, when I reconnected with Tammy, she told me that I should have stayed and fought them. I went from being angry to transparent in my thinking—I needed to change my thinking and return home.

I no longer was angry with them or wanted to kill them; I wanted out of this life and this relationship. I thrived off well thought out street decisions because I never planned to lose to the streets: death or prison. I was masked, but I was far from stupid. I never wanted to be a fool, and I was quick to change situations when situations failed to make sense to my psyche—fighting them and not having my girl support my decision made no sense. After about a long month and a half (felt like two years) away from home, I decided that any opportunity to succeed and to figure my life out would come from my loving home that I chose to leave. I realized lust and sex drove me out of my home, but common sense and true love inspired me to return home.

I displayed some strong mental and internal will power, and it appeared that the storm was over and the tide was turning in my life. The only problem was that I still did not recognize this person staring back at me when I looked in mirrors. The mask controlled me to a degree, and I did not know how to formulate lasting change. I was determined to rise above the drama that plagued me throughout high school and returning home gave me time to reflect on past mistakes and challenging experiences. I learned how to implement quiet time, and I used quiet time to evaluate and to assess past behaviors; this gave me an opportunity to strategize and to plan for the future. I received inquiry letters from some major universities, so those thoughts led me to believe college might be a viable option.

This interest motivated and inspired me to take school more seriously because I wanted an opportunity to play football in college and to live within the diverse and stimulating college environment; this motivation minimized my poor decision-making for the remainder of my junior and senior year of high school. Tupac, the author of thug life was dead, and I tried to kill those thoughts and desires within me as well; Tupac died during my junior year, on September 13, 1996, the night of one of my Friday football games. Playing collegiate football was alive and well in me, so that dream of playing in front of ardent college fans and the potential payback from two fights during my junior year decreased my desire to be seen in the streets or at social gatherings.

Early in the year, Deon and I beat up Germane in front of his girlfriend's house ironically over another girl who was cheating on me with him. After the fight, he had threatened to kill me, and he attempted to hit Kelsie with his car as we strolled down Snowden Drive with Derrick Liles, AJ, and some other members from the Snowden crew. Then one night at the county fair, Rat and I got into a brawl with the McClain brothers, while about 20 spectators looked on—we embarrassed them, and there have been warnings of payback as they traveled out to Beddingfield one day in search of us; I mad a point to remove myself from campus. I was a little apprehensive about both situations.

I realized change does not stop consequences, and it left me secretly wishing I walked away from those fights. I prayed that God would calm the anger in the head and in the heart of my foes. We must be willing to walk away, to pursue peace and to earn extra days on this precious earth. I wanted to stray away from this violence, but my conflicted mask kept me taking one step backwards—never quiet out of the darkness—the light appeared distant. I had to appear in court during my junior year for a locker room altercation. My cousin Mike and I fought two twin brothers in the locker room for no apparent reason—we were trying to demonstrate our toughness in front of other classmates.

However, those brothers developed amnesia in the courtroom, and I am glad that they did; I sucker punched one of them as I offered him my hand for help—a complete coward move. I found myself masked in darkness the more I tried to crawl toward the light. Not knowing, the mind must completely change and be renewed before an individual can truly embrace the truth or that distinguished light. Without the truth in our minds, we cannot develop that light needed to understand our hearts; the heart is the key to changing destructive behavior because permanent change occurs in the heart. With all those outside temptations and pressures, I found solace in sports, and the possibilities of playing in the capacity of large college arenas.

I stopped trying to change, and I focused solely on sports. I minimized my interaction with girls to a degree, so I did not halt my positive progression in sports. The more I focused on sports, the more I employed rational choices in my existence. I refrained from running my mouth and convinced myself that fighting might lead to suspension and to an untimely death, which can keep me separated from football—my true love on this earth. Football became my god, and even though it pulled me from negative behaviors; it is not beneficial to make anything your god. I learned that replacing my negative behaviors with positive behaviors created positive results—mathematics. Even though I was still selling weed, I focused the majority of my time on sports to enhance my popularity. Sports became my savor, and inadvertently, I loved sports more than God and my family for the most part—it consumed my mind more than anything else—even sex.

I was viewed, as a legit running back during my junior year, but my touches were limited due to our high potent offense that featured top senior players. Our team was ranked fourth in the 3-A state ranking early in that season, and I averaged close to eight yards per carry; I displayed promise with my minimal offensive involvement. I received invitation letters from West Virginia, East Carolina University, and Fayetteville State University based on potential and speed; I clocked a 4.5 in the 40 yard dash my junior year. Mentally and physically, I felt stronger toward life. Life has multiple lows and highs, but successful individuals understand that both are part of the maturation process. Sports motivated me to maintain my eligibility requirements, so I earned grades sufficient for high school sports participation.

Varsity basketball served as an unexpected low because I anticipated instant success due to my performance on the junior varsity (JV) team. I emerged as a star and focal point on our JV team, averaging about 15 points per game. This success never truly won me favor with Coach Bean, and it seemed as if he made a point to break me mentally; he dictated my number of shot attempts, and he omitted me from taking the ball through my legs or around my back, limiting my offense and my overall effectiveness on the basketball court. I continued to toil in practice without complaining during my junior season because I thought my senior season would be different and would serve as my break out season.

In practice, I was the top three in sprints, and I scored at will during inter-squad scrimmages, but nothing appeased him—I grew frustrated and defeated. I supported the team, and I made a point to conduct myself in a positive manner; this small choice helped to improve my self-control in uncomfortable future situations. Sports helped to keep me sane, and it served as a balance from my masked identity. The problem was that sports presented a lot of disappoints, and a substantial amount of failures. Eventually, sports altered my belief in people and belief in fairness; those beliefs eventually led back to more negative actions and twisted values—it was hard to trust when I felt as if I was treated unfairly, even when I tried to do the right thing.

I learned that we must commit to doing right regardless of whether fairness finds us; it is about doing the right thing rather than receiving some fair reward. When basketball season ended, I wondered if playing professionally would ever come to fruition. My uncertainty had me in a state of confusion, and to soothe my concerns I returned temporarily to smoking weed. Sports gave me a positive outlet, but it also fueled my negative energy. Great things appeared to happen and quickly dissipate in my life because I proceeded through life with no specific purpose or direction; those who lacked vision will perish. When we mask ourselves, our lows have a way of defining us and controlling us.

I fed my mind with negative images, so I wanted back in the streets—selling dime bags of weed at breakfast during school and smoking dime bags of weed at lunch during a skipping class session with Mack and others. Irrational thoughts consumed my psyche and left me mentally depressed. I developed a love for making money, the smell of it, the site of it, and this admiration combined with attention inspired me to plot on evil endeavors. I kept money on me, my frugal ways taught me to never spend all of my money at once and to never spend more money than I made—I never fell for that capitalistic trap of spending majority of my money on depreciating items (i.e., shoes and clothes).

I was prone to flash my money around females, but in a strategic fashion, stacking two or three $20-dollar bills on top of an abundance of $1-dollar bills on the bottom. During my junior-year of prom, I was selling dime bags in the bathroom, and I did not care who knew it—I was loosing control. I never thought about the severity, or how dumb it was to sell weed at a high school prom. I was more excited about the people saying,

"James, you are a wild boy, and you crazy to sell weed at school." I viewed that as respect for my hustle, and it won me favor with those I respected.

Turning from a negative mindset to a positive mind state, and then regressing back to a more negative mindset can be more detrimental to a healthy mind than the initial negative-minded perspective. Normally, people become worse when they return to their negative behaviors or mindsets. My life became complicated due to poor decisions and to defiant behaviors. I wanted to be like Tupac, so after his death, I honored him by cutting all my hair off, sporting a baldhead for the next five years.

Tupac and the rap culture became another idol of mine, and I placed this image and lifestyle above the identity of self. I am aware that I am stating this again, but I lost myself, and the mask became me—I no longer knew anything else. In life, we cannot embrace fictitious characteristics and act rational because it requires an understanding of self to use rationality in unfamiliar situations. My life was simple, but very complex; my mind became an oxymoron—all I had to do was make above average grades and play sports, but I complicated it with drugs, girls, false identities, and acceptance—too much to bare and too many opposing charges (positive behaviors and negative behaviors). I wanted to be a thug, but internally, my soul desired to live a life exemplary to Christ; I recognize the paradox as I type, so please imagine the mental struggle I faced daily in this unrealistic world.

At times, I tried to use troublesome situations to evoke change, such as my run-in with law enforcement when Mack and I drove to an infamous drug turf called the "school yard" to sell some dime bags. I had to pull over on the curve to organize my bags. As I nervously positioned my bags in my lap, I noticed bright lights in my rear view mirror—it was the cops of course. The fear had me about to crap myself, but I became poised and creative as I heard their doors popping open. I informed Mack to be still, and I covered the weed with my football jersey in the front seat.

When they knocked on the window, they asked, "What are you all doing in this neighborhood?" I responded, "Sir, we are coming home from football practice and took the wrong turn. Can you please direct us out of this neighborhood?" He was convinced that we were lost, and he gladly pointed us in the right direction; and I pointed myself out of the drug game forever because I feared being arrested—no shame in the game for me—I had no desire to scheme through the judicial system.

Mack's arrest early that school year shunned me away from cuffs and prison bars as well, and it made me reluctant to engage in any criminal activity. I was back on my positive tip, but the past had a way of catching up with me. I attempted positive actions to find residual affects of past poor behaviors—running hard forward but no way to stop sins of the past. Rumors circulated in and out of my circle that Tammy was pregnant, and the regrets about running away flooded my mind—thinking that was a dumb idea—two kids prior to graduating high school at 17 years of age. I was shocked, even though I never practiced safe sex; I did not think I would have another child prior to marriage or graduation. Soon that shock turned into denial once again, and that denial turned into fear and instant rejection of her conceived embryo—it's not mine became my daily mantra.

I love my precious daughters, but fear limited any positive reactions during those delicate moments. Fear propelled me to repudiate the claims and any notion of having another baby, and I became upset and poignant as I reflected on our past relationship. I encouraged my parents to spend their hard earned money for DNA testing, and they did it without hesitating. Quality parents are always there to support their children even when we continue to disappoint them and to make bad choices. I witnessed the pain and fear in my parents' eyes. They thought another child at this juncture in my life would derail any plans of college—deep down,

I think we all feared that I will never amount to much.

My anger was not aimed towards Tammy; it was aimed more at myself. I was dead wrong for carrying on as if it was not my child because I knew it was probably my child; but I did not want the new responsibility. I know you all are probably thinking I should of thought about this prior to having unprotected sex, but I didn't—most 16-year old boys are not glad to be fathers—they just want the pleasure or thrill from having sex. Truth be told, a lot of us desire temporary fun or excitement without any harsh consequences—many failed marriages, terminations, crimes, and etc. are the result of this selfish way of thinking.

Consequences are not voided because we decide to rewrite the script; poor decision-making leads to unwanted consequences. I was stressed, and I felt defeated in my mind, body, and spirit. I conceded that my life was destined for poverty and failure, and I lost all hope in playing collegiate football. My parents were aware of my fragile state of mind, and they were convinced that I needed a change of scenery; and I was willing to try anything that might motivate and inspire me to find my true identity and accurate direction in life. I was shook about finding out I had another child on the way, shook about my run-in with the law, shook about potential payback from enemies, shook about my performance in school, and shook about this person I had become.

My parents decided to make a move to save their son from any more despair, so they reached out to their long-time friend, Bessie from Massachusetts who recently moved to Picayune, Mississippi; they asked if I could live with her for my senior year of high school. With no hesitation, Bessie agreed and was thrilled to have me move in with her and her family. We used Bessie's world to escape my self-inflicted problems rather than self-reflecting and acknowledging that the real problem lied within my poorly structured mental paradigm and dismal choices in life.

Running away from problems, never solve the problems, but in essence can create more problems. Change occurs in the thinking, and my thinking did not change, it just relocated to

Mississippi. I found myself smoking weed on a daily basis while living in Picayune; it was nothing to climb in a non-operating vehicle with the windows up while passing a blunt (weed in a cigar) back-and-forth among three teenage boys in the sweltering 90-degree temperatures during that hot summer.

I contemplated getting back into the drug game until I realized their legal system was vastly different than ours; weed convictions carry lengthy prison sentences, so I wanted no part of that game. I went to Picayune to graduate and to play football, but my mind succumbed to boredom; and that boredom produced negative thoughts and ultimately negative actions. I knew trouble was evident if I stayed in Picayune; so I blew off the chance to play for a nationally ranked high school football program, known for producing D-I football players—the coach wanted me there, but I was in a desperate search to save and to find me.

I also walked away from an opportunity to play high school basketball with Jonathan Bender (one of the top-ranked basketball players in the nation) at Picayune Memorial high school. I lacked the mental focus and self-control to survive there—I tapped out and had enough of that life. I begged for my disappointed parents to allow me to come back home, and I was truly determined to be better and to pursue positive living.

After two months, the Picayune experiment was over, and that chapter was closed to my life forever. Picayune football team was ranked third in the state, and Jonathan Bender went on to get drafted in the first round as the fifth pick in the NBA draft at the conclusion of that year (1998). However, I returned to NC with focus and determination on the football field and in the classroom, and I was very productive my senior year; but the past reared its ugly head again to halt my promising progression. When I left home and stopped attending school regularly, I was classified as a dropout in two classes. Those two teachers gave me a "F," which dropped my GPA to a 1.9 and made me ineligible to play sports for the fall semester. However, I did not get mad; I decided to pray for some kind of intervention or help. That help came.

Coach Johnson (head varsity football coach) pleaded with the instructors on my behalf, and those instructors gave me some projects to complete for a passing grade ("D"). I worked diligently to complete those projects, and both instructors were impressed with my effort and my overall quality. However, my new grades did little to improve my overall GPA, bumping my GPA up a minimal 0.2 points to a 2.1 GPA. My senior year, I learned the importance of setting goals, and I created goals to improve my GPA and to never engage in the sell of narcotics again.

My mind was more invested in things of substance, but I was not completely sold on this positive living perspective. During my senior year, the pursuit of positive living conflicted with my thug life persona, making me a little uncomfortable. The attention was still attractive, and I was not ready to let go of the acceptance and admiration from the in-crowd—just some of the negative behaviors. Occasionally, I smoked weed and hung around with street thugs to keep up my street credentials—I feared the label of being called "sell-out, uncle Tom, or fake."

Perception was everything in my unique subculture, and many people I knew died for the perception of this so-called realness or being down for the hood—ignorance. Even though I was still somewhat conflicted, I thought often about college. I dreamed of walking barefoot on some college quad, while bantering with college peers about some football game I played in—my pensive stare was always accompanied by a smile as I shut myself off to the world and thought deeply about this possibility.

I drew several scholarship interests after I amassed for 220 yards on 16 carries against Southern Nash high school, in a game that featured Julius Peppers, future UNC standout and NFL superstar, CJ Taybron, high school standout and North Carolina State University (NCSU) signee, and Cornelius Gary, future North Carolina A&T University standout. Fayetteville State University (FSU) and East Carolina University (ECU) were impressed by my performance, and they offered me official invites to their respective campuses. I grew more inspired when I thought about playing football in ECU stadium with 40,000 or more adoring fans screaming my name—thoughts galvanized me to run extra laps and lift weights on a more consistent basis.

When I thought about college, I thought about the fun, the freedom, the girls, and the thought of playing football; but, reading books and taking tests never entered the right or left hemisphere of my brain—not entering the hemispheres of creativity or reasoning. The idea of pursuing college was an excellent idea, but my thoughts and actions were not conducive to succeeding academically. I accepted the invite to visit ECU. Immediately, I fell in love with everything about their university: the food, the stadium, and the size of the campus—I was ready to sign a letter of intent that day if it was offered—they had me at "hello." Yet, I reluctantly went on a visit with FSU because it was not my type of school; and I lacked the interest to be there.

A part of me wanted to be near my hometown, so people from Wilson could observe my success and football prowess; that is an ignorant reason to attend a college or to do anything for that matter. I was fixated on impressing people from Wilson because a small part of my mind thought I needed people from Wilson's approval in order to be considered a valid success in this huge world. Methodist College (D-III) recruited me as well, but I thought I was D-I material; however, I graciously accepted an invitation to tour their campus and facilities.

The excitement I got from my college visits inspired me to increase my efforts within the classroom, but my extra effort became a futile attempt to raise my GPA. In the process of raising my GPA, I struggled to score higher than an 870 on the SAT, which had a maximum score of 1600, and the combination of a poor SAT score and a dismal GPA closed the doors on my desire to sign with ECU or FSU. There would be no scholarships and no big dreams of wowing thousands of ardent ECU fans with my athletic prowess.

I was depressed by this situation, and I was determined to focus my attention on dominating in basketball my senior year.

Yet, I destroyed my high school basketball career with spats with Coach Bean, the varsity basketball coach about dribbling the ball through my legs and behind my back; he wanted to control my game, but he crippled my game in the process—lack of confidence emerged from his sovereignty over my basketball play.

I was an aggressive and passionate basketball player, but his rules and limitations put a damper on my passion and admiration for high school basketball. I had to play within the parameters the coach set; some restrictions, however well intentioned, can place limitations on our development.

After playing basketball all my life, my coach drove me to quit one of the games I adored—never playing in another high school game or Wilson's popular Christmas tournament—something I dreamed about starring in since middle school. I never quit a sport, but my desire to quit made me strong and gave me fuel needed to succeed in a new sport—learning that change makes you stronger when you passionately search for something new. I decided to wrestle for the first time in my life, and this small decision developed confidence in my ability to leave my comfort zone and prosper in an unknown endeavor. I started 10-0, and I finished all matches with first round pins on the mat, earning the number one rank in my conference and my region—my speed and power overwhelmed my opponents.

I became the first wrestler to go to the state championship in five years, and the only wrestler from my high school that year; I wrestled at the 171-weight class and finished the year in the top-ten weight class (7th in the states). Determination, hard work, ability, and commitment made me a star in that unfamiliar sport. My senior year instructed me that talent alone does not open doors because my meager academic performance halted any talk of athletic scholarships so I decided to attend Methodist College (MC). I convinced myself that I would dominate; I embraced an imperious and arrogant attitude—I was a D-I prospect and MC was a little D-III school in my mind. Those thoughts entered my mind as I found myself attending my high school graduation—a graduation that my parents felt would elude me.

I was consumed with emotions, and I tried to stand stoic, as my eyes began to swell up with tears—high school was behind me, and now college awaits. I did not want this joyous moment to end, and I wanted to ride this positive momentum wave into MC. In my mind, I would be different at Methodist, no thug life, but the mask was still there and lying dormant in the shadows. MC was predominately populated with rich white students, and I assured myself that I would go there and be different in this unfamiliar school environment. Life is about discovery of self, and I discovered I wanted more of myself—the question was how do I get back to that hidden individual and put down my mask forever.

Lessons Learned

Life is full of choices. Sometimes choices are made from a dismal perspective of life to create irreversible problems. When we have no clue of our purpose or our direction, we tend to gravitate toward situations or behaviors that we feel will bring us happiness. There are many paths that we can find temporary happiness in, but temporary happiness keeps us searching and floundering around aimlessly toward nothing of substance for our individual lives.

The common theme or pattern in my life was to seek acceptance or approval from others; this pursuit led me to a masked identity, which triggered disconnect between my inner and outer world. I became a thug and an athlete, and my true identity became unfamiliar to me—I was clueless to tactics that were needed to bring back my authentic self. Life lessons can still be taught during our masked state of mind. I took calculated risks to produce winning results. Wrestling gave me the confidence needed to step out of my comfort zone, and hustling taught me to invest large sums of money to make more money (i.e., spend money to re-up on bigger purchases of drugs).

There were no nostalgia moments about my past criminal endeavors, but I believe it is imperative to extract anything positive from negative situations—this promotes awareness and growth. Up to this point, my life was predicated upon the opinions and thoughts of others, and that led to bad decisions; those bad decisions influenced me to mask myself as a thug and to emulate individuals who portrayed thug life. We must be aware of subtle traps in our lives. Adopting the opinions of friends and family members, finding happiness in temporary objects (i.e., money, sex, status, and etc.) or actions, and living in a nostalgic state of past successes. I was tired, and I wanted to remove my mask; but I did not know how to alter our most valuable asset— the mind. I thought my relocation to MC would alter my behavior, but I did not know that behavioral change starts in one's mind. Enforced, manmade change is temporary, but permanent change is godly change or the ability to shift one's outlook to a positive perspective of love and happiness.

Chapter 13

With No Mind, the Body Runs Nowhere Fast

Gunplay raises the stakes and changes the game

"One man with a gun can control a hundred men without one"

~ *Vladimir Lenin*

Arrogance can quickly label you a fool, and arrogance normally accompanies those who are wearing masks, pretending to be someone different than their self. I entered MC football two-a-days camp about 15 pounds overweight because I failed to commit to their summer workout program. From my point of view, I did not need to workout to earn a starting job on this football team; I did not think I had to put forth much effort to start at a D-III school. I ignorantly laughed at the notion of playing D-III ball at MC, believing I was too great for this school—ECU wanted me, so MC was small potatoes. However, to my surprise, I could not finish any of their designed football workouts during the first week of camp; and I ran one of my slowest 40-yard dash times ever, a dismal 4.7 seconds—performing poorly throughout the remainder of camp.

This pitiful 40-time shattered my overall confidence; and at the college level, the mental aspect is more vital than the physical aspect to a degree.

My lackluster 40-time, negative attitude, and poor physical condition quickly moved me out of favor with MC's coaching staff. Shane Ingram, a high school phenomenon from Chiefland High School in Florida became the featured freshman running back behind the returning starter, Mebane who was known for being a tough runner in between the tackles. Shane broke Emmitt Smith's touchdown record during the state championship game in the 1997-1998 high school football season.

He was much smaller than me, but he was very shifty and displayed a knack for getting extra yards after contact and making opponents miss in the open field. The coaching staff decided to redshirt me for my freshman year, and I took it personally, prompting me to come to practice high off marijuana at times, while displaying a nonchalant and a complacent attitude about the team, the coaching staff, and the entire football situation. Head Coach Sypult did not appreciate my negative demeanor toward his football program and his coaching style and decision-making.

Skill-wise, I showed a lot of potential on the practice squad by dominating the first team defense during inter-squad scrimmages and practices; I accomplished this small feat with a third string offensive line (less-skilled blockers). Arrogantly, I spoke out and challenged the starters during practice. I made a point to display my disapproval of my nonexistent playing time. I learned a valuable life lesson throughout my college football experience; talent does not beat character, and if people viewed me in a negative light, nothing positive would ever transpire in my life. My mind shifted away from playing football at MC because subconsciously, I thought I was primetime—still, D-I material. I contacted an assistant coach at NCSU about possibly transferring, so I sent him a highlight tape as he somewhat entertained the idea.

I strongly believed this opportunity would work in my favor. I rededicated myself to working out; I incorporated sprints up hills and with parachutes and committed myself to a taxing strength training regiment. This NCSU chance appeared to be promising for the upcoming 1999–2000 football season, but my mind also drifted toward late night partying and neglect of course work after the football season.

This shift in thinking brought back other illicit actions and regressive behaviors (i.e., sex, drugs, and thuggish attitude). At times, I partied about three days a week, and I began drinking excessively. I found myself staggering around campus dorm rooms; drunk off the ingested chemical components of Old English and Malt Liquor packaged in 40-ounce bottles. On most college weekends, I was drunk and high more than I was sober—this became a weekend ritual. The most dangerous behavior exhibited at MC was my constant affiliation with friends who had ties to the BLOODS street gang.

This street gang was well respected throughout the city of Fayetteville and at that time, BLOODS were not prevalent in my hometown (Wilson); Wilson consisted of neighborhoods clicking up as informal gangs, but no organized street gangs occupied Wilson in the late 90s to my knowledge. BLOODS were thriving and functioning in Fayetteville, and they were widespread throughout impoverished sectors of that city—CRIPS (rival gang) was well established there as well. I associated with Nate, Calvin, and Titus (MC basketball players) who were associated with BLOODS rather than my college football teammates. I distanced myself from the football team after Coach Sypult dismissed me for multiple infractions that I had committed that were deemed detrimental to the team.

I also associated with my college roommate, Bryan; we were both from Wilson, graduated together, and played JV and Varsity basketball together. Bryan was a laidback individual who did not take part in any thug behavior, but he would definitely cruise with us when we frequented nightclubs or parties, took trips to Myrtle Beach, or ventured out to other college campuses. Hot Boyz (popular rap group from New Orleans; Lil Wayne was a member) became our music of choice, and we became the "Hot Boyz" of MC and Fayetteville for that matter—our swagger was at an all-time high—we believed we were something of significance in every place. We were young, confident, handsome, and fearless individuals—I was regressing and returning to this thug character that I shelved back in Wilson.

Titus presented me with this .22 semi-automatic lifeless pistol. I was fascinated with the chrome and the light feel of his unregistered gun. I felt invincible when I clutched the black grip with my tiny and sweaty right palm—I became a god. I convinced myself that I was not afraid to shoot someone in any sign of trouble, and I embraced the idea that I may have to use a gun on someone one day—proudly embracing this mindset, thinking I was Bishop in the popular 90s movie *Juice*. I reiterated this self-confidence to Titus, so I ended up carrying the gun wherever we went (i.e., clubs or parties)—I was always strapped. Acceptance is a dangerous desire because I was willing to become a dangerous individual to fit in and be accepted by this crew as my football dreams begin to go awry and the team rejected me. I was willing to give up my freedom to be a thug and to gain a few cheers from some so-called college wannabe gangsters.

I entered local night clubs, Fraternity and Sorority parties, and any other various social gatherings around campus with the stainless .22 tucked on the right ankle of my Nautica boot—unaware of the crimes that might have been committed with that illegal gun. At that time, I was completely unaware that it was a felony to have a gun without proper registration—it never felt right, but the respect received from my crew was intoxicating.

I walked around with potential prison time in my immediate path; I went from football to an individual possessing murderous behavior and callous intentions. I donned red laces in my Nike sneakers, wore red shirts, and red bandanas that hung from my back right pocket to imitate members of my crew and their adopted BLOOD dress code. My parents were oblivious to my new dress code, so it probably never crossed their mind that I embraced a gangster lifestyle that was foreign to them and Wilson in 1999.

I thought I had arrived, and my thoughts were far from playing collegiate football. As far as I was concerned, I had a legit crew and a gun, so I maneuvered throughout Fayetteville with no fear, not rationalizing that inexperienced individuals with guns create violence rather than deterring violence. This mindset can lead to a premature death rather than some type of longevity to this existence. This gun gave me flashbacks about the first time I shot a .38 revolver at Happy Village golf course; it stood adjacent from a neighborhood field. At 15 years old, my former friend Boot placed the powerful revolver in my hands, and the cold pistol came alive for me as I felt the awe in which neighborhood onlookers now held me.

I realized that I had the power to instill fear in people, and that this gun had the power to take someone's life and to change their place in history forever. In my young mind, I really thought I was a god while clutching that revolver—I felt immortal. I fired shots at some designated trees, never thinking about the fact that those bullets could have hit someone or something of vital importance. This past experience heightened my interest in guns. I thought guns gave people the power over others. During those dark days at MC, I became a walking zombie and was led by others decisions. I had no sense of real direction and purpose; I was more dangerous than a real thug because I wanted to prove myself as being real—my new god (gun) provided me with the confidence needed to go anywhere.

I wanted to be known as a thug, and I started claiming "Thug Life," feeling like I was the reincarnated Tupac Shakur. I strived to show no fear, and I felt like I did not need anybody from my family to try to persuade me to seek a relationship with Christ. I believed in God, but I was done with all that religious talk. I was burnt out from church, and I felt like some Christians were too judgmental and too hypocritical. In my opinion, some of them spoke godly, but lived questionable lives. College was a mentally confusing time for me, and it was the first time I did not care about living anymore—I woke up some mornings wondering why I was still here in the world. I gave up and wanted out, but God kept me here for a reason.

I had no desire to keep living, and it was the darkest and unhappiest time of my life. I believe that I was miserable with living because I made sports my life and my god, while the recognition from others served as the stabilizer to my decision-making process. I thought playing professional football was my ticket to a world's acceptance and a joyous life. I had no other options toward acquiring happiness and felt lost without football—I never viewed education as my ticket to acquiring joy—without football, I felt subjected to a life of crime. I had no desire to be a dope dealer, but I sought toxic admiration and approval from campus gangsters to add to a shaky and already dangerous mindset.

I wanted to fit in and to feel connected to a clique because I was not comfortable in my own skin; I never truly figured out what James was passionate about, so I gravitated toward sports and toward being a thug—in my mind, I had nothing else. I lost touch with reality, and I did not know who or what I was becoming in this complex and unforgiving cold-blooded world. My mask was all about posing as a BLOOD or some developed thug character from popular gangster flicks and intricate street corners.

We knowingly entered clubs in Fayetteville where known CRIPS hung out with poor security (e.g., broken medal detectors) at the door; I concealed our .22 in my boots with a clipped blade behind the designer buckle on my belt—I was ready for war or any imposing threats—no love for the cops due to our brainwashed philosophies and rhetoric. I became powerful and invincible with hollow-point bullets that I kept loaded in that low-powered .22 handgun.

As I reminisce over this situation and a myriad of other situations, I know that God had angels watching over me because it was suicidal to walk in some of those establishments as an outsider with opposing gang colors on—I was only caught up in one club altercation, and I had to run one time for my safety as I found myself dodging through traffic once again on Ramsey Street in Fayetteville. I had two unforgettable instances in college that changed my perspective and outlook on life forever. A person's worldview can shift positively or negatively in critical or crisis situations.

These noticeable and critical situations played a crucial role in the permanent separation from my mask, and my eventual shattering of this thug life or tough guy persona. One night, Titus, Calvin, Nate, and I decided to visit some girls that we had met at the local mall. These girls lived in a rough urban trailer park, and we were all a little reluctant to visit with them at their place of residence—our hormones clouded our judgment, and our smaller heads decided for us—a pistol and knives to tote settled our nerves.

It can be extremely risky meeting ladies in any unfamiliar ghetto. Friends shared stories of robberies and homicides from girls luring gullible guys to their residence, especially in impoverished ghettos. When we arrived to the girls' locale, the situation appeared relaxed and chilled—no worries appeared in the horizon. However, the girls became real secretive after several minutes into our visit, whispering, and making phone calls in their backroom—I grew uneasy about this peculiar circumstances. About 20 minutes later, the girls received a random and a firm knock at their door like the police, but instead, it was several guys conversing on the other side of the door—the chatter incited fear and paranoia of a setup in my brain—thinking somebody might die tonight. I was convinced that this might be my last night alive.

The guys entered their habitation in an imperious manner, and we (our crew) all locked eyes with them, to create a hostile and a tense environment. Titus spoke and addressed them with no fear as these young boys abruptly began to sit down with some of the girls in the domain. He let them know in so many words that we do not want any problems, but we can also provide problems—these younger boys appeared shook as if we had an

AK-47 sprawled across our laps. Titus words provided us with a psychological advantage—leadership 101, speak with confidence and fervor because people must view an individual as honest and inspiring prior to accepting them as a credible leader—Titus was viewed as the unspoken leader within our crew. Eventually, we left their house without incidence, but it made me question my sense of direction and purpose in life quite frequently after that; I was wondering if my next mishap would bring death or prison.

True self-discovery and mask removal commences with well thought out questions, and I begun to ask myself very specific and goal-oriented questions, prompting me to perform an internal inquiry about my stolen identity. I continued to hang with my informal college BLOOD gang because I felt like these guys were my extended brothers, a family who loved and understood me. We exhibited some unique qualities, and we explored this world blindly. Calvin was always trying to convert me from a Christian to a Five-Percent Nation (religion of Supreme Mathematics), but I never bought into his very entertaining mathematical philosophy of me being a black god.

I was not living a godly life, and I felt strongly that I was hell bound; but I never doubted the gospel of Jesus Christ. Honestly, I had no desire for religion and felt unworthy to serve—I was on the losing team and living for Satan. I am not ashamed to admit this fact because acknowledging it helped me change my life. There were times when I thought we would die as a crew, until the unforgettable incident after the 1999 Aggie-Eagle classic basketball game in Greensboro, NC. This game drew an enormous crowd filled with beautiful ladies, so Bryan, Nate, Titus, Tavis, Calvin, and I went to the arena dressed in our club best attire.

When we arrived in Greensboro, the night appeared to be drama free—our passion was aligned with meeting new and pretty girls—no fighting was on our agenda. I was still flagging (wearing gang apparel) with my red colors as an initiated BLOOD member—oblivious to the real BLOODS or gang bangers in the murderous city of Greensboro. For the most part, we were relaxed during the game, and Bryan and I spotted some friends from Wilson and began to converse about some potential parties at North Carolina Central University (NCCU) in Durham, NC.

Durham is known for violence, and it is one of those cities in NC that people tended to respect or fear to some degree—people got shot and robbed in neighborhoods near the NCCU on the regular—this fact heightened my awareness and brought about delusions of getting shot. However, I felt confident as long as I had that concealed .22 because I was not afraid to use that gun; I was all in—anything for my brothers. On that particular night, we packed in and traveled together in Titus's red Ford Explorer. Too many immature minds can create a pernicious environment that can result in poor resolutions and actions.

I was a little apprehensive about heading to NCCU after midnight. We were headed south on I-85 around 1:00am—nothing positive or wholesome happens at that time of night. Furthermore, nothing positive or wholesome was on our minds. When we arrived at NCCU, we walked around campus and hung out with some girls in their dorm room; but there was no party on campus, so we decided to head back to Fayetteville after a few hours of joking around with some random young ladies whom we met on campus.

We were about an hour or so away from Fayetteville, and we all appeared exhausted. As we walked in the silence of the night toward Titus dented Ford explorer, I thought I saw some guys sizing us up with menacing stares. I fought off fear with the grasp of my gun within the external pocket of my leather Member's Only jacket. My new god, a .22 pistol, was there to assist and to calm me immediately when I reached out to it. I wonder now how many men died secretly believing that their guns would save them; such deadly false realities are made every second of every day.

As we began to load into Titus outdated SUV, we began to carry on a tiresome conversation about our blurred alcoholic memories of that night. I was tired from the constant cogitating over my life—I didn't feel right and new I had to change my approach on life. I could not run from the stressful thought of living a pointless life. I conceived to the idea that I was wasting space and failing to live up to my God-given potential—whatever that was. I became poignant as I reflected on my past meaningless sex encounters. I was overwhelmed with regret that night, regretting all of my past fights and acknowledging how I allowed the desire to be recognized control my life. Sitting in that vehicle and thinking about how much I hate my life and wondering why my mind would not stop spinning.

My mind was cloudy due to sleep depravation, alcohol, and some paranoia, so I was antsy to leave Durham, noticing guys parlaying in dark spots throughout campus and Titus's clock as it switched to 3:54 am. I attempted to lay my head back on the headrest, trying to prepare for some much needed rest when I noticed someone sprinting in the dark toward our vehicle screaming and maneuvering in a sketchy fashion. I had no time to think, so I became reactive and reached for the stainless .22 inside my warm coat pockets—fear shocked my mind and numbed my body. Titus yelled out, "James shoot that nigga," and I nervously clutched that .22 and was locked in on him as he continued to gain ground and move closer—I kept referring to Titus words over and over in my mind "shoot that nigga."

My heart was racing and thumping fast inside my chest, and the faster he ran, the faster my heart pounded against the inside of my chest—no time to think, but it was time for reaction. My arm now raised and left eye squinted, nudging my index finger closer and closer to that hair-pressure trigger. I felt all the eyes on me in the jeep. The plethora of eyes were piercing my skin and adding compiled pressure on me. I was a man of my word, so I had to shoot and honor my word among my boys. We must be careful about what we say, but we do not need to feel compelled to honor negative words and negative actions. I was poised to shoot as he continued to move swiftly through the faint night toward our vehicle.

The moment stood still and a deafening sound fell all over the

SUV, and Titus broke the silence with, "don't shoot, don't shoot, that's my boy." I faintly heard some edgy sighs, but I sat motionless and paralyzed with an unfamiliar and unsettling emotion of fear— fear of self and fear of being around them. Titus and my hesitance to shoot saved my future and potentially saved that young man's life. Calvin referred to me as hard, but he had no idea that that situation changed me forever.

I realized the underlying seriousness of that situation because I allowed peer pressure and the desire to feel accepted propel me to possibly claiming someone's life. I realized I was not built for the streets and this thug mask did not mesh well with my personality and character—I wanted out, no more of this thug life. That entire drive back to campus, I reflected on the thought that I could have killed somebody and spent the rest of my life in prison with grown and aggressive men who would have viewed me as prey.

I became contrite about my thug style demeanor and attitude toward life. The conviction was too much for me, so I was driven to change my thinking and to embrace a change of scenery. I kept apologizing to God, and asking for help; I cried out and said, "God I cannot change without your help, please God change me." It felt as if my spirit hovered outside of my body and looked down at an unrecognizable individual sitting in that vehicle on that fateful night. That night would be the last time that we all hung out together, and my ambitions shifted completely away from the desire to be a thug. It was soul-searching time, and my soul needed a cleansing and some spiritual healing. I understood that I needed to be proactive in my thinking, in order to change my habitual behaviors and negative perpetual way of thinking.

Lessons Learned

"If you don't like something, change it. If you can't change it, change your attitude. Don't complain."
~ *Maya Angelou*

Change of physical location does not mean a change in personality or behavior. I thought that a change of venue would change my thug behavior and masked persona. My change required a different way of thinking, not relocation to MC. I adopted and embraced this perpetual way of thinking that football would give me a more positive outlook on life, but when I lost football due to my arrogant attitude; I lost my insanity and regressed to my masked thug demeanor. When we fail to recognize and to change toxic behaviors, we might attempt to hide those behaviors by running away to different locations.

Most people find themselves revisiting masked behaviors when temporary changed behaviors fail to give them that satisfaction desired in their individual lives. All my life, I was chasing acceptance and approval from individuals whom I regarded as significant in this world. MC was my change. Nothing substantial ever materialized, so I reverted to my masked persona because it felt more natural than my hidden identity and my true potential. When masked identities bring you to a fork in the road, you change or die; I arrived at my fork when I set out with murderous intentions that night at NCCU. When we face a crisis, we need to create a contingency plan and be willing to shift prototypes for living.

Chapter 14

The Decision

What's Next?

"Be the world you want to see"

~ *Mahatma Gandhi*

After that night at NCCU, I minimized my contact and engagement with my MC crew because I did not trust myself around them—this masked person frightened me. I confined myself to the light green walls of my dorm room as "what if " and "what next" scenarios ran wild in my mind. I was repeatedly haunted by that night, and I constantly fought nightmares and periodic flashes of that incident. The gun goes off in the dream, and the unknown victim is left bleeding and twitching on the sidewalk; and as soon as I am slammed into the black and white police car, I awake to heavy breathing and soiled bed sheets from my pouring sweat. I was terrified of the mask I wore—I no longer desired to posture around with my so-called gang. I was determined to keep a safe distance from them because I lost control and no longer knew the evil deeds I was capable of partaking in.

This fear caused me to shutdown mentally and physically. I did not know what to do, and I did not know how to remove this sealed thug mask I created. I stopped going to my college courses, and I isolated myself from the nightlife and withdrew more and more from everyone at Methodist—no dating, no hooking up, and no partying—fear shut me down to the world of Fayetteville. While I was trapped and surrounded by my thoughts, I decided to explore the possibility of joining the armed forces—something I was strongly and ignorantly against because I heard some people say that, "The military is no place for a black man."

I dispelled that notion because I believed anything was better than my current mental and physical state; I needed to get away because my current location was not working. Privately, I consulted with an Army reserves recruiter, and I successfully completed the ASVAB (military entrance examination). I scored fairly high on the exam, and this gave me some options into some great career fields. However, the Army recruiter at MEPS (military entrance personnel) was trying to influence me to be a fuel tanker, to probably help fill his quota, prompting me to reject an acceptance into the Army reserves. God works in mysterious ways because obstacles create even greater opportunities. This roadblock led to an exit strategy out of NC and to an even greater opportunity.

I never had a desire to acquire a position that could place me in the heart of a war, or a position I lacked passion for. I wanted to secure a job synonymous to a job in the civilian sector because I wanted to acquire some transferrable skills for the civilian area. I prided myself for thinking two steps a head or being forward-looking, even when I pursued negative endeavors. When I left Fayetteville for MEPS (Raleigh, NC) in there military issued van, I continued to ponder over the decision to serve part-time in the Army.

Inspiration can sometimes come from subtle encounters, but we must seek the underlying messages in those encounters or any encounters for that matter. I started a conversation with some young lady on the van whom I viewed as gorgeous, but the conversation diverged to an unforeseen conversation about the benefits of the United States Air Force (USAF) when compared to other military branches. I grew intrigued about the USAF during our stimulating conversation, and I completely forgot about her beauty and thought more about this unique branch of service. We might walk into situations with one perspective, but we should always open ourselves up to multiple perspectives; this level of thinking leads to untapped inner potential.

I was determined to find myself and to find peace in this complex world, even if I had to relocate to a distant place to find my peace and to rediscover my hidden identity. I felt out of place and detached from my loving family because the guilt and remorse made me feel ashamed and unworthy of their love. I needed to do something that would make me proud and ultimately make them proud—others' love and acceptance no longer fueled me. I knew I had to change my mindset and remove this thug life mask before I could do anything to appease them or strive toward future successes in this life. I concluded that:

> *"One bad wheel does not stop a well-designed car;*
> *we just need to fix our wheels, gas up our cars,*
> *and enjoy the ride. Success follows the determined*
> *drivers. We must be determined to press the gas and*
> *drive."*
>
> *~ James Williams*

I turned my back on God and family—I felt hopelessly alone. I had to save myself, so I shifted gears and explored all possible options that led me back to a decision to serve my country for four years.

I sought a branch that challenged members mentally and physically, while providing members with usable tools outside of their military service. I needed something that I could embrace with an open-minded perspective, so I opposed any branches that would lead me to shooting guns in the front lines of a war. I needed plausible change, and I decided that a violent position in the service could feed that masked thug—a mask that I was attempting to bury. USAF became the most viable option for me. I admired the idea that people perceived USAF members as intellectual individuals, that beautiful females were among the ranks of Air Force enlisted and officers, and that this branch of service had an easier basic training than other than other branches of service. Many people, including me, thought that the USAF provided careers similar to those sought after in the civilian sector with the added attraction of the distinctive uniforms.

I enjoyed the opinions and perceptions of civilians and other service members, but I know wholeheartedly that all branches have intelligent individuals and attractive females. My parents were unaware of my decision, and my MC crew was completely oblivious to my decision to enlist as well; but I did not care, my mind was made up. In my mind, I had no other recourse because I no longer recognized the individual I had become. I was done with college, and this dream of being a collegiate football player or some NFL draft selection. I was in search of my true identity, and this previous life led me to darkness and to a masked thug persona. My true potential was out there somewhere, and I was on a mission to find it.

I was tired of wasting my parents' hard earned money so I could pursue a floundering football dream. I was also tired of living a lie as a wannabe thug and tired of being unhappy and miserable in this short life. I decided to come home from college to inform my parents about my horrible grades and my decision to join the military. This overwhelming information served as my shock-and-awe campaign. They indicated that they felt I was probably not performing up to par, but they did not foresee this odd scene playing out.

My mom was stunned and confused about my ungoverned rhetoric because she had a strong desire for her sons to graduate from college and lead a more productive professional life. My dad was supportive of my decision to serve our great county. My father proudly and honorably served in the Navy, so he thought the military might build character and help me to mature in and improve my overall decision-making ability. Eventually, my mom came around, but she still longed for the day to watch one of her sons proudly cross some graduation stage after completing our bachelor's degree. My mom lived for that moment because she forfeited her pursuit of a four-year degree.

I was unsure about my decision, but I decided it was the best decision at that time in my life. I was very observant, and I saw how Deon, Torey, and Tony benefited from their military service in their respective careers. Deon went from stints in the Wilson County jail system to visiting extravagant countries while serving sea duty on the USS Enterprise (naval carrier). Torey and Tony also witnessed different parts of our world during their military service, so I was sold on the idea that the military could positively change my outlook on life. I had an opportunity to remove this mask and to find out more about my true individuality.

This awareness brought excitement to my spirit as I daydreamed about the possibilities that a military career could offer me: responsibility, maturity, and freedom—not freedom from my family, but freedom from myself and freedom from the pursuit to please others. I no longer desired a life of crime, but I would soon learn that change is a process and no one changes over night.

I had four months before my military departure, and I did not want to take any chances of messing up this favorable USAF opportunity by residing in Wilson and associating with individuals pursuing negative tasks or living in a state of inertia. I sought refuge in my Uncle Kent and his Mayflower trucking business, so I worked and moved furniture for the summer, relocating families' household goods from coast-to-coast. I was overjoyed with the opportunity to travel America and to see places considered foreign to me—not realizing the hard work that this job entailed.

I have been blessed to visit every state from trucking and living—minus California, Hawaii, and Alaska. This trucking experience taught me a lot of things I did not know about myself.

I realized I had the ability to work long and strenuous hours, but I recognized that I strongly disliked physical labor outside of the structure of a weight room. Manual labor was no passion of mine. I learned that there were exciting cities and states far away from my little existence in Wilson, NC. I learned to appreciate individuals from different ethnic groups, cultures, and religions or beliefs from my broad travels across America.

I unloaded and loaded furniture from middle class and upper middle class residences, and it gave me an opportunity to evaluate and to understand the benefits of college degrees. My interactions with some of those college-educated customers taught me that a college degree could enhance the overall quality of life. My perception of life was shifting toward an acknowledgement that I had the ability to even the playing field with a college degree.

I was convinced that fairness does not find the idle thinkers or complainers. However, I was still displaying flashes of thug behavior, and I found myself carrying blades and my uncle's gun from time-to-time in dangerous cities (i.e., Memphis, Little Rock, Seattle, and Dallas) to potentially combat myself against some unsavory looking characters or threatening situations that I voluntarily placed myself in.

I wore red bandanas when I traveled to Dallas and Seattle, though I knew none of the BLOODS' deep-rooted street codes, just a few hand signs I had learned from my former crew at MC. Some people say I was lucky, but I do not believe in luck. I strongly believe God saw a fool (me) whom he had greater plans for and prevented me for underlying evil elements within those dangerous locales. It could have easily been my last days wearing gang attire and breathing on this earth, if some authentic gang members of different sets approached me with bad intentions.

I did not know these cities, but at times, I walked around with a halo over my head like I was an immortal god. The residual effects of my mask made me unaware of looming dangers, and the evil I could have brought to my uncle and me in those treacherous cities. However, my ignorance did not stop me from absorbing vital information from people I encountered throughout my travels. I saw a lot money enter my uncle's rough hands from accepting truck contracts. Mentally, I registered that taxing physical labor is required to receive an abundance of cash without a college degree. I desired to make a lot of money, but I want to make stacks of cash with minimal physical exertion, unless I was playing some professional sport.

A six-figure income was nothing for my uncle during those lucrative years of hauling furniture across multiple time zones, but my uncle worked extremely hard for those wages— nothing came easy. He spent countless nights on the road, and he worked from sunup to sundown on many occasions, missing a lot of family holiday gatherings. My uncle is a proud and very hardworking man who believed in providing quality service to his customers. He made sure I worked hard throughout the day because he was trying to teach me a valuable lesson about hard work, character, and integrity. My uncle decided to pay me $500 a week for my grueling efforts and positive attitude toward working and servicing his distinguished customers.

The required traveling was exciting at times, but I knew that it was no way I could pursue a career as a truck driver. I admired this engineer we packed and moved from Colorado because he had an enormous house that was filled with extravagant materialistic items. This man took the time to discuss the benefits of his engineering degree and his life's choices, and I used our conversation to ignite a passion toward enhancing my mind with applicable knowledge. He also inadvertently guided me to the idea that life is about receiving and giving back to other people. I believe people should make a point to share knowledge to breathe life into others, and I am so thankful that this individual took it upon himself to share his precious jewels of knowledge to motivate and inspire me to seek more out of life. He had a profound impact on me.

I adjusted my perspective from a thug—and sports—attitude of making irrational and illogical decisions to viewing education as a potential key needed to unlock hidden doors that might be pivotal to my future triumphs. The main problem was I lacked the confidence needed to find those educational keys for unlocking my secret doors. My fictitious thug mask became my comfort zone because I was afraid to step outside that unrealistic world on a consistent basis and abort my thug mask.

The USAF gave me an opportunity to seek a new world from multiple perspectives and to regain control over my hidden identity. I no longer would be identified as an athlete or by the pseudonym of "J-Roc" tattooed on my chest, as I watched my past life boxed into a basic training locker within my dorm barracks—switching street clothes for BDU's (battle dress uniforms) and dress blues (formal dress uniforms). No more first name recognition—it was trainee Williams and the digits of my social security number in this new world of USAF— this all started on August 25, 1999 in San Antonio, TX.

Lessons Learned

When life smacks you in the face, you must be willing to proactively fight back and to seek resolutions to created problems or to unpredictable roadblocks. I sought refuge in my thug persona, and my thug persona failed me—no peace—just added turmoil and guilt. There are always hidden gems that can aid us from dismal situations, but we must be willing to uncover rocks and to dig deeper for those precious gems. I found people who challenged me directly and indirectly to want more out of my life. A rare encounter with a woman on a military van shifted my thinking to survival and to an enhanced vitality; she inspired me to pursue the USAF.

My uncle taught me to work hard and to choose another path not as arduous as his trucking career and lifestyle. A random customer from my trucking escapade taught me to embrace applicable knowledge and to pursue a sound education, most importantly to view the world from an open-minded perspective. It is vital to embark on our individual life's odyssey with multiple perspectives and with a willingness to learn from others; this approach gives individuals an opportunity to discover their hidden individualities and to unmask to their authentic prospective. I was able to remove my mask, but the removal left me unsure of myself and unsure of my direction. Life is unpredictable and the unexpected offers many blessings in the process.

Chapter 15

True Love and New Beginnings

Thank God for Toya

"Destiny is no matter of chance. It is a matter of choice. It is not a thing to be waited for, it is a thing to be achieved"

~ *William Jennings Bryan*

Prior to arriving in San Antonio for basic training, I became nostalgic about wearing civilian attire and growing facial hair, but thoughts of the past quickly transitioned to thoughts of the future, prompting a Kool-Aid smile on my face as I walked boldly with my luggage into Raleigh/Durham airport. I reminisced on past mistakes and thought about how I dispelled the young black male statistics (i.e., dead or serving time in prison). I also found it funny that I was entering the military after I joked on kids in high school for wearing the ROTC uniforms. God seems to have a way of making me eat my words.

I paced anxiously through the airport, excited about the positive possibilities that the military might have to offer. Within a month of basic training, the military blessed me with an unlikely gift. I had a rare and brief encounter with a woman who would rock my world and inspire me beyond my wildest imagination and passionate dreams.

In basic training, I formed a strong bond with a group of military brothers who flew in with me from NC. Fortunately, six of us ended up in the same basic training squadron, and ultimately, four of us ended up at the same technical (tech) school for job training at Sheppard AFB in Wichita Falls, TX. We bonded as military brothers, and ironically, it made basic training enjoyable and the days in basic training flew by. We spent our time discussing past relationships and conversing about our player days as civilians. Marriage was the last thing on our minds, and it was hard for me to even fathom the idea of marriage. I stated vehemently that, "There is no way I will ever get married" while laughing and slapping high-fives with other trainees within our sleeping facility. We were young and consumed with the idea of having fun throughout our military careers.

Yet, we wanted to make sure everyone succeeded and graduated basic training within their scheduled time, so we worked together by ironing each others' uniforms, shining each others' boots, and tightening the corners on each others' sleeping bunks—collaborating for unified success. USAF trainees attended church to gain some separation from our mundane downtime in the dormitory, to pursue spiritual growth, or to enjoy the company of women in the church pews. One day after a Pentecostal church service, Bruce, Bethea, and I were on our way back to our dormitory when we stumbled upon a flight (group of trainees) of beautiful women trainees. My eye was drawn to a gorgeous and a confident woman. She was light complexioned and had a nicely shaped body. She was very appealing to my eyes.

I became fixated on this sexy and angelic woman as she proceeded to speak; however, nothing that came out of her perfectly shaped lips made me think of angels relaxing on clouds while playing violins to the rhythm of heavenly hymns. She was annoyed by the way we had bumped into her and her flight of girls, and immediately, I could tell she demanded respect. She told us in so many razor sharp words that we needed to move out of their way, and she stood still as if she expected an apology from us. I was stunned because I had never had a woman utter offensive words to me in that fashion before. The more she spoke with that northern accent, the more I desired to get to know more about her.

So, I elected to apologize on the behalf of my group, and then, I playfully introduced myself to her and her girls while maintaining my focus on her. She responded with "My name is Toya," with an annoyed facial expression, while she continued to stroll toward her destination. I was hoping that she remembered my name, and I prayed that she thought about me long after our encounter; I sure thought about her. Toya had me fascinated, and I was willing to do anything to woo her. Her beauty and straightforward communication style drew me toward her and had me wanting to know more about her.

I had never met anyone like her, and thoughts of her sent me to a fantasy world of positive "what ifs." Toya became an uplifting thought in my life because thoughts of her heightened my positivity. Positive thinking attracts positive results, and positive thinking restores confidence. I regarded Toya as out of my league, but the more I thought from an affirmative perspective, the more I expected favorable outcomes.

When I was in middle school, I learned to perceive sex as a real man's way to parade his masculinity; I never considered sex as an extension of love. In my opinion, young people who engage in sex tend to devalue the act when they become adults, viewing sex as selfish pleasure, not as a form of commitment. Toya was no exception to this rule because I lusted for her; however, there was something vastly different about my encounter with her. I desired to know more about her, and it was much deeper than her pleasant appearance and seductive body. I attended and scanned church services in hopes of seeing her with some halo hovering above her head in those well-crafted pews. In my young brain, I was still a playa, so I did not focus solely on Toya; but she occupied my mind long after she left my presence. No women had ever captured my attention and my mind like her.

Beauty and sex are like parts of a resume to most men. They can get you in the door, but they are never the deciding factor to gaining a man's heart. Marriage was still a distant thought for me, but I envisioned her in my future in some capacity. The more I thought about her, the more I would pursue and make comments about other girls to detract or interrupt these unusual feelings I had about her. Honestly, I did not want to be vulnerable or to open myself up to being a victim of failed love.

I was afraid of falling in love; love can still be intimidating to me at times—nothing last forever because death is imminent. Love brings extreme excitement and joy, but love also opens us up to heartache and heartbreak. I have lost a lot of friends and family members, and some deaths leave empty voids in our lives—never to be filled again. Meeting her opened my mind up to the idea of falling in love, in the past, I fell in love with sex; but it was difficult to allow myself to be vulnerable to love. My new growth taught me to pursue love and to be open to new experiences that are opposed to my old way of thinking.

We should seek the good in all situations, even situations deemed as bad or extremely challenging—there is always a lesson to be learned. My negative and positive situations inspired me to witness the love in all people and eliminate prejudgments. We must avoid all prejudices based on manmade categories such as ethnicity, socioeconomic status, gender, sexual preference, color, education, and etc. of people. Military and relationships formed in the USAF helped me develop this beneficial concept toward people.

Toya and I continued to communicate throughout my final weeks of basic training at church services on Sundays, and the more I spoke with her, the more I recognized the honesty, strength, and power within her. I could relate to her personal struggles in Newark, New Jersey and Durham, NC, and I loved her overall realness; she spoke her mind, even if it hurt my feelings. She informed me about some guy she was dating back in Durham, but I operated on fate and believed it was a reason why we met; I thought it was destiny, and he was just a temporary obstacle.

I never planned to be vindictive, but I felt a connection with her that I could not explain. I tried to respect her relationship as much as possible without leaving her alone, but I was determined to remain her friend with a hidden agenda of luring her away from her boyfriend. I expressed my big ambitions of playing professional football after my four years of military service, bragging about how I was a big time high school and college football player—but she cared nothing about football or professional athletes. She was not impressed that I played college football, and she definitely was not impressed that I use to sell drugs or any of my past thug behavior. She dated tough guys who came from much tougher environments than I was accustomed to; she actually had a former first love and boyfriend who was killed for his pursuit of street life, so being a thug was not impressive to her.

Toya emphasized how dumb it was to act hard while joining the military to become a productive individual; she made me think, and she made me wiser—I respected what she had to say. In so many words, she taught me never to regress, instead to move forward and be better. She validated my unmasking as a thug and assisted my substantial growth in the process. She helped me discover the thinker, the dreamer, and the goal-setter within me. Toya adored the loving side of me, and the glimpses of intellectual brilliance that I exhibited.

She encouraged and inspired me with her clever words and purposeful questions. I felt comfortable and natural with the short span of time I was around her. I was comfortable opening up emotionally (i.e., smiles and hugs), and I was able to live my life without the pressure of being someone different from my authentic traits and inner voice. I was not prompted to use vulgar language to impress her; on the contrary, she corrected my improper grammar or poorly phrased speech. I felt driven toward pursuing positive successes when I was around her; but I was still confused about my authentic being. When I was around my basic training cohort, I bragged about past negative behaviors and past years of being a star athlete to raise my level of recognition among my band of military brothers—doing what I was accustomed to, to validate me.

However, I noticed an evolution in my thinking and temperament when a training instructor confronted me in a deliberate and confrontational manner. He stared at me and proceeded to belittle me in front of other trainees while some of his warm spit rested on the side of my face and lip. Instantly, I became enraged, and I lost all of my military bearing, reverting to past combative mannerisms—slouching shoulders, posturing in a fighting manner, and acting nonchalant to his utterance.

I started to lose self-control, and my reactive state of mind had every intention of taking a swing at his chin. However, I shifted to a proactive state of mind and thoughts of failure started to cloud my mind. I fought to reverse those negative thoughts by visualizing myself walking throughout the base with my dress blues and graduating from basic training. I was able to escape that confrontation by reminding myself why I joined the military: for progress and growth in every aspect of my life.

An instant calm and peace came over me, so while the spit from his mouth clashed against my youthful and bronze skin, I came to military attention (straighten the body for a sign of respect) and stated, "Trainee Williams reports as ordered and apologizes for this mishap sir." In that moment, I transitioned from a reactive boy to a proactive and rational-thinking man, and I knew that change occurred within me—the masked no longer enslaved me. I felt proud of the subtle shift in my thinking and aggressive attitude, and I was very thankful for the influence that Toya had on my life during our brief but special encounters. I graduated from basic training and shortly after, I departed for tech school (Sheppard AFB) in Wichita Falls, TX, so I would be separated from Toya for a month. Her tech school was at Sheppard as well.

Leaving basic training was a bittersweet moment for me

because I was happy to graduate and leave but drew poignant as I thought of Toya. Bruce and Bethea would join me at Sheppard, making the transition a little smoother. I was focused on receiving my tech school training as a dental assistant, but I was also excited about the freedoms that tech school provided.

We could play basketball, chat with girls, attend the BDU club to party, and walk without being in a flight or around drill sergeants. Tech school was similar to the college learning environment, but military assessments were more stressful; failure of tests meant reclassification to another job or career. I studied hard and passed every test in my Air Force dental assisting program, but I utilized my spare time flirting with girls within my medical squadron.

Even though I engaged in this behavior, my mind was never far from Toya; I sent her letters frequently from tech school to her basic training squadron. I had some mental masked pitfalls in tech school because Bethea and I represented "BLOOD" on occasion; he was a member of that gang in Fayetteville, so we meshed well together. Bethea and I formed a small crew with Gary from Baltimore (B-More), Henry from New York, Tarvis from Mississippi, and Bruce from NC, and we made a point to represent for the east coast around base and at the BDU club.

The old me loved the idea of a crew and a position of power. I was no longer an advocate for "thug life," but the competitive side supported this power position. Change does not occur over night and that is a profound lesson to be learned as we maneuver through this intricate world. I found myself bouncing around and throwing up gang signs when popular songs came on and riled up the crowd like *Make 'Em Say Ugh* from Master P on base and in the local clubs we frequented. The mind must completely be renewed and ignorant actions must be replaced with sound actions before change will remain consistent and permanent.

This was the first time my mind had an opportunity for some clarity because I had no girlfriends, no active past friendships, and no real hang ups hindering me from seeing the hidden me. At this time, the discovery of my identity was the primary focus.

I quietly rested on my pillow and stared off in the dark corner of the room at night, trying to pinpoint my values and my purpose in this crazy and complex world. I forgot my values or had no real values, so I adopted the USAF values: integrity, service before self, and excellence in all we do.

I incorporated these values into my character and my daily routine; those values made me question certain day-to-day decisions and revisit my reasons for joining the military again. I chose to be a productive and positive citizen—that's why I joined. Finally, Toya arrived at Sheppard AFB about a month into my tech school experience, and even though I had been involved with some other girls, Toya was the only woman I wanted. I was relaxing near the lounge area within my dormitory when she gently tapped me on my shoulder; she said, "hello," and I was filled with excitement and joy. Nobody else mattered on that military installation in that very moment.

I went from using all of my time to hang with my friend to employing all of my time to hang with her in tech school. Inadvertently, Toya taught me about self-improvement because she critiqued my dress and manners. Her approached challenged me to think and self-reflect about my actions because I sought actions and behaviors that aligned my thinking with positive living. Her actions were subtle, and her comments were brutally honest.

She also did not put up with my subterfuge when I tried to avoid her questions. She challenged me to think before I spoke. She was a tough woman, and I needed her tough attitude to challenge me to be greater. At this time, we were hanging out but not dating. We had a break from each other during Christmas and New Year's break, so I went home with the belief that it was nothing too serious between Toya and I; yet, I found myself thinking about her and wondering about her actions over the break.

I bought a Mitsubishi Mirage over our break, so Bethea, Bruce, and Shaka decided to ride with me from NC to TX. During this long two-day drive, I could not distract my mind from thinking about her; no woman has ever consumed my thoughts like that.

In January, Toya and I returned from our break, and I built up the courage to ask her to be my girlfriend; she loved the idea. Dating her boosted my confidence because I pursued someone I deemed of high quality and virtue. We went on a lot of dates together, and this was new to me; sadly, I never treated other girls with as much respect as her.

My relationship with Toya was less about lust and more about developing an authentic relationship. This relationship taught me how to treat people in general because I learned to open up and show genuine emotions when conversing with diverse individuals. My tech school training was getting ready to conclude when I received orders to Holloman AFB in New Mexico as some cruel military joke; I selected all east coast locations on these so-called assignment relocation dream sheet. The dilemma was that Toya received orders to Beale AFB in California, and I was perplexed by this prospective separation from one another. I knew Toya for only four months and dated her for about a month, but it was something special about her; I knew she was meant to be in my life.

I concluded that the smart move to make was to marry this woman or take the risk of never having that relationship with her. I decided that Toya was the one. I knew we were probably too young and too immature to be married, but I felt strongly that God sent her in my life for a reason—I could not let her go. I was resolute in this guilt feeling, and I was not going to allow any unbelief deter me from my developed conviction. My mind was made up, she was the best person who came into my life, and I needed her love and strength for individual maturation. Being around her made me authentic, I did not have to hide this humble, intellectual, and inspirational person behind a masked thug demeanor; I yearned for this feeling for years and now I have it.

I did not want to return to the same cycle of progression to regression. I wanted to seize the initiative and to make her my wife—change or conform. I felt it was the right thing to do, and I knew in my heart that Toya would marry me—no arrogance, just understanding timing and our current state of minds. True leaders know when to act and expect positive results; I evolved to a true leader. I was reserved to the fact that some people perceived me as an idiot for marrying a woman a barely knew, but those people could not live my life. Sometimes our best choices come from the strong undeniable belief of knowing what to choose, even if it is not the most popular response. Sometimes intuition is more advantageous than a person's deductive reasoning or sound logic. Toya presented me with hope, and she brought positive change to my life; I needed both to help me successfully stay unmasked and find my purpose.

At 19 years old, Toya and I walked hand-in-hand toward the ticket box to see "Scary Movie," and I gingerly walked as I complained about some constant knee pain from a prior basketball game on base. I scored buckets like Michael Jordan in his prime prior to our venture to the movies as a side note. Toya proceeded toward the ticket box unaware that I collapsed valiantly to one knee and with a ring case that rested on the palm of my extended right hand.

She soon noticed that I was lagging behind, so she turned around in an abrupt manner to see what was ailing me. Inner confidence exuded to my exterior as I boldly said, "Will you marry me?" Time stood still, as I stood superbly confident that she would utter the word "yes." I was very auspicious about this surreptitious relationship, but thoughts of my family clouded my mind as I waited patiently for a response. My family will think I am crazy. What will my mom and dad say? What will Deon and Mack say? In my opinion, Toya was worth any backlash or rejection from my family. I grew more confident in my choice because it was to appease me and no one else. This was a significant shift from my many years of living to appease others.

As my mind drifted off and dreamed on to brighter horizons, Toya face swelled with great pleasure and yelled a fanatic "yes." I knew my life would never be the same, and I knew I was destined for greatness and was led to find my God-given purpose. We promptly got married a week later in the Wichita Falls, TX local courthouse in our casual civilian attire. Toya's orders were swiftly changed to Holloman AFB, NM, so I departed with fervor toward my new journey, knowing that my wife would join me once she finished her training. Toya and this marriage gave me reasons to love and to believe in myself again, and this union galvanized me toward a passionate pursuit of self-development. I saw the world from a new and rewarding perspective. I was confident about being a strong and positive man, no longer a weak man hiding behind an unnatural mask. I unmasked that person forever; that chapter was closed, so on to new discoveries and to plentiful opportunities.

Lessons Learned

The law of attraction belief is that likes attracts to likes in this convoluted universe. Toya and I were alike; we had challenging backgrounds and struggles with being accepted and recognition by family members and friends. Magnetic fields are strong, and it is impossible to pull strong magnetics apart. Our minds are our most valuable asset to formulating behaviors— positive or negative. When I embraced a negative way of thinking, I produced negative actions: fighting, selling drugs, having sex in middle school, leaving home at 16 years of age, dropping out of school, producing two children out of wedlock, and participating in a BLOOD gang lifestyle that almost claimed someone's life.

However, my decision to join the military led me on a new odyssey with a more diversified perspective. I developed a zest for life, a passion for self-development, and a desire for authentic admiration from someone I could trust. I believe that God sends us blessings when we least expect them; but those blessings can be in ways that we reject because we do not pay attention to those subtle messages or signs. I repudiated any notion of serving my country or any hint of marriage, but I ate those words and enjoyed every taste. We must set sail for new journeys, but it is germane to trust our intuition in unique or challenging situations over the sound reasons of others—new pursuits present unimaginable successes.

Chapter 16

Unexpected Success Breeds Unimaginable Success

To Whom Much is Giving Much is Expected

"To accomplish great things, we must not only act,
but also dream, not only plan, but also believe"
~ Anatole France

The next three years at Holloman AFB, NM positively changed and charged my life forever. During my time at Holloman, I realized that being black does not hold me back from being a successful man in white America, and I realized being "thug" or being "tough" does not make me a real man—a real man is willing to accept feedback and help from other individuals—even individuals who come from different cultures, ethnic groups, genders, and beliefs. I adopted an optimistic approach toward life, and I sought to find the real beauty or pleasant qualities within people rather than assuming an individual was a racist or an evil person. I made it my prerogative to seek the productive and positive attributes in people and this philosophy minimized any negativity and evil dwelling internally and externally in my life—I sought the good in everyone. I was determined to spend my time wisely at Holloman by finding my individuality and making something positive with the remainder of my short existence on this earth.

I developed arduous work ethic in my dental assisting profession because I was determined to become one of the best dental assistants in our dental clinic. My supervisor, Sergeant (Sgt.) Chapman inspired me to search within for my greatest potential by setting objectives and working toward them daily. Her commitment and dedication to my self-development as a person and airman created a tenacious attitude toward the pursuit of excellence.

I never witnessed the difference in her fair skin color and bright blue eyes; I saw a person with a genuine heart and sound wisdom, caring for my individual triumph. She shared the importance of returning to college and pursuing a college degree, and I needed to hear those encouraging words after my previous failure at MC. Her interest in my life galvanized an inner drive that challenged me to step outside of my comfort zone. Sgt. Chapman spent her feedback sessions encouraging me to dream bigger than completing my CDC's (proficiency assessment of my military job).

I became motivated to enroll in some college courses and to receive additional training in my military job to become a dental hygienist within our dental facility. This was the first time that I set a long-term goal that included an enhancement of my mental, and I became auspicious about my military career and my quest for higher learning. I was always curious about the possibilities that a college degree might offer me since my trucking odysseys with my uncle but no one within my immediate family ever received a bachelor's degree and provided me with a true measuring stick. I experienced individuals who labored in factories to make adequate money without fancy college degrees. My street IQ taught me to be a little paranoid, and that paranoia translated to being very observant of my surroundings. I observed how enlisted members went out of their way to salute and to respect officers on base, adhering to military protocol.

The officers appeared extremely happy, and they seemed to do very well financially when compared to my rank as an E-1. Some officers were only a few years older than me, but they made twice as much and appeared to perform less strenuous work. This spurred me to ask some random officers about their military careers and what it takes for an individual to become an officer. One officer looked at me and informed me that it requires a college degree, so his statement reinforced my decision to return to college to further my education.

God aligned me with the right people, and they appeared to position themselves in my life at the right time. Those people inspired me with the right words needed to generate a profound belief in my academic abilities. I did a lot of thinking and daydreaming in those days, trying to envision my life years ahead, and I started to truly believe that a college degree might provide me with the tools needed to establish wealth throughout my existence. I remember watching my wife being brought to tears because I brought home an 80-hour check of about $120 dollars due to child support garnishments—this unexpected incident challenged my ego as a man and belief as a spiritual being.

In the past, I would have folded mentally, but this unfortunate event challenged me to stay on top of my child support obligation and be a better father—I did not complain, but instead, I searched internally and acknowledged the errors of my ways. A calm resolve came over me, and I realized that somehow I would be able to take care of Toya; and I was willing to do whatever it took to support my beautiful wife and fulfill my child support obligations. My wife charged me to be the best father I could be, even from a distance; she also encouraged me to continue taking pride in my work and in my academic pursuits.

One year into my military assignment at Holloman, I was promoted to a dental hygienist and received my own DTR (dental treatment room). I also enrolled into undergraduate college courses at New Mexico State University. I gained life-long confidence from enrolling in college and seizing the initiative on positive alternatives. I replaced a thug mindset with a learning mindset, and I was dedicated to learning in all facets of my life—no more shortcuts. I wanted to earn everything; I viewed hard work and completion as my reward. I learned how to invest in my mind, how to be patient, how to appreciate and love others, and how to discover God's will for my life.

I thrived in college, spewing rhetoric from Socrates, Plato, and Sun-Tzu—Philosophy was my favorite course. I developed an obsession toward school and toward acquiring new knowledge. My perspective on life became more focused on growth, and my faith grew stronger through manifestations taking place in my way of life: praying and receiving the woman of my dreams, earning a 4.0 GPA my first semester in college, and receiving a promotion within my first year at Holloman. However, I still felt a little empty on the inside, and I could not quite figure out why until Mack came to visit us in New Mexico. At this time, Mack was a devout believer, and I viewed him as a seer; I sought his spiritual guidance and advice when it came to understanding God.

He spent his visit discussing his relationship with God, and it intrigued me, even though I fought against his religious talk. Mack's timing seemed to be perfect because at this time, my life was improving personally and professionally but I still struggled with a quick temper that affected my relationship with Toya at times. I still retained aspects of the hip-hop culture in my speech and my actions. Perception creates a form of judgment, so we must be mindful of our image being presented at all times. My brief time in the military taught me how to leave some people from the past in the past and how to embrace diverse individuals with contrary lifestyles and beliefs.

I learned that some people were meant to be in my life for a season, so it was my job to absorb all blessings that arose from those seasons and unique relationships. Mack was a positive example of a true believer in Christ. At that time, he did not partake in alcohol or frequent the club scene. I envied him because he was in his early 20s and had this inner peace and calm resolve that I strongly desired. Mack read his bible and took copious notes on scriptures to develop a more thorough understanding of what he was reading, treating it like an intense college course. Mack spoke in a meek and polite fashion, and he viewed the world from a loving and a godly perspective. I had more happiness and more love in my heart, but I was far from viewing the world as my twin.

I spouted more profanity than a rated "R" flick, and I fought bottled up anger. From time-to-time, I punched holes in walls to mitigate my anger rather than communicating properly and appropriately with my wife—pouting like a little kid over a video game or cream-filled Twinkies. Something on the inside of me was yearning for more, and I needed something to inspire and to guide me. I wanted a relationship with God, but I had no idea of how to pursue it. I strongly desired to change my interior as well as exterior.

I was the quintessential airman at work, but I was not that constructive outside of their extended view—the interior was still suffering and needed to be fixed. Success cannot be achieved when the interior lacks substance; the exterior will eventually deteriorate. I knew that eventually, the underperforming interior would have harmful influences on my relationship with Toya and other relationships. Toya was my catalyst for change, but a mere mortal can only inspire and provide me with temporary happiness—I yearned for permanent peace and fulfillment—something greater than a human.

While Mack was there, he continued to share his spiritual experiences with me rather than preach to me and judge me. Yet, I attempted to belittle his spiritual pitches when his messages challenged me, but secretly, I latched on to every word he spoke. I displayed a stoic facial expression as a defensive mechanism because I acted as if I did not care to here his sage advice. Deep down, I was tired of living empty and with no guided purpose. I was too weak mentally and emotionally to exhibit emotions to other people who were not my wife, but I soon learned that real men cry and share their emotions with love ones. At this stage of my life, I was not too fond of portraying mushy emotions and behaviors, so I refrained from giving hugs and expressing heartfelt "I love you." I was brainwashed to think that those behaviors made me inadequate.

I was convinced that it was time for me to dedicate my life to living as Christ because I yearned to live with a purpose much greater than my selfish pursuits of acquiring worldly things (i.e., house and cars). My belief was that my growth needed to be a physical, mental, and spiritual pursuit, and my spiritual pursuit was to live as Christ and to follow instruction from the Holy Bible. My belief is not to judge or to condemn other people's beliefs, but live with fervor toward Christ's philosophies and teachings.

I knew it would be a challenging process, but I was ready to pursue that spiritual walk. I wanted a complete transformation and grew tired of regressing back to thug behaviors in settings relatable to my lived thug culture. I expected to feel overwhelmed by some magical spirit when I decided to commit myself to that spiritual journey. I thought that my spiritual journey would give me the power to never want to commit a sin again. This idea was so far from the truth and completely unrealistic.

Spiritual growth required me to seek God daily through prayer, scriptural reading, spiritual self-help books, and fellowship with other brothers and sisters of this similar faith. This renewed mind and balance toward thinking enhanced my faith and minimized my unbelief and worrying about daily obstacles and challenges. Growth is the pursuit of perfection, but perfection does not exist. In my opinion, perfection is the aim of daily improvement. I was trying, but I was far from the finish line—the race is not given to the swift.

I am convinced that temptation arises daily, and we all fall short daily in subtle ways (i.e., overeating, failure to take care of our temples, or exaggerating our anecdotes). True believers, not religion seekers keep pursuing God and never rest on the appearance of being viewed as holy. We all have a spiritual journey, and our journeys require undeniable faith. I am not writing this book to sway people to believe in God, but I will tell you that it is imperative to believe in something greater than yourself and to have strong faith; we all believe in something. My spiritual connection drove me to inner peace and to greater self-discovery of my hidden potential.

Yet, change was not coming fast enough for me, even though I continued to flourish within my military career. I had problems embracing this new non-threatening outer appearance. I did not want to come off as fake or as someone who failed to keep it real among individuals who displayed mannerisms and styles from hip-hop culture. I was aware that I needed to abandon nostalgic thoughts about past negative actions that I perceived as cool. I wanted to be different, even if it did not come off as so-called cool.

I strived to improve my character, my mind, my personality, my speech, and my zest for living. I forced myself to apologize when I offended someone even if I felt or new that I was right; this humbled me and taught me to discuss topics from multiple perspectives. I sought advice from people whom I viewed as sages; I also welcomed unwarranted sound advice from unique settings. This Air Force chief challenged my profane words on the basketball court one day with a subtle statement and a thought-provoking question.

He stated in so many words that intelligent individuals expand their vocabulary rather than employing ignorant profane words as fillers in sentences. He said, "What words would you use to replace those swear words?" I pondered long and hard on his question, and I had no response to his well-structured inquiry. His unusual challenge prompted me to examine my rhetoric and to study prolific speakers such as Dr. Martin Luther King, Bill Clinton, and Ronald Reagan, to practice pronouncing my words correctly, to increase my vocabulary, and to eliminate profanity from my speech. Welcoming inquiries into our lives can force us to improve problematic areas or to acquire new skills. Nightly, I would reevaluate my decisions throughout the day, and challenge myself with self-imposed questions.

The nighttime gave me an opportunity to envision the future and to play out favorable outcomes over and over in my mind until it became my lived reality. My inner confidence grew in the wee hours of the night and in the right hemisphere of my brain as I continued to dream big. Everything is conceived in the mind, and we should speak boldly to generate that inner belief in our hearts. God spoke the world into existence, and the bible concludes that God made man in his image. I strongly believe that we are born with speaking power, so I was determined to speak my inner world into existence to create a successful reality.

I gazed in my transparent bathroom mirror and repeated these phrases, "I am intelligent," "I am handsome," "I am funny," "I am loving," and "I am a true child of God" nightly for 30 minutes at a time until I believed every statement. Over time, I developed a high-level of confidence from these exercises, self-reflections, and daydreaming episodes. Overtly, I acknowledged my flaws and my weaknesses, and I worked daily to address those issues and to create constructive actions to mitigate poor decision-making.

I grasped how to manage my USAF career, how to communicate and manage healthy relationships, and how to function as a loving husband and father—being a great husband and father is perpetual—no mastery skills will be presented in this book because I am no master in these areas. My fervent prayers helped me to manage the complexity of marriage, personal change, military career, and life in diversified NM.

I had to work hard to balance the demands of life. I was pursuing a bachelor's degree, building a spiritual relationship with God, and challenging military career while bringing a new child (Jay) into our world. Paranoia challenged my love and trust in Toya at times, stemming from poor self-esteem within intimate relationships. I was paranoid that Toya would leave me for someone smarter, more attractive, or perceptually better than me according to societal standards. My mirror exercises gave me the self-assurance needed to combat those feelings of paranoia.

The more I began to pray, to meditate, and to focus on improving me (i.e., mentally, physically, and spiritually), the less jealous and paranoid I became, and the stronger I grew within. God gave me the motivation I needed to gain control over my being; my mind was shaping a new reality of external rewards and successes. I was inspired to work on rewards that impacted my physical structure. I ran and worked out to lose some excess weight that I had packed on around my mid-section. Poor dieting and beer consumption contributed to this increase in body fat, (20 percent compared to 10 percent entering the military). I also used combative situations to improve my attitude when interacting with difficult supervisors. I had a challenging NCOIC (MSgt. Kelly), and she tried to make my life hell within those structured walls of the small dental facility.

I seized the initiative in this situation, and I viewed it as an opportunity to practice positive communication and to understand a person who failed to connect with me on a personal and professional level. My situations became opportunities for inner growth; inner growth made me more and more auspicious about endless possibilities. I attempted kill MSgt. Kelly's evil with kindness, and no matter how upset or frustrated I gained by her comments, I responded in a courteous and favorable manner.

Eventually, I lost about 15 pounds of fat, and, as proof of the law of attraction, MSgt. Kelly was replaced with MSgt. Salley, who adored me. I sought positive endeavors and positive outcomes found me. I was able to generate small wins throughout my military experience, and those small wins were huge for fortifying my inner beliefs. I was very appreciative for those small wins. Winning becomes contagious because my wins drove me to desire greater successes: I set my sights on earning two associate degrees, a bachelor's degree, Airman of the Quarter, Airman of the Year, and Below the Zone (earn stripe early).

Minor successes galvanized me to raise the bar and to set my sights on lofty goals of graduating with honors and of training my body to play professional football after concluding my military career. This newfound confidence and identity propelled me to seek the best out of my short life, and it inspired me to enroll in and complete two associate's degree programs (Community College of the Air Force/CCAF and New Mexico State University/ NMSU) and a bachelor's degree program (Park University) simultaneously before my scheduled discharge from military service in 2 ½ years—tough feat but I yearned for this challenge.

I enrolled in three college courses scheduled for eight weeks, and I will be lying if I say that the intense workload did not intimidate me at first; however, I convinced myself that if I completed this daunting task, I could reach unimaginable heights.

After I completed those three courses: Philosophy 101, Legal Terminology 103, and Arts 111 during the spring semester of 2001, I grew addicted to learning new theories and thinking on a more critical and creative level. Socrates and Plato abstract way of thinking influenced me to adopt an open-minded viewpoint toward vitality rather than viewing the world as concrete or black and white.

I created a positive outlook on life, and I focused on thinking in a slow and meticulous manner. First, I learned to smile more and to hold myself accountable for my decisions. Secondly, I learned to manage and control my temper as well as misguided rhetoric with internal questions (e.g., "What is the benefit of getting mad? Does it promote growth? What is the best solution to this situation?")?

God surrounded me with an excellent apparatus of tactical relationships, and I used those to influence me in a positive mode. Sgt. Chapman constantly encouraged me to take more college courses, so she served as an impetus to my success as an airman, a dental hygienist, and a college student. When I started my college summer semester in 2001, I loaded up on college credits to expedite my completion of two associate's degrees by taking 12 credits, working full-time, and helping raise a five-month old. Even though GPA is not the most accurate indication of learned information, I earned a 3.5 during that loaded summer session;

I made a "C" in Psychology—the last "C" I ever made in college.

During my fall semester in 2001, I intensified my passionate pursuit of learning by taking a course in the morning during work hours (NCOIC approved this course), a course at lunch, a course after work, and an online course while still maintaining my military obligations and family duties. I did not believe in wasting my time on excuses and complaints because excuses and crafty complaints never solved problems. I had a goal, so I used these issues to push me harder toward my set goals and objectives. I took it upon myself to read a book on substance abuse, and I employed that new knowledge with my street knowledge of substances to take a CLEP assessment of a Substance Abuse course for three additional elective credits.

This academic opposition was not easy by any means, but I evolved as a thinker, a leader of my life, and a hard worker throughout this laborious endeavor. I finished the semester with a 3.7 GPA at NMSU, and I went on to complete over 37 credits my first year back in college. I was focused, and my diligent works and faith kept me in an academic zone like Michael Jordan on the basketball court in a NBA finals game.

I remained engaged throughout the entire degree process. I earned "A's" at NMSU and Central Texas College, and these feats gave me inner confidence to believe that I could excel and graduate from any college with high marks and high honors. With the credits that I received from Methodist College (9 credits) and USAF (30 credits), I was able to obtain an associate's degree in dental assisting from CCAF and an associate's degree of Arts from NMSU with honors in 2002.

At this time, I had about 1 ½ year left to serve in the USAF, and I was convinced that my body had some years of football left. Realizing that collegiate football would no longer be a viable option, I focused my attention on playing professionally. I knew this goal was a long shot; yet, this newfound inner peace and self-confidence had me believing this lofty goal would be my reality. I was living and thriving in my inner world, so I was determined to find somewhere to play professionally—you only live once ("YOLO" as todays generation states it). Balancing workouts, family, school, and work became the new challenge and opportunity for growth. I convinced myself that I had to do it—make it work . . . make it happen James—my mind spoke back to me.

Motivation can sometimes lead us into dangerous waters if our bodies are not ready for new tasks. My motivation drove me to insane workouts by benching too heavy and squatting too heavy, while imploring sprints after those strenuous workouts. In my opinion, this made my body susceptible to injuries. I was naïve about my physical condition, and I trained as if I was in peak condition or back in college. I was benching 365 pounds, squatting 585 pounds, and leg pressing about 1200 pounds. In my mind, this was how Barry Sanders trained, so I needed to train in the same fashion. I assumed that heavy weight equaled high-performance on the football field.

I informed military members that I was going to play professional football when I separated for a unique mental advantage; the more I spoke it, the more the dream came alive within me. The belief prompted those strenuous workouts, which contributed to a sport's hernia surgery, the first of nine surgeries throughout my short time on this earth. Prior to separating from the USAF, my left knee was scoped twice, and my right knee was scoped once. The irony is that my surgeries enhanced my motivation and faith in playing professional football. I had no fear of the unknown; I just believed in my self-created inner world—I became king in my mental world and ruled over all outcomes.

Playing flag football and basketball for my medical squadron kept me elusive and confident in my athletic abilities; I scored early and often in flag football and some players called me Marshall Faulk because I left opponents hugging air and tracking my long gone cleat prints toward the end zone for six points. I also started as point guard for our medical squadron basketball team, and we went on to win the base championship. I scored my first game winner for that highly talented basketball team. These sport experiences helped me maintain my hand-eye-coordination, balance, and overall agility.

While I was maturing under the tutelage of Sgt. Chapman, she received orders for relocation. It was a great season for her, and unselfishly, I was happy for her and her family. I was blessed with a new supervisor, Sgt. Prosper who played a crucial role in my continued maturation process. Sgt. Prosper ended up becoming a great friend and mentor to me. Sgt. Prosper designed an award-winning conglomerate of my military accolades, community service, and self-improvement (i.e., college achievements), and his well-written package helped me win "Airman of the Quarter" twice and "Airman of the Year" for my medical squadron.

My wife was also a recipient of "Airman of the Quarter" for her outstanding service, and Holloman AFB recognized our collective accomplishments with a well-written article in the base newspaper. I was elevated to extreme happiness and a sense of achievement, and I realized my potential was limitless. I was no longer trapped in the perpetual mindset of a thug. Toya and I also earned "Below-the-Zone," which gave us an opportunity to tack on senior airman (E-4 rank) six months early—increase pay and responsibilities. I was extremely proud of Toya, and I could tell that she was very proud of me as well. We pushed each other to soar higher in our personal and professional endeavors. A relationship is worth investing in when both parties grow together and make each other better.

The last year of my military contract, I spent majority of my free time playing in three-on-three Gus Macker basketball tournaments with Fennel, AJ, and Kevin. Fennel and AJ became life-long friends and extended brothers who taught me how to smile and how to grasp enjoyable moments from everyday. We traveled throughout New Mexico (i.e., Las Cruces, Albuquerque, and Roswell) to play in that popular Midwest basketball tournament, and this helped me maintain my competitive edge over opponents.

I also learned how to maintain a balance between competition and sportsmanship because I adopted Fennel and AJ's smiles and pleasant personalities—winning us awards for showmanship and sportsmanship. We were likeable figures, and people who did not know us began to root for us. This unusual encounter taught me that authentic love rewards me back with genuine adoration from others. I was determined to remain likeable, and I desired to embrace my hidden self rather than that fake "Thug" demeanor—I detested the masked thug.

I understood that it was nothing real about being a thug because we are born as beings destined to spread and to share love with others. AJ and Fennell were positive individuals with a peaceful resolve toward living, and they had no desire to engage in violence, drinking, partying, or detrimental behavior that I was accustomed to. Believe it or not, most of us mirror the behaviors of the company we keep, and I had some constructive company around me. They played a crucial role in the burying of my former thug mask because I wanted to see the world from a broader, more loving perspective; they reinforced and added to my inner world of peace and happiness, to connect me with an external world of love.

Two years embarking on my spiritual journey, I was still evolving and transforming into my true potential. I specifically noted two years, so individuals can comprehend the fact that change requires a lifetime commitment; change follows us to our coffins—perfection is only found in death. I loved being around AJ and Fennell because they held me accountable any time I acted ugly or displayed a bad attitude on the basketball court, improving my self-control and self-awareness.

I began to understand and to visualize all of the favorable outcomes that could arise when I exhibited a positive attitude. Success is predicated on our awareness and conceived reality—power of thinking. Basketball was my self-therapy to compounding academic stress, and self-therapy is needed in taxing situations;

we must diligently find a productive self-therapy that works for us. We should never waste our time thinking and overthinking something difficult in our lives; we must break away and relax our minds, returning with a fresh and a responsive mind. I sauntered around with my preset degree course curriculum in my pocket for inspiration.

Occasionally, I retrieved the worn document from my pocket to don a smile that traveled my thoughts away from the present and to a future graduation stage. I envisioned myself with a Park University cap, gown, and cum laude cord draped over my shoulders, as I nervously waited for an applause from the audience. When I snapped back to my external world reality, I gazed over the lined through course curriculum to observe how many courses I completed and how courses remained for this elusive bachelor's degree. Graduating with a bachelor's degree was a huge deal for me because I would be the first in my immediate family; the two associate degrees were much appreciated, but my mother had an associate's degree—she wanted more, and I wanted more.

At that time, I had not walked across a stage and heard my name called since high school, and I did not want high school to be my last applause or the last time celebrating a graduation ceremony. I yearned for that day and wanted to receive those claps—positive praise was my new vice—not recognition from a masked thug persona. I worked hard to finish the semester with a 4.0 GPA, and I cried as I realized I would soon be a college graduate—an accomplishment that I could not envision as I reflected on my old mistakes and my old way of viewing my existence. On May 11, 2003, two months shy of the conclusion of my distinguished Air Force career, I walked enthusiastically across the ceremonial stage at Park University's commencement ceremony, where the degree of bachelor of science in management/computer information systems was conferred upon me. I graduated cum laude; my GPA was 3.7.

My family was overwhelmed with joy because they lived through the nightmare and witnessed first hand my metamorphosis to a productive citizen and even better person. Prior to entering the military, I am sure my parents had their reservations about me succeeding in the Air Force and returning to college. My wife's beliefs in me as a student, a provider, a husband, and a father encouraged me beyond doubt, so I knew she relished in my transformation as well; she observed a change in my speech, noting that I had eliminated profanity from my vocabulary. She also saw that my destructive attitude, and poor decision-making and actions had diminished.

It felt great to dispel some stereotypes that plagued my psyche and a large portion of black males having two kids in high school, selling drugs, running away from home, dropping out of college, and associating with a gang. My commander awarded me with an incentive flight that gave me an opportunity to fly in a T-38 with an Air Force fighter pilot because he was impressed with my military accolades and degree accomplishments.

I served as a co-pilot with Major Barnes. As we soared in the T-38, we climbed to a gravitational pull of four G's (gravity force), and my mind climbed with the jet, dreaming on how high God might allow my untapped potential to take me. While I was daydreaming and enjoying the mountain-view from my small cockpit window, Major Barnes maneuvers propelled me to share my lunch with a designated vomit bag—my stomach could not handle flying upside down and freefalling steers in the compressed New Mexico air.

My military memories were filled with formidable obstacles and accomplishments that expanded the borders of my inner world, and my military experiences inspired me to remove the thug mask completely. I now desired a more positive outlook and to engage in constructive actions. I found peace and identity in the military, but now, I was in pursuit of my purpose. Change was happening for me, as we prepared to separate from the military, but my experiences and my spiritual faith taught me not to fear this major change in our lives. I was very optimistic about finding a great paying job and playing professional football in the NFL.

I believed that I would acquire one of those worthy goals, and I was supremely confident that I could utilize my college degree to land a great paying job while continuing to pursue professional football. Three weeks prior to my honorable discharge, I was derailed temporarily from training and working toward my football dream because I had a third knee surgery to repair my meniscus in my weakening left knee. This was the second time the doctor had to scope this knee.

Toya did an excellent job budgeting and managing our finances prior to separating from the service. She managed to build up a sound savings account; it was significant because we had no jobs lined up. I stepped out solely on faith of playing professional football and landing a quality job. Toya thought it was a little foolishness, but she believed in me; and her belief forced me to work harder to be the best at everything I did.

It is crucial to have a friend or a love one who believes in you. We were aware of monies needed to place Jay in daycare, food, shelter, and other necessities, but the poise I gained through my military and life experiences prepared me mentally for the daunting task of separating from the military and reentering the civilian sector. I never complained, and I viewed every challenging obstacle as an opportunity for personal maturation. Overcoming obstacles can be used to lead us to our purpose in this life. I trained myself to find some level of peace within unexpected storms, so I viewed unexpected storms and set obstacles as issues one must endure prior to achieving ultimate success in this dynamic universe.

Lessons Learned

Life has a purpose, and we are all designed for greatness. Greatness arises from unexpected circumstances and lofty dreams that are structured within our inner world. It is imperative to build our confidence from within because a lack of confidence leads to the inability to generate the proper momentum needed to pursue set objectives or goals in our individual lives. I faced a traumatic situation of possibly shooting someone that prompted me to change or die masked to a thug life or ignorant way of thinking; change became the only viable option when I generated some self-confidence in my inner world. Once we attempt to seek positive change, we create a foundation that is welcoming even of more productive change.

I used the diverse world of the Air Force to observe the world from multiple perspectives rather than a thug-minded tunnel vision. I sought and accepted advice from anyone opposed to my beliefs or overall way of viewing life, if they sought to make me a more astute individual, a more logical or a more resound thinker. The pursuit of knowledge transitions to the pursuit of understanding, and it is crucial for us to comprehend who we are and what purpose we have in this enormous world. When we can answer those two questions with affirmation, we will have a doorway that opens up and leads us to self-discovery and inner peace. I stood affirmed in my direction and with fervor toward learning novel life theories and ideas, so my journey was formulated around how to make those theories or ideas applicable to my purpose, my true identity, and my true potential.

Chapter 17

Who Am I?

Finding Tranquility became my Mission

"Peace cannot be achieved through violence, it can only be attained through understanding"
~ Ralph Waldo Emerson

When we moved back to Wilson, NC, I was humbled by our living arrangements in my parents' 1970 singlewide trailer. It was rent free, but we were not used to living in those poor conditions. We only had to pay taxes on the property, so it was a huge benefit— still a mental adjustment though. The trailer was not in the greatest condition, but it was clean and rodent free. I was astatic about moving back to Stantonsburg, NC because a part of me expected people to embrace me with love upon my arrival; but there was no fanfare outside of my family. Living at a distance and not coming home often brought me more fanfare from family members because people do not have access to you everyday. This makes me think about how some guys go out of there way to gain the attention and interest of some beautiful girl; he treats her as a princess until she becomes his queen. When she becomes his queen, he decides to scale back on vacations and love notes. Some ladies are not exempt from this example because they treat their kings like lost puppies on long dark roads in search of their owner once they receive their interest.

Some people would be like, "Oh you back in Wilson, well, welcome home," and they proceed to make way to their autopilot lives of working and setting their sights no farther than Wilson. I invented this determination that made me believe I could acquire whatever I set my visual perception on, such as working at BB&T (local bank in NC area). Prior to this focused drive to work at BB&T, I worked as a temporary (temp) employee at Leiner Pharmaceutical for $9.75 per hour, and I worked diligently making generic Naproxen, donning full personal protective equipment (PPE) while sliding heavy barrels of powder between mixers.

I also decided to enroll in Central Michigan University master's of administration degree program to challenge myself further, while taking advantage of Uncle Sam's GI Bill benefits; we needed that additional income to cover our bills. Advance education and distinguished military service had me desiring a white-collar gig, where I had to dress like a businessman on Wall Street. For many years, I envisioned myself wearing suits while watching the world past in my rearview mirror.

On my days off from Leiner, I bottled up my confidence and left my house in search of that envisioned dream of fancy banking job because I thought that being a businessman was I; and I thought BB&T was that job for that particular dream. I dressed for success, and I strolled into BB&T hiring center with a smile on my face and a sells pitch about my abilities and credentials in my back pocket. I waited in the lobby, and I requested a chance to meet the hiring manager to shake their hand; I made up in my mind that I was willing to return everyday and to sit for hours for this chance.

Without much resistance, the hiring manager came out to meet with me briefly. I gave her a firm handshake, and immediately, I provided her with my resume and my persuasive pitch that highlighted why my military experience made me a valuable asset to BB&T. I believed that my newly minted degree and high level of confidence would open any shut door for me, even when she stated that they were not hiring at the time, so I still left that encounter with no job or job interview but with a sense of satisfaction. While I waited for a personal phone call from BB&T, I shifted my focus back toward training and chasing my set football dream of playing professionally.

I thought I was skilled enough to play in the NFL, and I thought the NFL was a part of God's master plan for me—our plans are not always aligned with God's plan or will for our lives—peace can be found in any pursuit though. I viewed football as my lottery ticket to instant success and money; my degree was viewed as a backup plan to professional football failure. I thought playing professional football would validate my success and give me a chance to prove any doubters or haters wrong. It was a selfish reason to seek the NFL, but that reason drove me toward that lofty dream for many years. I believe some of our dreams or prayers never come to fruition because our motives are wrong.

I understood that faith with the wrong motives produce unfavorable outcomes. However, God's plans were greater than my well-thought out vision of playing on Sundays when people fry up chicken wings and smack bottle of beers together to praise their favorite teams or favorite players. Still recovering from my third knee surgery, I decided to tryout for the Fayetteville Patriot's arena football team, but I ran a dismal 4.78 and 4.73 in the 40-yard dash. Coaches who invited me were not impressed, and I walked away with no contract in my stubby fingertips.

This was a depressing experience, but shortly after that disappointment, I received a phone call from BB&T to work as a temp in their loan services department for $10/hour and no benefits. I was a proud man who served honorably in the USAF with mounting bills and a large family, but I was happy to earn that low wage and work for that company. At that time, I was about a year into my master's degree, and I was thriving in the classroom among my distinguished cohort. I was the youngest in this non-traditional master's degree program (Seymour Johnson Air Force base, NC); I spoke confidently and lead teams that consisted of assistant managers, managers, and police chiefs within those intimate classroom settings during our eight-hour Saturday and Sunday class meetings.

Utilizing this imbued credence that I can accomplish dreams of any sort due to this constant flow of success, I down played my previous poor arena football tryout and worked even harder by running sprints up stadium stairs along with more strenuous strength training workouts. After a year of dedicated training, I attended a pro-day tryout in Greensboro, NC, and I ran a 4.58 (second fastest among skilled players) in the 40-yard dash during frigid weather—running in biker shorts and no shirt—less was best for my psyche.

I was satisfied with my elite time, and I was sure that my time and outstanding drill performances would get me some attention from AFL and CFL scouts in attendance. To my surprise, nothing transpired, and I grew frustrated as Deon and my late friend, Mike Honey tried to encourage me to not focus on this camp as my answer to the league. Mike was murdered two years later by an off-duty police officer in his former home; the story told remains suspicious to me.

Mike and Deon encouraged me to speak with one of the CFL team scouts, so I obliged their request to mitigate my level of frustration. The stout and arrogant scout crushed my spirits even more by telling me at 24 years of age, I was too old to play without current football footage—give it up was his thought process. Instantly, I felt helpless, but I gathered myself and dismissed his comments by stating, "All I need is the faith of a mustard seed and God will open a door for me." I still believed in the unimaginable idea of playing professional football, and I knew deep down that I would play professionally one day. I found peace in this joyless situation, and I was determined to work harder and be ready when another opportunity presented itself. I learned to disregard the bad in situations and to extract the positive lessons I learned from those experiences. I was convinced success was found in circumstances I might have decided were bad in the past.

I focused on turning a negative into a positive, and I truly believed I was destined for prosperity and a multitude of successes. However, I found myself revisiting clubs when I moved back to NC, and the club scene attracted old demons, yearning the spotlight, drinking until intoxication levels, and parading around at times as a tough guy with my shirt off in the club. No shirt on and rocking back in forth on the dance floor with a drink in my right hand became a recurring theme when I trooped out with Deon, Torey, Tony, Lex, Chub, and others to the club.

It felt wrong internally, and it was contrary to my new, godly lifestyle. I found myself reverting to sinful behaviors. Living for God has setbacks, and I made it difficult at times by failing to cutout negative influences (i.e., club, drinking, and people who promote wrong desires). The club scene gave me a feeling of nostalgia when I was masked as a "thug," but eventually, the love for the club no longer felt natural; I felt out of my element many nights, but the alcohol gave me the ability to cope in those diverse club locales and to manage those uncomfortable feelings.

One night at a bootlegger house, I received an offer from an old high school buddy to travel with him to move a package of pure cocaine, and this offer came at a time when Toya and I was struggling financially. With no hesitation, as I became semi-immersed in the club scene and negative culture, I kindly declined his offer. I was not a thug, and that life was dead to me; I desired God's will not a quick fix to a temporary problem. Most problems are temporary, but sometimes we panic and amplify our problems by making impulsive decisions; those impulsive decisions can lead to major and sometimes irreversible consequences.

I learned to welcome challenges and apply the work needed to overcome those challenges—there are no easy routes to success—success requires hard work. His offer was never an option in my mind, and his impressive jewelry and expensive name-brand clothes never tempted me during our conversation—thug life was dead to me, and I was dead to it. About a year later, my friend found himself hemmed up on trafficking charges and received 30 years in federal prison while in his early 20s. I minimized my circle of friends and left some friends behind because they were out of season and not conducive to my constructive atmosphere and growth.

I tried to keep it real and take some friends to a local Turkey Bowl game on Thanksgiving, but they were still trapped in the street hustle lifestyle. I love these guys to this day, but they stashed some drugs in my family vehicle during the game; I was oblivious to their actions. I was only privy to this information when I had to leave the informal football game or social gathering—they made a dash toward my car to retrieve their illegal property. This experience taught me to watch the company I keep and to forget this so-called street way of keeping it real.

My vehicle became the official family vehicle, and I never allowed individuals pursuing opposing lifestyles in my vehicle again. I was not going to allow poor decisions to impede my evolution process. I also became cognizant of whom I allowed to visit my place of residence. As a family man, I did not believe people need to hang around and over my house, and paranoia from my past life made me keep people at a safe distance.

My experiences in the military taught me that triumph comes from hard work, and I employed hard work in my graduate program, physical training, and employment with BB&T. I detached myself from old friends and old neighborhoods, and I did not care that some probably perceived me as weak, fake, or a sellout. It made me feel like a change had actually occurred because I had no desire to act hardcore or be perceived as a thug.

I craved acknowledgement as a scholar, and I wanted to be known as an astute and an intellectual individual. I found a home and a new class of friends in graduate school, and those friends desired the same interests and had fervor toward lifelong learning—I found tranquility in those graduate classrooms. The program stimulated my intellectual development and taught me to think in a critical and creative manner. I continued to win favor and acceptance among my sagacious and professionally accomplished constituents.

It was a little intimidating to verbally communicate lessons learned in collaborative presentations or lead discussions about the principles of accounting with individuals managing million dollar firms. I surpassed my expectations of maybe getting a master's degree and being content with a bachelor's degree; I developed a passion for research and expressing my thought through scholarly writing. School became my niche—something that I was great at—only if they paid high salaries to be a lifelong degree-seeking student; and I am sure I am not the only nerd that thought in this fashion.

I made phenomenal headway at BB&T as a temp, and I was being sought after for a full-time position. Now, I had to find an avenue to market me as a serious or legit football player, so I decided to spend $250 to play for an unorganized semiprofessional football team in Goldsboro, NC that could only muster up about 16 players to play in competitive contact football games. Most players played both ways, consisting of offensive and defensive linemen that weighed only 220 pounds—100 pounds lighter than opposing players on the line.

Our 16 players were definitely dedicated to the will to compete and win. I played tailback, linebacker, defensive back, kick returner, and kick-off-gunner to assist our team, due to the paucity of players. The experience was great for me because I learned some invaluable tips from Montrel, the all-time leading rusher for NC high school football and Hampton University hall of famer.

I never dropped eye-popping statistics playing on this team, but this experience taught me how to make big runs with minimal offensive line blocking. It also forced me to work harder on refining my fast twitch muscles and expanding my muscle mass to absorb power shots from tacklers. My work ethic was impeccable;

I lifted weights before work, performed foot drills during lunch breaks, and ran stadium stairs, hills, and 200-meter sprints after work concluded.

I enhanced my catching abilities by having Deon throw me football passes while my friends (Maurice and Twig) held and fought with me at the line for 10-15 seconds before releasing me to run my route to concentrate on catching passes. This trained me to focus on catching the ball after becoming extremely fatigued. I worked myself into tip-top physical conditioning, and this process instructed me on the significance of performing grueling workouts and the importance of pushing myself beyond the limits—no boundaries to triumph. I worked strenuously on my take off in the 40-yard dash, and I consistently clocked (hand-clock) a 4.40 in the 40-yard dash—above average for NFL running back standards. My football prowess improved to match the progression of my on field experience.

An accumulation of football successes, arduous work ethic, academic achievements, and vocation success brought me renewed self-assurance. I started to tap into unimaginable potential, and I believed that I could do anything as long as I had oxygen entering my lungs and life in my body. I took a part-time position to teach computer and business courses at Wilson Technical Community College to support passion and curiosity raised within me to teach adult students. Those adult students challenged me, and those challenges were similar to the opposing obstacles felt on the football field. Teaching trained me to relax and to compose myself when I communicated with random people—humility was the key to building a successful learning environment.

I made it a point to meet random people and to start new conversations for two reasons: the more people you know, the fewer strangers you know and diverse individuals broaden my horizons through those unique communication experiences. I no longer became nervous during my job interviews; on the contrary, I viewed job interviews as an exciting chance to sell myself to people who did not know me—interviews were fun. When BB&T

gave me an opportunity to interview for a full-time position, I wowed Debbie, the hiring supervisor with my responses to her open-ended questions and with my level of comfort throughout the entire interview process.

Debbie's facial expressions highlighted her interest in my presentation during the interview session. She displayed a smile throughout many portions of the interview, so I used her genuine interest with specific phrases and topics as points of reference to develop a common ground and favorable conversation. I became very loquacious throughout my years of maturation; far from the masked stoic thug persona I projected.

I also became gregarious within those years, socializing and mingling with all types of people and in all types of settings (i.e., elevators, airplanes, buses, and etc.)—I developed a profound love for people. A few weeks later, I received a formal notification that BB&T offered me a $28,000 salary, I was overjoyed and excited about the opportunity to work for a respected company in Wilson County. The low salary did not derail me from accepting the offer because I was determined to make the most of this opportunity. Prior to accepting this job offer, I completed my master's degree and strutted proudly across Central Michigan University graduation stage in Goldsboro.

Opportunities were surfacing in all aspects of my existence, and the greatest opportunity of my football career was waiting for me via email in the midst of all these perceived blessings. Faith and endurance made me a humble individual, and it assisted in my evolution as an educated, spiritual, and athletic 25-year old man. I received an email about the formation of a new arena football team in Raleigh, NC. The email stated that the team was seeking former college players and former NFL, AFL, and CFL football players.

The Raleigh Rebels (AIFL) was a new professional arena football team that entered the Raleigh area to capture a former arena fan populous, which supported the Carolina Cobras prior to the team's relocation to Charlotte, NC in the early 2000s. I was not a huge fan of arena football due to my prior tryout experience with the Fayetteville team, but my father reminded me of all my hard work and other opportunities that can come from playing on this professional football team. He also informed me to pursue all opportunities and to never close doors. His words ignited a fire in me and created a belief that God placed this chance in my path for a reason—galvanizing myself to capture this unique blessing and to make the most of this situation.

I entered the tryout thankful for a chance to compete for a position on a professional football team, and I knew this was an opportune time for me to display my football mastery in front of guys whom I watched play on TV for Duke, UNC, and NC State. When I arrived, I was a little dumbfounded by the former college Division I, ex-NFL, ex-CFL, and ex-NFL Europe football players. Yet, I was committed to being conspicuous and doing my very best during this tryout. I felt this tryout was ordained by God, and I performed as an individual charged by a higher power and with a specific purpose, running 4.5 seconds in the 40-yard dash, benching pressing 225-pounds 19 times, and catching 11-13 passes once I removed my $75 gloves.

I dropped my first two passes when I believed those gloves gave me an advantage in catching passes. When I removed those gloves and trusted solely in my football abilities and God, I caught my next 11 passes. I know some of you think it is a coincidence, and you might be right; but I believed it was my faith that gave me leverage during the catching drills. I was impressed with my overall performance, so I exited the tryout proud of my exerted effort in the small dome arena. As I proceeded to leave the workout facility, I galloped away with a smile on my face and accepted that at 25-years old, the game I love might be over for me. And, I was fine with that conclusion and understood I had other practical options in my future—no longer needing to rely on football for my prosperity.

I reflected on some of the accomplishments within my 25 years of living, four college degrees, a loving family, an adjunct teaching job, and a full-time position as a white-collar employee at BB&T. Secretly, I was becoming more and more passionate about my adjunct teaching position, and I thought that my master's degree would give me an opportunity to climb the corporate ladder in BB&T's management development program; so either way I positively welcomed and embraced the arena football outcome— professional contract or no professional contract. While I was pensively thinking about my professional life and the football tryout, Coach Gibson summoned my presence, and immediately, an inner peace came over me. I sat down and chatted with him, and I instantly thanked him for the opportunity to tryout for his team.

He smiled and offered me a contract without spouting off a lot of rhetoric. Personally, I did not care too much because I was stoked at the chance to play professional football and to improve my marketability to professional agents and NFL scouts—playing the game was the only thing that mattered to me at that point. During the inaugural season, team checks were scarce because we did not have a home arena; we played all of our games on the road. Late night practices were the biggest issues for me. I traveled an hour to practice and an hour from practice every night for 9pm-11pm workout sessions. After arriving home, I slept briefly and woke up early the next morning at 6am for a brief workout prior to starting my 8am-5pm shift.

I was humbled and thankful for having the opportunity to travel from state-to-state to display my athletic abilities in front of ardent fans. Some teammates moaned and groaned about the minimal pay and lengthy travels, but I relished in this opportunity, utilizing it as my missed college football experience days—never complaining and enjoying every short-lived moment.

I appreciated the moment, and I flourished in this sport's atmosphere. Spiritually, my faith continued to grow because I dwelled on the fact that I asked God for an opportunity to play professional football and the unimaginable possibility happened. I exhibited faith of a mustard seed and displayed no unbelief about playing professionally. I did not worry or complain at all about playing professionally because the dream was living and blossoming in my inner world; I surmised that all my dreams would come to fruition. I understood that I would never be content with settling for mediocrity; my tranquility came from stepping outside of my comfort zone and aiming for the so-called impossible, everything was possible in my inner world—all I needed was to believe.

I enjoyed the two years that I played for the Raleigh Rebels; the relationships, the struggles, and the triumphs on the football field made me believe I could achieve any lofty goal, especially goals requiring intellect and wisdom. Mentally, I had to adjust to the politics and to the business factors that accompanied playing professional football. The only success was current success in that world, and past accomplishments were irrelevant when winning comes first.

Every week, Coach Gibson invited bigger football players to come and to compete for my position, so it forced me to stay sharp and to play injured. I received multiple cortisone shots in both of my shoulders, in my right hand, and in my right knee to reduce the inflammation from the constant banging around on the football turf, which helped to alleviate most of my pain—this was a short-term solution to my multitude of injuries because surgery followed some of this short-term resolutions. I worked hard to earn the starting fullback position—undersized at 205 pounds when compared to the average 225-260 pound fullbacks in our football league.

I earned my job when our starting fullback walked out of the practice arena because he grew angry with the coaching staff. This unique way to earn this position taught me how to fight to the end to retain my starting job; I never lost my job to those newcomers my first year—my little frame fought painfully to keep my job. I had my most memorable game in the playoffs against the Canton Legends in Canton, OH. My wife, Deon, and Carlton (old friend) were there to witness my first and my last professional touchdown. Coach Gibson called for a typical counter play to catch the defense off-guard, so we could pick up five yards for a first down. I focused solely on not fumbling the football and attempting to fall forward to gain positive yards. However at the snap, the defense overplayed the right side of our offensive line, I noticed the defensive shift to the right; so I stepped back to reverse to the left side of the play with quickness and power to evade the clutches of those pesky defenders for a 25-yard run toward the end zone.

I cherished lasting memories from my arena football days: signing autographs and interacting with the fans on the field after games, bantering with teammates on the bus and in the locker room, and enjoying the competition on the field against the opposition. Yet, all great things must come to an end, and professional football ended for me in the middle of my second football season and under the helm of my new coach, Coach Folmar. He was renowned in arena football leagues, and he demanded big time players with big time names to market his teams—this is some of the politics of professional sports. He had a smart business approach toward his recruitment of known players from the Raleigh/Durham area, such as big name players from NC State and UNC to gain a greater backing for our home games in Dorton Arena (Raleigh).

I lost my starting position to a former NC State standout, Cotra. Cotra had amazing quickness, speed, power, and size. I competed in practice, but I lost my passion for the business aspect of arena football. Playing arena football was becoming stressful and less fun, so I altered my ambitions and plans toward the pursuit of a new direction. About the same time, I hit a crossroad as I was attempting to enter BB&T's management development program, Debbie (supervisor) became opposed to this idea. She wanted me to wait five years before seeking management opportunities, but I found her request ridiculous. The management program accepted people with undergraduate degrees and no experience; I had a master's degree and respectable experience in many industries.

I grew frustrated with BB&T because I did not recognize growth potential; and Debbie appeared irritated with my attempt to climb the corporate ladder. She had no formal education, but performed as my supervisor—my mind opposed this odd situation. Soon, I found myself at the unemployment line with a business suit and a hand full of resumes when BB&T terminated me from my position. I lost respect for this well-respected firm because I associated her actions and behaviors with the face of the organization. BB&T is a sound and a fair organization, but that leader was not a valid representation of their quality organization. Working random jobs (e.g., fixing displays at Lowes, delivering oxygen tanks and hospital beds at Family Medical Supply, selling knives for Cutco, and supervising 57 employees at Stock Building Supply) eventually inspired me to pursue a career in teaching at a known charter school in Wilson.

At 26 years of age, I felt compelled to teach, and I had no idea where this opportunity would present itself; but I trusted that somehow God would open a door. While I was working out at World's gym one day, I spotted Dr. Wilson riding a stationary bike, so I decided to chat with her about my life and her charter school (Sallie B. Howard). Dr. Wilson demanded that I apply for her technology instructor position at her school, so I dashed to my car to retrieve a resume I had tucked in a folder on the passenger seat of my Mirage to hand deliver her my resume. I saw opportunities in every conversation, so I always kept a resume on hand—folders in my car and in my trunk contained a stack of my professionally designed resumes. Remember, we bring blessings and opportunities to our lives, so it is imperative for us to open our mouths and to pursue conversations with random people.

I felt God nudging me toward a career in teaching, so I was excited about an opportunity to educate kids about life and technology. When Dr. Wilson called me to set up an interview, I knew I had the job in the midst of our conversation. It was a gut feeling because I thought I was being led to teach and lead others to greatness. I received a contract two days later to teach at Sallie B. Howard; my oratory skills were used in a fashion to connect with the panel and buy into my teaching and leadership philosophies—comfort in myself made me a master interviewer. I grew to love myself throughout my evolution process, so I learned how to tap into my inner self and let my positive energy flow into others. I loved teaching at Sallie B., but I was not brought there to retire as a teacher or to work for multiple years. I believe God directed me there to find my passion in teaching, to develop an effective communication style with challenging students, and to enroll into a doctoral program. Dr. Wilson inspired me to pursue a doctoral degree—something I never fathomed.

A month into my job at Sallie B., I enrolled into a doctoral degree in management/organizational leadership (DM) with University of Phoenix (UOP). I had no experience managing or facilitating classrooms with hyperactive and aggressive students, so I utilized street knowledge and real-life examples to connect with them and to reach them on a much deeper level beyond the classroom. This approach worked and eliminated any classroom issues or distractions.

I mastered classroom management, and I taught middle school students who were perceived by many as the toughest students to teach. Middle school age is a confusing age for many students; they can easily move in a positive or a negative direction. I was not the greatest deliver of content because I had no formal training on how to instruct a class. My success came from my passion toward attempting to save my students from poor decision-making. I did not want them to repeat my mistakes of sex at a young age and getting involved with street life.

I gave these students a lot of genuine respect because I saw my two out-of-wedlock daughters in a lot of my students. Some of these students came from one-parent households and had part-time fathers, so their lives were similar to my daughters'. These students would listen attentively to my words, and I spoke as if I were going to save all of them from abusing drugs, dropping out of school, and having babies as teenagers. Tears filled my eyes many days because I realized I was not Jesus and could not save the world, but I still tried. It was 2006, and my life flourished that year. Toya and I bought our first home, I developed a passion for teaching, and I unofficially retired from the going to the club after engaging in an unscheduled street fight at a Raleigh nightclub called Black Tie.

I was too old, too mature, and too accomplished to place myself in situations to fight. I had to avoid situations that brought any negativity to my life, so I decided to eliminate liquor and beer from my life about two years later. The fact that it took me two years to stop drinking hard liquor and beer should prove that change does not occur overnight, and we will always have weak areas to tweak and correct—changes conclude at death. At that time, I thought I was done pursuing football, but my students convinced me to keep working out and to keep the door ajar. Once again I began to train with sprint drills and route running, but I was derailed by a foot surgery and another knee surgery that year, bringing my knee surgeries to four and a sum of surgeries to six.

Toward the end of the year, Dr. Wilson informed me that she was taking the school in a new direction that did not include me, so I willingly left my position there. I had to adjust to this reality as my wife and I traveled to Las Vegas for a vacation. We were just one year into a $1500 monthly mortgage. I also was very comfortable at Sallie B., so I had no intention of leaving; but I trusted that God had a better plan for me.

Sometimes, we need to be pushed out of situations, so we can walk toward our true purpose and direction. Even though I was unhappy, I heard a quiet voice say, "Every year you will receive an increase" and immediately, any worries over money, paying bills, or finding a job dissipated—to this day, every year I have received an increase. Throughout the summer, we received checks from Wilson Technical Community College that they forgot to send and ironically, child support checks with claims that I paid too much.

Those checks covered our bills and amounted to more money

than I would have earned at Sallie B. during those summer months. We never missed paying a bill, and we were never late paying a bill. Later that summer, I was driving around Rocky Mount searching for employment, and I spotted a sign that read Rocky Mount Preparatory School (RMPS). I had a gut feeling that I should hand deliver a resume, and the closer I got to the school, the more I envisioned myself teaching there. I walked in that school suited and booted with a fancy resume in one hand and a personality full of charisma on my face; I wowed the office staff with my confident demeanor, so they introduced me to the leader of the school. I met Mr. Pitt, the headmaster of the school, and I exchanged pleasantries with him; he stated, "You are the guy we were looking for." I signed a contract with them a week later to serve as a technology instructor, middle school basketball coach, and high school track head coach.

The next three years of my life would be spent mastering my abilities as a teacher and communicator at RMPS (2 years), Wilson County Schools (1 year at Elm City and Toisnot Middle), and UOP (2 years teaching online). Football was vastly becoming an after thought, as I developed a more profound admiration toward academia. I loved interacting and engaging in classroom discussions with middle school students, but I had a strong desire burning inside me to instruct full-time at the collegiate level. I put in resumes at local community colleges, but no one was taking the bait. Academia was an unfamiliar world to me, and I did not have the proper key (Ph.D.) to occupy unlock doors to assume a position as a professor.

Jocelyn (Joce) was born in 2008, the second year of my doctoral program, and she would become the last of my beautiful children to be born into this complex world. Joce's arrival brought joy to my life, but it also generated poignant memories of Jas and Tia's births. I regretted not being in the delivery room when they were born, and I wish that they were afforded the same life experiences and lifestyles as Joce and Jay. I took care of them financially, but I did not have the opportunity to tuck them into bed every night while reading fascinating bedtime stories; I also had to be cautious with my fashion of discipline. Time spent with them was precious, and I had to raise Jas and Tia differently. I love all my children the same, but relationships are skewed when family dynamics are altered by past selfish decisions of instant sexual pleasure.

Toya was unexpectedly laid off from her pharmacy technician position after delivering Jocelyn. Toya did not complain about the layoff, but instead became proactive and sought to enhance her knowledge by adding to her professional repertoire. She made the conscious decision to enroll in a master's degree program at UOP. She used her time wisely, and her graduate program completion date appeared to be synonymous to my completion date of my doctoral program. We saw an opportunity for us to participate in the same graduation and share the commencement stage two years away in May 2010.

During my doctoral residency in 2008, I met Dr. Roberts, and he painted an unbelievable picture about a potential career in the world of higher education; he truly believed I could be a successful professor at major universities—speaking life into my inner belief and unimaginable dream of being a scholar. Dr. Roberts served as my major professor in my DM program, so he provided me with sage advice on my writing and challenged my thought process during the completion of my dissertation. While I shifted my focus from playing professional football to academics, I received three official invitations to work out with the All-American Football League (AAFL) in Houston, TX, Atlanta, GA, and Knoxville, TN. The AAFL was a new professional league that sought players with bachelor's degrees, so I believed in the league and thought I had a legitimate chance to make the team.

I accepted those invites and worked out at all three respective locations, but the desire was long gone by this time; and I realized that football was a younger man's game—the fire fizzled out and the dream was forever lost. I performed very well at those tryouts, but watching Stefan Logan (Detroit Lions KR/PR) run a 4.3 in the 40-yard dash; and noticing how previous surgeries and nagging injuries limited some of my maneuvers and speed bursts my decision to abandon this dream forever. I was proud of those opportunities, and I was pleased to receive some interest to tryout for some CFL team four years after one of their scouts told me I was too old to ever play.

I confidently walked away from the idea of playing professional football at the age of 28, and it felt as if I could live and work toward my true purpose on this earth—to serve and to teach others. I thrived as an educator, and I excelled within my doctorate's program. I became a life-long learner, and I realized football was not in God's plan but my plans. God had a greater plan in store for me that would inspire me to soar to even greater heights because I became more addicted to reading books, studying research, and learning from professors, other student learners, and sages from different walks of life.

My focus shifted from being an aggressive football player to a proactive thinker and leader; the more I absorbed information, the more wisdom I obtained. Training myself to relax and to stay calm—I became slow to anger and quick to spread love to others—Christ like was my spiritual journey. When I changed my outlook, I developed a knack for learning new things while Dr. Roberts inspired me to be an accomplished professor and a distinguished scholar. I could see clearly that my true identity was to be a writer, a researcher, and a professor, not a "masked thug," not a professional football player, and not even a middle school instructor. Being good at a task or job does not mean that it is your true passion or purpose in this short life; don't waste your time on things because you are great at them. When you feel like you should pay your employer or customers to perform your job, you have found your true calling in this world.

Lessons Learned

Pursuit of happiness is closely related to the pursuit of peace, but both endeavors require a form of self-discovery prior to being captured. Without capturing happiness, it is impossible to live in tranquility; I was in search of both of those fleeting goals. I sought happiness in professional football, and I received temporary happiness and peace in arena football and in my dreamed businessman profession; but they were short lived and ended abruptly. However, those were ideas I conceived as happiness and peace, and they failed to connect with my authentic identity and inner potential. Many people attempt to find happiness from other people's perspectives of happiness, so they chase and accomplish those noble perspectives of happiness to find stress, misery, and a heightened level of unhappiness—no peace can be found in that quest. I bucked back against the preconceived apparatus that dictates happiness and success, and I searched for common themes in my personal and professional experiences.

The recurring theme appeared to be my love for teaching, inspiring, entertaining, and enhancing the minds of people. While playing football, I adored the interactions with the fans, the chance to encourage and instruct my teammates; and while working in various professions, I appreciated management roles of advising, inspiring, and motivating people—teaching was my contentment and roles of instructing was my peace. I knew my identity and my peace, but now I was being led to my God-given purpose; so the odyssey was to be continued.

Chapter 18

Obedience Leads to Blessings

Unshakable Faith

"Faith is taking the first footstep even when you do not see the whole staircase"
~ *Dr. Martin Luther King, Jr.*

In 2010, Toya and I completed our advanced degree programs at UOP, and we were presented with a rare opportunity to graduate together in Raleigh, NC at the University of Phoenix commencement ceremony. Our graduation was one of the major highlights of that year, and it is a moment that I will cherish for the rest of my life— joy overwhelmed me as I watched Toya proudly glide across that graduation stage. Once the graduation ceremony was over, I was driven even more to obtain a position as a professor at a well-respected university. I phoned Dr. Roberts for his sage advice on this matter, but I quickly found out that I needed research publications and a PhD to acquire such a prestigious position as a tenured-track professor.

I grew discouraged about this new information because I thought my doctoral degree would suffice and pop open some of those closed doors to a career in academia. During that time, I was working at Elm City and Toisnot middle school as a business education instructor; I rotated days between both middle schools. I believed deeply that somehow I was destined to be a professor, so I decided to walk away from teaching and to walk toward obedience and believing that I was destined to teach and to present knowledge to the world.

I knew that my career as a middle school teacher was done, and God was pulling me in a new direction. This new direction required crazy faith in myself and in God. I forfeited my rights to a new contract with Wilson County School system, but I had no job or no sound backup plan setup for my family and me. I was operating solely on faith because I felt strongly that my next blessing or opportunity would pull me away from Wilson, NC forever. Dr. Roberts believed in me, and he felt led to find an appropriate PhD program for me. Dr. Roberts researched feasible PhD programs, and he continued to encourage me by feeding me with sound advice and words of wisdom throughout this process.

This is a man in charge of running a major academic program, but he sacrificed his valuable time to assist me in my time of need—angels are all around us, but it is our job to open our eyes and find them. Closed eyes cannot see, so we should NEVER view the world from a single-minded perspective (e.g., do not trust them because they do not believe in God or do not trust them because they are not black). I constantly expressed my passion and desire to join academia as a professor, and I informed him that I was willing to relocate for a chance to establish a career in that well-respected profession—determination to succeed superseded any trepidation that built over my current job situation. Dr. Roberts was a library of knowledge for me while exploring this arcane and unfamiliar world, so I clung to his every word.

I grew frustrated about the time and money I spent pursuing my DM degree, but immediately, I acknowledge that negative energy and redirected those negative thoughts into positive thoughts and constructive actions. Without my DM degree program, I would have never met Dr. Robert's, who inspired me to aim for a career as a professor and to develop the confidence to write scholarly and succeed in any PhD program. Something positive can be found in all negative situations, but it is our job to be proactive and to seek those opportunities—an exploration for hidden answers provide that arcane information.

My major issue was that most universities already accepted applications for their fall semesters of 2012, and I sought an application in May from these distinguished universities, about three months past the due date—it did not look great for me. A small window of hope presented itself, and I never wavered on my faith; I believed something would work in my favor. I notified Toya that I needed to work toward a PhD, and it might require us to relocate. She was excited about the move but leery of my decision to return to college.

She did not understand the difference between a PhD and DM—neither did I for that matter at that time. However, she believed in me and supported my dreams of being a professor; she trusted in my decision-making and knew it was in the best interest of our family. People striving for success need to align themselves with people who believe in them; and Toya was my biggest cheerleader and my greatest supporter.

Faith kept me poised because we still had a house under mortgage, financed cars, child support, and other miscellaneous bills. One day toward the end of my contract with Wilson County schools, Dr. Roberts called and recommended Iowa State University (ISU) as a possible school to pursue for a PhD in Hospitality Management, and I was dumbfounded about attending a school in Iowa, even though ISU had one of the top PhD programs. Iowa was never on my radar, and I had no desire to move to the Midwest and leave the east coast. Blessings or opportunities do not come in the fashion that we desire; it comes in the best form for our individual maturation and successes—our job is to trust that form.

My passion to become a professor was much stronger than my desire to stay on the east coast, so Ames, Iowa became a desirable option; I soon fell in love with the possibly of becoming a Cyclone. Once Toya confirmed her commitment to this possibility, I let Dr. Roberts know we would be willing to relocate for a scholarship in ISU Hospitality Management PhD program. Dr. Roberts wasted no time contacting Dr. Bob, the department head of ISU's Apparel, Events, and Hospitality Management (AESHM) department; and I assume Dr. Roberts spoke favorably of me because Dr. Bob requested that I call him the next day—giving me time to research Dr. Bob, his faculty, and his recognizable program.

I used that day to perform extensive research on Dr. Bob and his distinguished faculty, and I knew his presence in the academic and professional realm of hospitality. I wanted to be a professor badly, and I aligned my faith with dedicated hard work to force closed doors to open. I knew that if I believed in a dream and utilized actions to support that belief, those dreams would come to fruition. God seemed to place the right people in my life during the right seasons, and I knew God would continue to align me with the right people to mentor me and to groom me for future triumphs. I spoke with Dr. Bob over the phone, and he was interested in meeting with me face-to-face to discuss some potential options as a teaching assistant (TA), the only caveat was that I had to be accepted into the program.

I had to take the GMAT, an assessment that I despised when I took it seven years earlier in 2003. I also had to enroll in some summer courses offered in their distance PhD program as a non-degree seeking student, which prompted me to spend $2,000 of our saved money—with no job to recoup that substantial sum. Bills were still there, but I saw past our current state and saw that God would not present an opportunity without some resolve to my current obstacles. Obstacles and barriers appeared daunting, but I honestly had no worries—my focus was on ensuring that I do not blow this chance with ISU—viewing this as my one shot to the world of a professor. In my inner psyche, I could not fail, so I believed that I would not fail in landing a scholarship to seek a PhD at ISU. I visualized myself shaking hands and communicating in a way to win them over, Dr. Bob and the lovely staff at ISU.

In the midst of this major decision, Toya and I decided to celebrate 10 years of marriage with a cruise to Bermuda; the trip gave me a chance to clear my mind and to generate positive thoughts prior to departing to ISU to meet the faculty and to take some summer courses with no reprieve from doctoral studies. As I gazed out at the massive body of water from the cruise ship, I visualized taking classes and thriving among my fellow future ISU cohort. Visions and previous experiences made me believe that God was pushing me toward the life of being a scholar.

I acknowledged that true blessings come through hard work, unshakable faith, and extreme dedication—an ultimate resolve of focus toward a set goal. Toya and I enjoyed the cruise, and the cruise gave me confidence before heading out to Ames, IA. After returning from the cruise, I scheduled an appointment to take the GMAT and received a dismal score—a little below the recommended score. Negative thoughts clouded my mind as I proceeded to drive away from the testing site. When I acknowledged the negative thoughts, I begin speaking life into this unfortunate situation; I kept repeating positive words of success, and the more I spoke, the more those negative thoughts dissipated.

Once again, a calm came over me as I spoke those positive words, and a small voice said, "Everything will work in your favor." I never worried about that test score again, and my attention shifted back toward selling myself to the ISU faculty. I flew into Des Moines, Iowa with a mission, and I came with my game face—all business . . . I had to earn this scholarship. I utilized the 35-minute drive toward Ames thinking and playing out conversational scenarios in my mind; I also envisioned myself smiling and interacting in positive manner with my future peers. The next morning, I entered ISU campus on a mission, exuding tranquility in my disposition, and as I spoke, it felt like I was destined to be there—I knew that I would receive a scholarship after the first day around the faculty and my graduate peers.

I knew God had his fingerprints on this entire episode; I knew it was mine and nobody could stop this progressive movement.

I knew Ames would be our future home for some years, and I visualized myself teaching courses, presenting and publishing research, and graduating from ISU before receiving the official confirmation letter from Dr. Bob. I successfully completed those two summer classes, and I worked extremely hard to prove that I belong among those accomplished students who were more knowledgeable and distinguished in their hospitality careers than I.

I was impressed with those distance students because they held positions as GM's, Presidents, and managers. Continuous interactions with them in the classroom enhanced my self-assurance in ISU's PhD program; and I continued to boost my self-confidence with the help of my extended family (Liz, Michael, Don, David, Suzanne, Ryan, and Barry). I admire those non-traditional PhD students because they do not have the luxury of leaning on professors and other graduate students as many traditional PhD students do.

I flew home from ISU supremely confident that we would be relocating to Ames, IA, and about two weeks later I received an acceptance letter and full scholarship to boot. I believed and I received, so we promptly placed our house on the market and trusted that our house would sell in a reasonable time—the reasonable time became 17 months. My salary was cut to $14,000 annually, but I was willing to do whatever it took to turn this endeavor into a final triumph as a professor. My uncle Kent served as another angel during this time because he utilized his truck to move us for half the cost of other commercial truckers—saving us money that we would need to manage accumulating bills.

Goodbye Wilson, I was being obedient and was leaving my comfort zone for a predestined blessing with unshakeable faith. Officially, I enrolled in the PhD hospitality program in fall 2010 with credits from the summer and credits from my masters and doctorates programs to eliminate a year off my course work. I started the program with straight A's, and I was driven to gain the most from this experience from the start. I taught whatever Dr. Bob asked me to teach, and I made a point to represent ISU and publish research for every conference (i.e., graduate and professional conferences). I was overjoyed to be there because I was grateful for the opportunity. The PhD process felt natural and not too challenging for me. I was passionate about the reading, research, and teaching, so it came with less effort than playing football or attempting to be this masked thug. I never donned a mask to develop ardor for researching and teaching—it was my identity, it was REAL.

When we pursue anything to appease people or to achieve a title, I feel we are attempting to mask our true identity; the thought of being called a doctor does not excite me. Serving and inspiring others ignite me everyday and fuels me to deliver the best quality instruction within my classrooms—not the opportunity to brag about my degrees or titles. My first year in the program, I understood my true purpose and identity, so I was determined to graduate in 2 years and to acquire an assistant professor position somewhere on the east coast after completion.

I reiterated this belief to my wife, and I spoke those words with conviction. My visions compelled me to believe because I saw those things happening vividly, over and over in my mind. I saw it when I walked around on campus, and I lived those accomplishments in my daily thoughts and nightly dreams; I knew that those dreams would come to fruition.

I started my PhD in Hospitality Management on August 2010, and I graduated with a teaching excellence award and PhD on May 4, 2012; and six months prior to graduation, I signed a contract as an assistant professor with James Madison University (JMU), located in Harrisonburg, VA. Throughout this entire process, God sent me two great mentors, Dr. Roberts and Dr. Bob who continue to encourage me and to provide me with beneficial advice about submitting publications, teaching, and improving my career as a tenured-track professor. I acquired a congregation of ISU peers

(Kelly, Jay, Queena, Anh, Fatimah, Derrick, Aja, Katerina, and the entire AESHM graduate students, staff, and faculty) at ISU who constantly encouraged my heart toward personal and professional triumph.

My two years as a graduate student at ISU, I compiled 10 publications (one article in the Journal of Leadership Studies, "Youth Sports and the Emergence of Chameleon Leadership"), Certified Hospitality Educator (CHE) licensure, and graduated with a 3.92 GPA; I also took the time to play running back for the 2011 National Champions Des Moines Blaze (Ranked #1 in the nation for semiprofessional football). Nothing can stop a train when it generates force (identity), motion (unshakeable faith), and guided steam (God and self)—blessings or opportunities will follow that obedience and unstoppable focus.

> *When I stand before God at the end of my life, I would hope that I would not have a single bit of talent left, and could say, "I used everything you gave me"*
>
> ~ *Erma Bombeck*

Lessons Learned

God's love is absolute, and it does not give up on the low or so-called societal failures. I started this book standing over Speedy after my punches drove him to the ground, and my right hand became unusable due to my apparent fractured knuckle; so I proceeded to kick Speedy violently—this young and weak masked thug was not walking in spiritual obedience or purpose. Later in life, I decided to become obedient and pursue a Christ like life, and even though I get weak and falter at times, I am committed to serving something greater than myself. We become consumed with guilt of shortcomings and sins, and this guilt can force us to run away from our God-given purpose.

We compare our lives to others, depicting all of our flaws and thinking others are better—no one is perfect and no one is without sin or fault; so it is imperative to focus on improving ourselves rather than comparing ourselves to others. I never allowed my guilt of poor judgment to deter me from pursuing or believing in God; we are imperfect people, but it is our choice to turn from our imperfect ways and to pursue righteous living that gives us the strength to serve others graciously. I am convinced that we might struggle with some sins until the day we expire, but I know if we acknowledge first the kingdom of God; God will align us to his will, and the true purpose for our lives.

This acknowledgement and vulnerability will provide us with the apparatus to unmask from false identities. My beliefs may be different from your beliefs, but I charge you to hold tightly to the belief in yourself. If you give up on yourself, you are sure to fail in this life. The power in the belief of self is greater than the thoughts of others, so never stop believing in your abilities and any unimaginable dreams. I knew a dentist in the military who worked very hard within his skilled profession, but he hated his job with a passion.

The sad part is Americans view him as a success because he can call himself a dentist and make vast amounts of money. How can a person be a success and hate what they do for a living? As stated in the introduction, to me those individuals are masked in a career to appease their parents or set standards by our society, but they are no different than a masked thug—one is legal and one is illegal, but both are not tapping into their true potential and tranquil state—both lack authenticity.

It is impossible to unmask without discovering our true identity, and we need to unmask before we can tap into our true potential. Today, I wake up thankful for God's grace, mercy, discovery of self, and multitude of blessings and future blessings. I thank God for the blessings and perceived bad situations (i.e. pain for multiple surgeries, relationships, and critical issues that may arise) because God is great in every occurrence and lessons are learned in every situation—positive or negative.

Our perceptions are shaped according to our realities, so we should mold them carefully. I have developed a genuine love for people and an appreciation for people with unique personalities (i.e., different sexual preferences, beliefs, and cultural upbringings), forcing me to broaden my perspective. I will end this book with the following statements: when we find peace, we will find happiness; when we find happiness, we will find our true purpose, passions, and true potential in this existence. This mantra shifted my focus and galvanized this inner center of solitude that led me to remove my mask, and mature from a boy to a man and from a thug to a scholar.

Timeline

"Our greatest weakness lies in giving up. The most certain way to succeed is always to try just one more time."

~ *Thomas Edison*

- 5 – 9 years old: 10-15 scheduled fights; tested for special education
- 13 – years old: Lost virginity at a skating ring; sold crack cocaine
- 13 – years old: Broke hand fighting; questioned by police
- 15 – years old: Cynthia claimed that she was pregnant
- 16 – years old: Fatherhood; Tia was born; ran away from home
- 17 – years old: Second child was born; Jas; period of selling marijuana
- 17 – years old: Colleges stopped recruiting me for football
- 18 – years old: Graduated from high school and enrolled at Methodist College
- 19 – years old: Started hanging with BLOODS; pulled gun on a person with bad intentions

- 19 – years old: Joined USAF; married Toya
- 21 – years old: Re-entered college; Jay was born
- 22 – years old: Graduated college: two associate degrees
- 23 – years old: Graduated college: bachelor's degree; honorably discharged from military
- 25 – years old: Graduated from grad school: master's degree; signed arena football contract
- 26 – years old: Retired from arena football
- 26 – years old: Enrolled in doctorate's program with UOP; first time teaching middle school students full-time
- 28 – years old: Met Dr. Robert's (Major Professor)
- 30 – years old: Graduated from grad school: DM; Accepted in ISU PhD program
- 32 – years old: Graduated from grad school: PhD; signed contract as an assistant professor-tenured track

Poems

TODAY I SHED A TEAR

Today I shed a tear while standing strong, proud, and bold as a
    black man with no fear;
Even though I look around and found no other young black males
    standing near
None to follow and none to cheer;
Walk with my head down to see some roll dice, pass a blunt, and
    sip some beer
So today I shed a tear, the picture is clear;
Some have no regard for the law, quick to embrace and celebrate
    their flaw;
No longer fighting for injustice and education, too busy
    gangbanging and trying to break their brother's jaw;

No regard for life, viewing violence as fun;

The black community is facing tragic situations: HIV, STD's, MTV, and obesity, to black males pulling guns, with no hesitation to add to this self-destructing generation;

I keep moving alone without fear, watching my unchained black brothers in the rear; so today I shed a tear.

WE SEARCH

We search for peace, we search for opportunity; we search for love, we search for unity;

We search for many things to hide the depths of our internal pains, protruding our veins, driving us insane;

Searching like a lost puppy because we search in vain, we search without evolving;

We search without ever calling a name so great because subconsciously we are content with earth being are heavenly state;

Blindly ignoring the fact that we all have a death date, thinking life is about finding that one true soul mate;

We search and we search, keeping God confined to the brick-and-mortar building of a church;

We search and we search for the same fate of returning to the dirt; ashes to ashes and dust to dust;

We search and we search, forgetting that God is a must.

Contact the Author

Twitter: **UnmaskYTP**,
website: **www.unmaskyourtruepotential.com**,
email addresses: **will22ja@jmu.edu; jamesw45@hotmail.com**